MEMOIRS
OF A MAN

Grenville Clark

MEMOIRS OF A MAN

Grenville Clark

COLLECTED BY

Mary Clark Dimond

EDITED BY

NORMAN COUSINS

AND

J. GARRY CLIFFORD

W · W · NORTON & COMPANY · INC ·

NEW YORK

Library of Congress Cataloging in Publication Data
Main entry under title:

Memoirs of a man, Grenville Clark.

  Includes index.
    1. Clark, Grenville, 1882–1967. I. Clark,
Grenville, 1882–1967. II. Dimond, Mary Clark.
III. Cousins, Norman, ed. IV. Clifford, John Garry,
ed.
KF373.C53M4   340'.092'4 [B]   74-20778
ISBN 0-393-08716-6

E. M. Forster quotation from "What I Believe" in *Two Cheers for Democracy*, copyright 1951, published by Harcourt Brace Jovanovich, Inc.
Excerpt from Richard D. Heffner, "The Legacy of a Great American," *McCall's*, April 1967, used by permission.

Published simultaneously in Canada
by George J. McLeod Limited, Toronto

PRINTED IN THE UNITED STATES OF AMERICA

1 2 3 4 5 6 7 8 9 0

To the principle that the strength of a nation rests on the vigor and integrity of individual citizens.

"I believe in aristocracy, though—if that is the right word, and if a democrat may use it. Not an aristocracy of power, based upon rank and influence, but an aristocracy of the sensitive, the considerate and the plucky. Its members are to be found in all nations and classes, and all through the ages, and there is a secret understanding between them when they meet. They represent the true human tradition, the one permanent victory of our queer race over cruelty and chaos. Thousands of them perish in obscurity, a few are great names. They are sensitive for others as well as for themselves, they are considerate without being fussy, their pluck is not swankiness but the power to endure, and they can take a joke."

E. M. FORSTER

Contents

Acknowledgments xiii

Foreword xv

PART I *Introduction*

Norman Cousins, Grenville Clark: A Man for All Seasons 3
J. Garry Clifford, Grenville Clark and His Friends 9

PART II *Portraits*

Joseph S. Clark, Memories of Grenville Clark 33
Louis B. Sohn, Grenville Clark: As Seen from a Co-author's Perspective 45
Samuel R. Spencer, Jr., Grenville Clark 53
W. Averell Harriman, Tribute to Grenville Clark 59
John J. McCloy, A Tribute to Grenville Clark 63

PART III *Legal Friendships*

John M. Korner, Grenville Clark: A Lifelong Friend 69
Henry Mayer, Grenville Clark 74
Cloyd Laporte, G.C. 78
Henry J. Friendly, Grenville Clark: Legal Preceptor 88
Lyman M. Tondel, Jr., Grenville Clark: Some Stories and Personal Recollections 92
Lloyd K. Garrison, Grenville Clark 98
John M. Dinse, A Vermont Lawyer's View 102
James P. Hart, A View from Texas 105

PART IV *Civil Rights*

Louis Lusky, Grenville Clark, 1882–1967 109
Francis E. Rivers, One Man's Conception of Grenville Clark 113
Roger N. Baldwin, A Memo on Grenville Clark 120

Jack Greenberg, Grenville Clark   122
Charles E. Wyzanski, Jr., Grenville Clark and the Harry Bridges Episode   124
Robert H. Reno, Grenville Clark and the Uphaus Case   127
William Worthy, Grenville Clark: A Vignette   132

PART V   *Educational Friendships*

Harold W. Dodds, My Friend Grenville Clark   139
John S. Dickey, Conservation by Conversation   146
Erwin N. Griswold, Grenville Clark: Notes   155
Kingman Brewster, Jr., Grenville Clark: Operator Extraordinary   159
James B. Conant, Grenville Clark: Stalwart Defender of Academic Freedom   161
William L. Marbury, Grenville Clark   163
David F. Cavers, Grenville Clark and the Development of the International Legal Studies Program at the Harvard Law School   165

PART VI   *Family, Friends, and Neighbors*

Mary Clark Dimond, A Daughter's Viewpoint: Lighter Moments— And Many Exposures   171
Elizabeth Jay Hollins, My Father's Friend   183
Paul Dudley White, M.D., Memories of Grenville Clark as Patient and Friend   190
Lewis W. Douglas, Grenny in the 1930s and 1940s   195
Lyman V. Rutledge, Reminiscences of Grenville Clark   200
Edric A. Weld, A Dublin Friend   204
Grenville Clark Thoron, A Small Boy's Grandfather   206
Lewis B. Hershey, Grenville Clark and Selective Service   209
Edward P. Stuhr, The Clark Family Financial Conferences   211
Mary Kersey Harvey, No Nobel Peace Prize Was Awarded in 1967   214

PART VII *World Peace*

Harry B. Hollins, Grenville Clark and the World Law Fund   221
C. Maxwell Stanley, Tribute to Grenville Clark   226
Simeon O. Adebo, Grenville Clark, the Great Internationalist   229
Sir Alexander J. Haddow, Grenville Clark   232
Einar Rørstad, Grenville Clark as I Met Him   234
Stanley K. Platt, Grenville Clark   237
The Rev. Gerard G. Grant, S.J., Recollections of Grenville
    Clark   239
Muhammad Zafrullah Khan, Grenville Clark   241
I. A. Richards, The Princeton Conference of 1946   243
Patrick Armstrong, An Incident in England   245
Stringfellow Barr, The Governed Temper   247
Carlos P. Romulo, Grenville Clark   249
Alan Cranston, Memoir of a Man   252

PART VIII *Important Letters of Grenville Clark*

To Theodore Roosevelt, November 19, 1914.   267
To Wendell L. Willkie, March 18, 1941.   270
To Harry S. Truman, June 2, 1945.   276
To Frank B. Ober, May 27, 1949.   279
To Allan Knight Chalmers, May 2, 1960.   292
To John F. Kennedy, November 22, 1960.   297

About the Authors   303
Index   311
Illustrations appear between pages 176 and 177.

Acknowledgments

Not more than two months after the death of my father, Grenville Clark, I was seated in the corner office level with New York's skyline with Norman Cousins, editor of the *Saturday Review*. We were silent for the moment. He had just asked me had my father suffered at the time of his death and I had replied briefly to this—not all truthfully, for Norman Cousins cared very much.

Next, I handed him a list in my handwriting on yellow legal paper of names of friends, former colleagues, and some family of Grenville Clark with the volume *T. E. Lawrence by His Friends*. My thought was that there be a similar book providing a portrait of Grenville Clark much as the parts of a mosaic together portray the whole. Norman liked the idea, glanced at the names, commented "Good list!", and agreed to write an introduction, edit, and guide the project.

It is now some time since I left that office to go out into a gray and chill Manhattan day, grateful and inspired. Norman Cousins has been true to his word and here is the book.

My father, Grenville Clark, died in 1967. To me he was a gentle, very sensitive, honest, and generous man of formidable intellect, perception, and humor. As a daughter, I was prejudiced, but many other persons of substance and intelligence felt as I did. The admonishment of my friend Edgar Snow that same winter was, "You must not let the life and accomplishments of this man go by default." His papers needed to be gathered, sorted, catalogued; a biographer needed to surface, equal to the task. Projects to his memory needed to be activated and a biographical publication appear before the public as soon as feasible. Wherefore, this collection of "sketches" was the literary form chosen for a more immediate publication, and I set about gathering these.

It all took longer than we thought, and not every author pursued was captured. Even now we might not have succeeded had it not been for the support and effort at initial stages contributed by Robert H. Reno, a good friend and lawyer of Concord, New Hampshire.

Mrs. Ruth Wight, Grenville Clark's secretary for almost two decades, was just embarked in 1967 on the enormous five-year task of collecting, sorting, and classifying the more than one million pages of the Grenville Clark Papers which now reside at the Baker Library at

Dartmouth College. Some material was drawn from these. As recently as the summer of 1973, Mrs. Wight typed the whole manuscript for Professor J. Garry Clifford of Connecticut University, who spent this same summer at meticulous editorial work on the collected monographs and choosing a handful of representative letters written by Grenville Clark with which to conclude the volume.

Jon Dunn reproduced and somehow revived the old photographs for publication here. Miss Helen Domann typed the many letters necessary for bringing the "sketches" together. Mrs. Frieda Bader xeroxed, filed, mounted, sorted photographs and the sketches, and often did it again, and then did it all over once more.

Copies of all contributions went to John S. Dickey, whose enthusiasm for this book never waned for a moment.

Members of the Board of Directors of the Grenville Clark Fund at Dartmouth College, Inc., gave me steady encouragement. These people are F. William Andres, Joseph S. Clark, Norman Cousins, John S. Dickey, Leo Gottlieb, Erwin N. Griswold, Anthony Lewis, H. Carl McCall, Dudley W. Orr, Robert H. Reno, John K. Schemmer, Samuel R. Spencer, Jr., Homer C. Wadsworth, and Ruth N. Wight.

Thanks, of course, go from me to all of the authors, many of whom were so patient, good-natured, and then productive following the repeated reminders which came from me to cross their busy desks.

My husband, E. Grey Dimond, with his general philosophy of "You can do it—so, do it," to which admonition he added humor and affection, never allowed me to falter in this endeavor.

To every one of these people and more, too, I wish to express my very sincere gratitude for making the book possible.

MARY CLARK DIMOND

Foreword

Grenville Clark had printed his early ideas on a solution to end war between nations of the world in 1939 and his continued work in this field culminated with publication of his book in 1958, *World Peace through World Law*, written in collaboration with Louis B. Sohn. This book will remain a classic.

Whether he would have left this plan, based on concepts of law in the Western world, unchanged if he had completed his next step, which was a trip to the People's Republic of China, will never be known. His final illness and death in 1967 stopped this phase of his education. What is known is that he fought throughout his life to do what was right and of greatest service to all of mankind.

Grenville Clark contributed in many areas other than that of world peace, and in each of these "as a private citizen."

This book's theme for emphasis is that an effective private citizen and public servant need not hold public office and may still be a person of great influence on public policy though little known to both public and press. A democracy needs such citizens to survive. Our America today requires a Grenville Clark, who never wavered from honest dedication and who knew that participation by private citizens is necessary to the security of democracy.

MARY CLARK DIMOND

PART I

Introduction

GRENVILLE CLARK:

A Man for All Seasons

Norman Cousins

———— ◆ ————

Grenville Clark made one think he would have been much at home with Americans like Madison, Franklin, Jefferson, or Adams. He had the breadth of outlook, strong rationalist strain, enlightened purpose, and intellectual versatility that one associated with leaders of the Philadelphia Constitutional Convention. He had the gift of leadership. He knew how to draw people together of widely varying viewpoints. He never held public office and was not popularly known, but it is doubtful if any other private American contributed more to the peace in the past half-century. If the United Nations ever achieves the maturity of a workable government with adequate, responsible powers, the inspiration of Grenville Clark for making it possible will have been a key one.

I first met him in the little town of Dublin, New Hampshire, not far from picturesque Mount Monadnock. He was a tall, strong-framed man in his early sixties. He also possessed an unforgettable square jaw that blended perfectly with fierce jutting eyebrows. The year was 1945 and the occasion was the little-known Dublin Conference. Clark had joined with the late Owen J. Roberts, associate justice of the Supreme Court, and the late Robert P. Bass, former governor of New Hampshire, in inviting forty-eight Americans to Dublin, where Clark lived, for the purpose of considering the revolutionary situation in the world represented by the development of atomic weapons. I did not know much about this unassuming New Englander, but from other delegates I learned of his Wall Street law practice, his work on the Harvard Corporation, and the fact that he had been adviser to four presidents on matters of foreign policy and national defense.

Grenville Clark made the opening presentation at the Dublin Conference. He was looking ahead twenty years or more. He said he thought it unreasonable to assume that the wartime alliance between the United States and the Soviet Union could hold up under the pressure of events. He forecast a struggle for the balance of power under conditions of uncertainty and insecurity for both countries. He saw the emergence of a world atomic armaments race. Despite published assurances to the contrary by U.S. government spokesmen, he anticipated the development within a few years of nuclear weapons by the Russians, and by other countries within a generation. He said it would be difficult to keep the atomic armaments race from leading to a world holocaust unless strong measures were taken to create a world authority with law-enacting and law-enforcing powers.

He believed the moment in history had come for creating the instruments of workable law. He spoke of the need for a world government which would have "limited but adequate" powers. It should be "limited" in the sense that it would not interfere with the internal functioning of nations. It should be "adequate" in the sense that it would be able to deal with the historic causes of war and would seek to insure justice in the relations among nations. In short, he proposed world law as the only alternative to the existing world anarchy.

Listening to Grenny Clark that day in Dublin was an unforgettable experience. He was then, as he was until his death in 1967, a magnificent example of the man of reason joined to the man of good will. He summoned historical experience, always giving proper weight to his analogies, always making the essential qualifications. The political philosophy reflected in his talk placed him in the tradition of John Stuart Mill, the Physiocrats, the leaders of the Philadelphia Constitutional Convention, and jurists like Oliver Wendell Holmes. When he spoke about the need for world law, he was not merely trying to prevent world war; he was speaking to a condition necessary for human progress.

As the result of Clark's leadership, the Dublin Conference produced a document that commanded international attention and served as the effective beginning for the world law movement in the United States and elsewhere. Men like Cord Meyer, Jr., Alan Cranston, and Kingman Brewster were inspired by Clark to labor diligently in the world law movement. Grenny was both architect and champion, a primary source of energy and strategy during these years, although, as was characteristic, he remained in the background and worked through those of us who were younger. His main work in the years after 1945 was that of a theorist for world law, one of the few men in the world who devoted full energy to those fundamental questions of planetary survival. With Professor Louis Sohn of Harvard University, he wrote the book *World Peace through World Law*, which addressed itself to the multiplicity of problems involved in the transformation of the United Nations into a source of enforceable world law. The book recognizes that a world legislature must be "weighted" in representation. The present one-nation, one-vote system of representation makes the enactment of world legislation cumbersome and potentially inequitable. The book, now in its third edition, presents carefully developed ideas that indicate the practicality as well as the feasibility of weighted representation. In 1959, the American Bar Association awarded Grenville Clark its Gold Medal, referring to *World Peace through World Law* as a "major contribution to world literature" on the subject of law and peace.

Grenny tackled the bugaboo of absolute national sovereignty in a way that would disarm even the most pronounced adherents of unfettered national determination. At the Dartmouth Conference between prominent Americans and Russians in 1960, I can recall the meeting reaching a point of tension-saturation. The Americans were steadfast in their advocacy of a plan for disarmament with full inspection and control. The Russians reacted sharply to what some of them described as a plan for violating the sovereignty and security of their country. The tone of the meeting was becoming harsh and strident. Grenville Clark, who until that moment had been silent, asked to speak.

He began by saying he accepted fully the sincerity of the Soviet delegates to reduce and eliminate the dangers of war. He spoke of the enormous numbers of casualties suffered by the Russian people in the Second World War, some twenty million dead.

He referred to the siege of Leningrad and the heroism of its people. He paid tribute to the Russian contribution to victory during the war. He spoke movingly and with great dignity. Then he told of the need to avert even greater wars in an age of nuclear weapons. He defined the basic principles that had to go into the making of a workable peace. He described the opportunity before leaders of public opinion in gaining acceptance for these principles. He called on both Americans and Russians to see the problem of disarmament in a larger and more historic setting than weapons alone. When he sat down, both sides gave him sustained applause. And from that moment, Grenville Clark's name was magic with all the Russians who had heard him and many who had not. He had demonstrated not just the power of logic but the prodigious force that is represented by an empathetic understanding of the next man's experience and problems. Even more, he had proved that even the most hardened positions tend to dissolve in the presence of honest good will and friendliness.

Grenny's last years were difficult. His beloved wife, Fanny, died very painfully after more than fifty years of a happy marriage. His own health, never robust, deteriorated. The world situation, for a time bright and hopeful in response to the vigor and rhetoric of President Kennedy, became dominated by Vietnam, missile crises, and overwhelming armaments burdens. At home, the cause of civil rights made headway only too slowly. Yet Clark was a congenital optimist. He simply could not believe that mankind would be so stupid as to blow itself up. He believed in the ability of men—and nations—to educate themselves to practical necessities. His favorite quotation was from Abraham Lincoln: "The people will save the government if the government itself will do its part only indifferently well."

So Grenny continued to work. Thinking it absurd not to include the world's largest nation in plans for nuclear disarmament, he tried personally to visit the People's Republic of China, and very nearly made it with the help of Edgar Snow. When the Cuban missile crisis in 1962 failed to galvanize the United States and Russia toward real and lasting disarmament, he thought in terms of long-range education. The World Law Fund, which he endowed with some $750,000, would begin this process of gradual education. And he continued to hope: perhaps his example as a private citizen seeking to effect change for national and international welfare would stimulate others. Several times his friends nominated him for the Nobel Peace Prize. He did not win, but he deserved the award.

His death in January 1967 at age eighty-four diminished us greatly. I often wonder how that grand old man would have reacted to the events of subsequent years, as the Vietnam war continued its ugly course, as the United Nations grew weaker, as Watergate left its scar upon America. Some might argue that the quiet and reasoned methods of a New England Brahmin were out of place in an age of Vietnam and Watergate. But I doubt if Grenny would have seen it that way. To be sure, it might seem incongruous that the man who wrote the Selective Service Act of 1940 should have resolutely opposed the Vietnam war, but Grenny saw no inconsistency. In his last months he wrote long and eloquent letters to President Johnson, Secretary McNamara, and Secretary Rusk, and had he lived longer he might have added his distinguished voice to Senator Fulbright's hearings on the conduct of the war. As a long-time champion of free speech, Grenny would have objected to some of the extreme methods adopted by opponents of the war; but at the same time, I think he undoubtedly would have shared their frustration at the lack of response on the part of government in Washington. Even in frustration, though, he would not have abandoned his principles. One can imagine him, during the Cambodia incursion of 1970, picking up the phone and calling an old acquaintance like Elliot Richardson or Erwin Griswold. He might not have affected policy in any substantial way, but he would have applied the strongest pressure against the policymakers.

One development that Clark would have applauded in recent years was President Nixon's initiative in ending America's isolation from the Chinese. Indeed, it was symbolic that his daughter Mary (and her husband, Dr. E. Grey Dimond), taking with them the Paul Dudley Whites, were of the first few physicians to visit China in 1971. Grenny would not have converted Chou En-lai to his visions of world government, but he would have had an impact on the Chinese leaders—as he has had on all others who knew him. Like Chairman Mao, Grenville Clark understood that a long journey always begins with a single step. In one of the sermons at the time of his death, a minister compared Grenny to a twentieth-century Tamerlane who did not wish to die so long as there was more territory left to conquer; the only difference being that Grenny wanted to stay alive until the world was secure from nuclear war. His wish was not granted. Nonetheless, we can continue his work and be guided by his spirit. This present volume of essays should recall the man and his deeds.

GRENVILLE CLARK AND HIS FRIENDS

J. Garry Clifford

Friendship is a thing most necessary to life, since without
friends no one would choose to live, though possessed of all
other advantages.

Aristotle

Grenville Clark's most remarkable quality was a capacity for
friendship. As a biographer who never met the man, after reading
through hundreds of boxes of correspondence, after interviewing
scores of persons involved in his work, I have been astonished at
the range and variety of those who called him "friend." And these
friendships are essential to any careful evaluation of the man and
his activities. Clark cared more for the cause than for personal
fame, and whether the cause was civil rights, world government,
or military preparedness, he religiously avoided the public spotlight. He worked through others because he believed more would
be accomplished that way. This technique became part of his personality, setting him apart from other private citizens who sometimes exerted large influence in national affairs. He was no Bernard
Baruch with a well-paid staff of public relations experts; rather, he
sought the role of "statesman incognito," a man whose name was
unrecognized by millions of Americans, but known very well to
thousands close to the seats of power. Both Grenville Clark and
his friends preferred this approach.

That Clark had impeccable Establishment credentials was important. Schooling at Pomfret and Harvard, membership in the Porcellian and Knickerbocker clubs, marriage to Fanny Dwight of Boston, the fact that both Franklin and Theodore Roosevelt called him "Grenny"—all had their formative effect. Clark's first important public activity, the Plattsburg movement, was very much an "elitist" undertaking, and nearly every friend that he recruited to shoulder arms by the shore of Lake Champlain in 1915 came from the same Ivy League background. His election in 1931 to the seven-man Corporation that governs Harvard University accentuated the Establishment image. Nonetheless, Brahmin ties and Wall Street connections did not mold Grenville Clark. Money and power did not corrupt. There was something about him, an independence of spirit, a dogged curiosity, a supreme indifference to ignorant criticism, that made him stand out, even to the point of being a maverick. At Plattsburg he avoided the shrill superpatriotism that motivated some of Theodore Roosevelt's followers, remaining aware at all times that the support of the Wilson administration was essential if the training camps were to succeed. On the Harvard Corporation he took a special interest in matters of academic freedom, and he hobnobbed with faculty as well as wealthy alumni. He startled conservative lawyer friends by organizing the Bill of Rights Committee of the American Bar Association in 1938, even more so by arguing that civil rights was as much a conservative cause as a radical or liberal one. This willingness to take unorthodox positions led Clark to associations that went far beyond Harvard or Wall Street, and only rarely did it cost him old friends.

His aversion for public office was another quality unique to Clark. In his long public career, from local politics in New York before his marriage to world federalist activities in the 1960s, he held only one official position—that of lieutenant colonel in the adjutant general's office during World War I. It might have been otherwise. There was a move afoot in 1929 to make Clark U.S. attorney for the Southern District of New York, a position his law partner Emory Buckner had held and one which Clark would have accepted. Political complications prevented President Hoover from making the appointment, however, and two years later when Henry L. Stimson offered him the position of assistant secretary of state, Clark declined because he had only recently joined the

Harvard Corporation and he wanted to spend more time with his family. He declined several lesser appointments when Franklin Roosevelt was president. And so the pattern developed. Had Clark accepted public office, he might have acquired a reputation comparable to Stimson or Elihu Root. But he did not. His decision to perform public service in a private capacity meant that he would have to work through others. He had to persuade private citizens to work with him—lawyers who opposed the court-packing scheme in 1937, ex-Plattsburgers who favored selective service in 1940, advocates of "limited world government" in 1945. He had to persuade men in public office to support his goals from within. And persuade these men Clark did, usually with a grace and personal touch that turned these political associations into genuine personal friendships. This volume of sketches testifies to his effectiveness.

Who were Clark's friends?

It would be a mistake to assume that his friendships were limited to public and professional associations. He was too old-fashioned and too gregarious for such narrowness. Several of his closest friends dating back to college days played little part in his public activities (except for Plattsburg). There was a small group of the Harvard Class of 1903, which included Delancey Jay, Philip Carroll, Richard Derby, and "Del" Ames, that dined without fail once a year on the eve of commencement. Neither a Supreme Court justice nor the president of the United States could intrude upon this yearly occasion. There was also Theodore Lyman, a Harvard professor and Clark's companion on several hunting trips in the Rockies, both before and after his marriage. Dr. Andrew Foord became a close friend of the entire Clark family after their year's stay at Kerhonkson in the Catskills in 1926. Edward M. Day, a Hartford lawyer and fellow patient at Kerhonkson, also became a lifelong friend. It was Day's suggestion that the Clarks buy stock in Aetna Insurance that led to an investment in Mrs. Clark's name which subsequently formed the basis of the Clark bequest of $500,000 to the NAACP Legal Defense Fund and $750,000 to the World Law Fund. And in what may have been a pattern of forming close friendships when he became ill, Clark acquired another good friend in Benjamin H. Long of Detroit while recuperating in Tucson in early 1942.

Membership on the Harvard Corporation brought numerous

friendships. Faculty friends like Ralph Barton Perry, Zechariah Chafee, Samuel Eliot Morison, and Alfred North Whitehead were particular favorites. Clark also came to know Robert Frost during these years, partly the result of helping the poet obtain a teaching position at Harvard during World War II. The stories are legend about Frost's visits to Dublin and his ability to talk nonstop into the late hours of the night. Among his colleagues on the Corporation, Clark became especially friendly with William L. Marbury, Henry James, and Henry L. Shattuck. His work in raising endowment for the divinity school resulted in close ties with Reinhold Niebuhr and John Lord O'Brian. Even beyond Cambridge, Clark's association with Harvard led to friendships with officers of other universities: Robert Hutchins of Chicago, James Phinney Baxter of Williams, Ernest Hopkins of Dartmouth, Kingman Brewster of Yale, Harold Dodds of Princeton, and John Dickey of Dartmouth. One of Clark's proudest moments was his honorary degree at Dartmouth in June 1953, a commencement which saw John McCloy and Dwight D. Eisenhower also receive honorary degrees, with Eisenhower making a ringing speech against those who would burn books—an obvious reference to Senator McCarthy. One suspects that Clark and Dickey may have reminisced about that occasion some subsequent autumn in a duck-blind on Lake Champlain.

The most interesting of his Harvard friendships was with James B. Conant. They first met in the winter of 1933 when Clark, in the course of interviewing candidates for the Harvard presidency, called upon the congenial professor of chemistry. Conant was not Clark's first choice for the position, nor did they always agree on university policy during the twenty years of Conant's incumbency, but Clark developed enormous respect for the man. Together, they set and maintained a standard of academic freedom that has lasted through these contemporary times of confrontation politics. Jim and Patty Conant became frequent guests at Dublin, and it was during one of their visits in September 1939 that Conant first encouraged Clark to write up his ideas on world government. And it was Clark who persuaded Conant to abandon his politically neutral role in 1940 to speak out in favor of selective service and other efforts to aid the Allies. The Ober correspondence in 1949 marked a high point in their relationship. Unfortunately, as Clark approached retirement from the Corporation and Conant neared the end of his presidency, two disagreements occurred—over raising money for a revitalized divinity school, and the Arnold Arboretum controversy. The divinity school matter did not affect their friendship, but the Arboretum affair did. The last time they met was at the Harvard commencement in 1953, shortly after Clark and his friends brought suit against Harvard for violation of a trust. Conant observed that such action was "dirty pool." Clark respectfully disagreed. It was not a bitter parting of the ways, and there followed occasional cordial letters about world peace and civil rights. Nevertheless, in the case of Clark and Conant, the Arboretum controversy ended a friendship. This was a tragedy for both men.

The practice of law produced even more friends than Harvard. The number of excellent essays in this volume make it unnecessary to dwell at length on these legal associations. Except for Elihu Root, Jr. Amateur painter, yachtsman, fellow Plattsburger, "Sec" Root throughout the years was closer to Clark than any other lawyer. Even more than Emory Buckner, who was a close second, Clark admired his diminutive partner. Contrary to some stories, it is a fact that when the Corporation was deliberating over the choice of a successor to A. Lawrence Lowell as Harvard president in 1933, the name that Clark kept pushing forward was that of "Sec" Root. He respected Root as a lawyer, and their military collaboration in two world wars cemented the relationship. When Clark joined Root as counsel to the Cleary, Gottlieb firm in 1954, their association was natural and fitting. The fact that Root did not take part in Clark's civil rights or peace activities did not lessen their personal friendship. Clark found it easy to let his hair down with Root, to sit around and "gas," as he put it, at the Dublin farm or in the office. They rarely wrote to one another, saving their news for face-to-face talks or phone calls. When Martin Mayer published his biography of Emory Buckner in 1968, he quite appropriately dedicated the book to the memories of Grenville Clark and Elihu Root, Jr.

Clark's first important public activity came in 1915 with the Plattsburg movement, and his collaboration with General Leonard Wood set a pattern for later activities. Although Clark genuinely liked the flamboyant ex–Rough Rider who focused national attention on the training camps, he did not always agree with Wood. In fact, it could be argued that Clark used Wood, letting the general attract crowds and controversy, while he planned the strategy and perfected the organization that culminated in success. On several occasions the two men exchanged heated words, with Clark generally disapproving of Wood's excessive partisanship. Once, in the spring of 1916, he walked out on the general for refusing to deal with the Wilson administration, and for several months he communicated with Wood only through intermediaries. Nevertheless, Clark, Delancey Jay, and the other young Plattsburgers applauded Wood's zeal, accepted his philosophy of a citizen's military obligation in wartime, and rarely challenged his leadership. Wood, denied any opportunity to command troops during World War I and thwarted in his quest for the Republican presidential nomination in 1920, came to regard the Plattsburg movement as his most important achievement. "Your views have been sound throughout," he grudgingly told Clark after the war. Despite his admiration for the prickly general, however, Clark was probably relieved when Wood became governor general of the Philippines in 1921. By then he had become good friends with another military collaborator, Colonel John McAuley Palmer, a leading Army intellectual whose views on military reform were similar to Wood's but whose personality was far more congenial. Palmer, who owned a small farm in New Hampshire not too far from Dublin, cooperated fully with the Plattsburgers both after World War I and during the campaign for selective service in 1940. As advocates of a citizen army, Clark and Palmer were more fitting symbols than the headstrong and politically ambitious Wood.

Charles C. Burlingham, who lived to be 100, also influenced Clark. One of the older patriarchs of the New York bar (along with Henry L. Stimson, Samuel Seabury, and John W. Davis), Burlingham looked upon Clark as a recapitulation of himself a generation younger—that is, the conservative and respected private lawyer who fought political corruption, upheld civil rights, and displayed an overwhelming devotion to maintaining a talented and independent judiciary. As late as 1951, then blind and infirm, "CCB" was writing letters to Dean Acheson and other Washington friends, hoping to obtain official support of a proposed trip by Clark to Moscow for private discussions with Premier Stalin. Their most important collaboration, however, occurred in 1937 when they served as co-chairmen of the lawyers' committee that opposed President Roosevelt's court-packing scheme. For both men, the objective was to protect the independence of the judiciary, notwithstanding their own support of the New Deal and their disagreement with some of the Supreme Court's recent decisions. Both men had voted for FDR in 1936, and they made it a requirement that anyone who joined their committee had to have cast a similar ballot. This studied nonpartisanship, combined with Burlingham's prestige and Clark's organizational talents, made the National Committee for Independent Courts perhaps the most formidable adversary that the Roosevelt administration had to face in 1937. It was characteristic too that once the fight had been won, both Burlingham and Clark managed to retain a cordial personal relationship with President Roosevelt. Clark never regretted his actions in 1937, even if it foreclosed any possibility that he might be named to the Supreme Court. And he always regarded Burlingham as one of the four or five greatest lawyers of his acquaintance.

Another older associate of large influence was General John J. Pershing. While Clark never knew Pershing as well as he did General Wood, or even General Marshall, he nonetheless made use of him. When the National Economy League needed prestigious national directors for its campaign to reduce veterans' benefits in the federal budget, Clark persuaded Pershing through his old Plattsburg contacts to add his name to such other notables as Herbert Hoover, Calvin Coolidge, Newton D. Baker, and Richard Byrd. Pershing's most important contribution, however, came in 1940. It was early July. Hearings on the Burke-Wadsworth Selective Service Bill had just begun, but no one in official position, from the chief of staff to the lowliest lieutenant, was willing to testify. The National Emergency Committee needed someone to capture headlines. So Clark dispatched John McAuley Palmer to the Walter Reed Hospital to request Pershing, then 80 and ill, to make a statement favorable to the draft. Palmer even offered to write something suitable. "I compose my own statements," the General of the Armies gruffly replied. Pershing's stated opinion that with selective service in 1914 "we could have ended the war earlier" received nationwide publicity, thus giving the campaign for the draft a momentum that it never lost.

Perhaps Clark's two most famous friends in high office were

Felix Frankfurter and Franklin D. Roosevelt. Moreover, his relationship with both men proved especially important in 1940 because it led to the appointment of Henry L. Stimson as secretary of war. Clark's acquaintance with Roosevelt dated back to boyhood in New York, and then at Harvard, where Roosevelt was a year behind him. They became fellow clerks in the Carter, Ledyard and Milburn firm in 1907, and historians still recount Clark's story about how FDR, in his disarming way, at that early date predicted his subsequent rise through New York politics to Washington and ultimately to the White House. The Plattsburg movement brought them closer together prior to World War I, as FDR, then assistant secretary of the navy, instituted summer training cruises on board battleships as the navy's counterpart to military training camps. When Roosevelt became president, Clark supported most of his New Deal measures (except the court-packing plan) and even helped draft the Economy Act of 1933. Roosevelt appreciated Clark's support. There remains a symbolic photograph of their relationship of these years—both men in formal attire sitting apart from the rest of the crowd, in the rain, at the ceremonies commemorating Harvard's 300th anniversary in 1936. Clark did not represent the majority of Harvard men (his membership on the Corporation notwithstanding) when he voted for FDR in 1936.

His relationship with Frankfurter took a different path. They were classmates at the Harvard Law School, but hardly intimates. And they used to drink beer and eat pretzels together as young lawyers in New York. Frankfurter, a bachelor on the prowl in those days, later admitted to Emory Buckner that he had a "boulevard crush" on Fanny Dwight before she became Mrs. Clark. Nevertheless, despite their old ties and wartime service together in Washington in 1917–1918, Frankfurter developed a much closer friendship with the jovial Emory Buckner than he did with Clark. Not until the 1930s, when Clark joined the Harvard Corporation and defended Frankfurter against President Lowell and others who criticized him for his frequent trips to Washington, did the two men begin to grow closer. Clark always tried to keep abreast of Cambridge affairs while on the Corporation, and the lively and intellectual Professor Frankfurter proved to be the perfect academic gossip. Moreover, many of Frankfurter's prize students had joined the Root, Clark firm and then gone into government service in Washington. And so the ties grew. Frankfurter, of course, served as a close adviser to President Roosevelt in these years, sending many law graduates into New Deal positions. It was a contemporary witticism that the most direct route to Washington after 1933 was to go to Harvard Law School and then turn left. Frankfurter, despite some misgivings, did not join Clark in opposing the court-packing plan, behavior which resulted in his being named to the Supreme Court by Roosevelt in 1939. The stage was set for 1940 and the Stimson appointment.

Clark's main objective in 1940, it should be remembered, was to obtain a selective service law. The secretary of war at the time, Harry H. Woodring, was an isolationist and opposed to such legislation. The solution was simple: get a new secretary of war. This meant working through Frankfurter and Roosevelt. With FDR, however, there remained a residue of resentment because of Clark's opposition to the Court plan. So Clark went to Frankfurter. They bandied names about and came up with Stimson's. Both had known the old statesman for more than thirty years, Frankfurter having first been drawn into public service under Stimson's auspices back in 1906. Clark knew and admired Stimson from Plattsburg days, and from their mutual association with old Senator Root. The choice seemed perfect, except for Stimson's age—he was seventy-three. Clark and Frankfurter then hit on the idea of a younger man as Stimson's assistant, someone who could relieve him of the more routine duties of office. A further canvass of names resulted in the selection of Judge Robert P. Patterson, a former Plattsburger and associate in Clark's law firm. Frankfurter then took it upon himself to suggest the ticket to President Roosevelt, whose eyes lit up when Stimson's name was mentioned. For two weeks there was silence. Then, on June 19, 1940, just as Clark and other ex-Plattsburgers were in Washington trying to find sponsors for their selective service bill, Roosevelt announced the selection of Frank Knox and Stimson as secretary of the navy and secretary of war, respectively. It was one of FDR's boldest moves in the months before Pearl Harbor, an appointment which had immediate and favorable impact on the selective service campaign, as well as important effects on the World War that followed. Frankfurter later told Clark that their little "conspiracy" was an "interesting illustration of Cleopatra's nose—the factor of contingency in history. If anyone were to tell me that it would have made no difference if FDR had appointed (Fiorello) La Guardia as secretary of war, as he so strongly contemplated doing, he might equally well tell me that 2 and 2 make 7."

An interesting footnote to this episode occurred in the 1950s, some years after Justice Frankfurter had told the story of 1940 to Samuel R. Spencer when he was helping Clark write his memoirs. The memoirs, as such, were never written, but they served as the basis for Spencer's doctoral dissertation, completed at Harvard in 1951 and thereafter available to scholars at the Widener Library. Frankfurter asked to see the chapter on Stimson's appointment, only to be shocked at his own candor in telling the story so completely to Spencer. He worried that people might misconstrue his relationship with Roosevelt, that perhaps his advice with respect to an executive appointment might be regarded as violating the doctrine of separation of powers. He wondered where Spencer's notes of their interview could be found. Spencer did not know the location of the notes. Clark could not find them either. At least twice a year for several years Frankfurter brought the matter up in letters to Clark. Then the justice forgot about it. Spencer's notes, appropriately enough, were later discovered in the Clark papers, and they are now in the Dartmouth Library.

Clark's relationship to Frankfurter and Roosevelt did not cease in 1940. In some respect the years 1940–1945 provided Clark with his greatest opportunity to influence national affairs. His success with the selective service campaign, his personal friendship with the president, and his close working relationship with Secretary Stimson provided him with greater leverage than he had had before or after. Yet what success he achieved during those years was limited, and he placed much of the blame on President Roosevelt. Clark's goals were threefold: a forthright interventionist policy against Hitler prior to Pearl Harbor; National War Service legislation to mobilize the home front during the war; and, after 1944, American participation in an international organization truly capable of preserving the peace. Each of these goals he urged upon Roosevelt, working in his usual fashion through Stimson, influential Congressmen, and citizen groups, and in each instance the president, despite assurances that he agreed with the objectives, failed to exert the power necessary to achieve them. So Clark became disappointed in Roosevelt the president, notwithstanding a real fondness for the man. To Clark, who always acted on principle, Roosevelt seemed to compromise too easily, to be more fox than lion. While such a judgment might underestimate the obstacles Roosevelt faced during World War II, it is one which more and more historians are coming to accept.

Although they remained close personal friends, Clark also had his moments of disenchantment with Justice Frankfurter after 1940. Their point of contention was usually civil rights. Clark was particularly upset at Frankfurter's decision in the Gobitis case, where the Supreme Court in 1940 upheld the Pennsylvania law requiring Jehovah's Witnesses to salute the flag in school. This was a case where Clark's Bill of Rights Committee had intervened as *amicus curiae*, and it pleased him when the Court overruled its own decision a few years later in the Barnette case. Clark always attributed Frankfurter's opinion in Gobitis to the atmosphere of national patriotism that engulfed the country (and the Court) after the fall of France. That Frankfurter spoke for the Supreme Court in 1960 in its refusal to review the case of Willard Uphaus also disappointed Clark. Nevertheless, despite these legal differences, neither man would let it mar their friendship. Always a welcome visitor in Dublin, Frankfurter would invariably greet members of the Clark family with a hearty kiss, be it at a Harvard commencement or in the Supreme Court dining room. The bespectacled jurist encouraged Clark in his peace work after 1945, and he was as voluble as Clark was self-effacing in praising his public activities. "He is that rare thing in America," Frankfurter described Clark in 1952, "a man of independence, financially and politically, who devotes himself as hard to public affairs as a private citizen as he would were he in public office." And Clark, after illness forced Frankfurter to retire from the Supreme Court in the early 1960s, quietly arranged through John M. Harlan to make certain that neither Frankfurter nor his wife Marion would have to worry about money for medical bills.

Clark's relationship with Secretary Stimson after 1940 was also rewarding. Still avoiding public office, he continued to give Stimson advice on such matters as officer training and national service throughout the war. He came to admire Stimson more than any other public official, and it is easy to understand why. Scrupulously honest, blunt, and nonpolitical, the secretary of war stood in direct contrast to FDR, who equivocated on issues which Clark and Stimson deemed vital. It was a great disappointment to Clark that the president, despite Stimson's constant prodding, did not strongly endorse national service until January 1945, by which time the war was nearly over. Clark and Stimson agreed on war aims, and they agreed on peace aims. Even in the middle of the war, when the killing of hundreds of thousands remained the army's highest priority, Stimson and Clark talked about the peace. Stimson's order to Clark to "go home and prevent World War III" was in direct accord with his later advice to President Truman to share the atomic secret with Russia after the war. Stimson's 1945 statement "The only way to make a man trustworthy is to trust him" was something Clark would say. It should be noted, however, that Clark did not have the same high regard for Stimson's closest adviser during the war, General Marshall. The two men had disagreed over selective service in 1940, and later they clashed over officer training and whether or not Marshall should make a strong statement in behalf of national service. The differences were not acrimonious, but they lingered into the postwar era. Stimson remained Clark's favorite. After the war he made many visits to Highhold, Stimson's Long Island estate, and he secured for Stimson a special doctor who eased his suffering from arthritis. Stimson died in 1950.

When Clark ceased his military efforts in 1944–1945 and began to concentrate on world peace, many of his associates saw the change as radical and inconsistent. Old Plattsburgers such as Kenneth Budd and "Archie" Thacher got crotchety and wondered why Grenny would oppose selective service in peacetime. Even Henry L. Stimson, who had urged him to "go home and prevent World War III," refused to become honorary president of the United World Federalists because such an action would be taken as a repudiation of General Marshall, Robert Lovett, Robert Patterson, and other wartime colleagues. Not even Howard C. Petersen, Clark's closest confidant in wartime Washington, would take part in federalist activities.

But the changeover from war to peace did not seem radical to Clark, nor did his style change. Some old associates, most notably

Douglas Arant, joined the federalist movement without hesitation. The new quest brought Clark new friends and colleagues: young men like Cord Meyer, Alan Cranston, Charles Bolté, and Norman Cousins; older men like Robert Bass, Thomas Mahony, William Holliday, and Fritz von Windegger. Clark neither altered his approach nor broke off old friendships. Warren Austin, with whom he had worked so closely for a National Service Act, he bombarded with letters and phone calls, hoping to persuade the U.N. ambassador that charter revision and disarmament were both feasible and necessary. He kept in touch (without much appreciable effect) with General Marshall and Dean Acheson. And surprisingly, he found a sympathetic ear in John Foster Dulles, that Cold Warrior of Cold Warriors. Dulles and Clark had worked together in Clarence Streit's "Union Now" movement prior to Pearl Harbor, and while Dulles became profoundly suspicious of the Soviet Union after 1945, he always shared Clark's ultimate goal of world peace under world law. Dulles had been impressed with *A Plan for Peace*. When the Ford Foundation in 1954 was considering a broad program of publicity for Clark's disarmament proposals, Dulles, then secretary of state, wrote a very strong letter to the Ford trustees to the effect that such efforts would not contradict the official government policy of "negotiating from strength." It was a private letter, written during the height of the Indochina crisis, and notwithstanding Ford's negative decision, Clark greatly appreciated "Foster's" help. Of course, he thought Dulles something of a hypocrite for not urging publicly what he advocated privately. Thus did he criticize all public officials.

Throughout the period after 1945 Clark became acquainted with well-known personalities who could further his causes, men who were not as close to power as Stimson or FDR, but influential nonetheless. There was Adlai Stevenson, whom Clark had known slightly in the 1930s in connection with the Bill of Rights Committee. Stevenson cheerfully agreed to take copies of *World Peace through World Law* to Moscow in 1958 and present one personally to Nikita Khrushchev. This association led to a fruitful correspondence and numerous phone calls when Stevenson became ambassador to the United Nations in 1961. An even more important friend during the Kennedy years was John J. McCloy, whose memories of Grenny dated back to the rifle ranges at

Plattsburg. As President Kennedy's chief adviser on disarmament, and a strong believer in Clark's ultimate goal of peace through law, the twinkle-eyed McCloy kept Clark fully informed of the complicated negotiations that led to the McCloy-Zorin agreement in 1961 and the Test Ban treaty of 1963. He also served as a conduit during emergencies, as Clark's telephone bill during the Cuban missile crisis can attest.

There were others during these years. Clark's two favorite senators after 1945 were Ralph Flanders of Vermont and his distant cousin Joe Clark of Pennsylvania. Both senators took a particular interest in matters of peace and disarmament, always providing the latest Washington information, and both men were frequent visitors to Dublin in the summer. Flanders' courageous stand against Joe McCarthy in 1954 was especially pleasing. A Dublin neighbor, Fredrick Eaton, became the ranking disarmament negotiator during the last years of the Eisenhower administration, and he too served as a conduit for Clark's ideas. And even if Clark did not know the people in power, he would write anyway. Or phone. Assistant Attorney General Nicholas Katzenbach probably never received a phone call as urgent or as angry as the one he received from Clark during the Selma riots in 1965.

Clark's peace work led to contact with several world leaders. One of the first was Lord Tweedsmuir, governor general of Canada, who gave Clark badly needed encouragement in 1939 when he wrote his first essay on world government, *A Federation of Free Peoples*. He particularly appreciated Tweedsmuir's response, for, as John Buchan, Tweedsmuir had been Clark's favorite mystery writer. Carlos P. Romulo became a particular favorite in 1945–1947 when Clark and Alan Cranston persuaded the Philippines ambassador to make several speeches urging reform of the United Nations Charter. Clark met Jawaharlal Nehru in 1949, was immediately impressed, and corresponded with him over the years in the hope of eliciting from the Indian prime minister a bold statement in behalf of disarmament and limited world government. Nehru never made such a statement, but the hour audience he gave to Clark and his wife in Delhi in 1956 remained an indelible memory for both. There were also contacts with the Vatican, and Clark played no minor part in the complex negotiations that led to Pope Paul's visit to the United States in 1965.

Probably the world statesman whose friendship Clark cultivated most successfully was Clement Attlee. Unfortunately Clark did not become acquainted with the former British prime minister until 1959, at a point when Attlee's leadership of the Labour party had passed into younger hands. A recent convert to world federalism, Attlee was on a lecture tour when he and Clark met. The two men, both the same age, hit it off immediately. Attlee paid a visit to Dublin, and the friendship grew. Then Clark began to plot. If Attlee could undertake another lecture tour in the spring of 1961, then Clark would arrange an interview with President Kennedy through the auspices of Joe Clark and John McCloy. Attlee could emphasize to the young president that nothing less than complete and universal disarmament could put an end to the Cold War. The desired interview took place, but Kennedy had his famous meeting with Khrushchev in Vienna shortly thereafter, and any spectacular move toward disarmament died aborning. Three years later Clark visited England. Through his connection with Attlee an interview with Prime Minister Harold Wilson was arranged, and Clark so impressed the British leader that he was asked to draw up a detailed proposal for disarmament that Wilson might put forward at the Commonwealth Conference of Prime Ministers in the summer of 1965. Clark drew up the proposal, but Wilson never acted. The problem of Rhodesia intervened, the Vietnam war grew hotter, and the opportunity passed. Clark nonetheless valued his friendship with Attlee, and he never ceased to laugh over the inaccuracy of Churchill's famous quip about his Labour rival: "He was a modest man with much to be modest about."

As Clark grew older, his activities involved him with persons of a more radical reputation. Norman Thomas and Henry Wallace, neither of whom Clark had ever voted for, became his associates in numerous peace and civil rights efforts. In 1949 the lawyers for the Hollywood Ten, screenwriters who were being blacklisted for alleged Communist sympathies, asked Clark to come out of retirement and head their defense. Clark declined, but he suggested other lawyers and he continued to offer advice. And there was his celebrated effort in behalf of Dr. Willard Uphaus, the silver-haired Christian pacifist whose summer camp in Conway, New Hampshire, had horrified the sensibilities of the state's attorney general in his investigation of subversive activities. Uphaus had respectfully refused to produce the names of guests who had stayed at his camp, only to be jailed in 1959 for contempt of court. Uphaus was languishing in the Boscawen jail when Clark decided to enter the case. Along with Robert Reno and Louis Lusky, he set out on the nearly impossible task of persuading the Supreme Court to reverse itself on a case it had already decided. The Court would not reconsider, but Justice Hugo Black was so impressed by their petition that he delivered a long and moving dissent, possibly Black's most eloquent statement in behalf of free speech. Shortly thereafter, partly due to Clark's efforts, the judge who had sentenced Uphaus released him. If any doubt remained about Clark's fraternization with radicals, the subsequent denunciations in the Manchester *Union-Leader* would punctuate that charge. Clark would only chuckle. He loved being an enemy of publisher William Loeb.

Another such friend was Edgar Snow. Never really a radical, Snow had shot to fame in the 1930s as the journalist who had "opened" Red China to the world. He had slipped through the Kuomintang blockade in 1937, traveled freely through the Communist stronghold in Yenan, became friends with Chou En-lai, Mao Tse-tung, and other Communist leaders, and wrote the classic account of the Communist revolution, *Red Star over China*. While never a Marxist, or even a fellow traveler, Snow was undeniably sympathetic to the Chinese Communists, an attitude that was often misunderstood in the United States during the era of Joe McCarthy and John Foster Dulles. It was not until 1963 that Snow and Clark became friends. Snow was living in Switzerland then, something of an exile. Clark had come to the conclusion in his study of disarmament prospects that it was sheer folly to proceed without including Communist China. Previously, he and Louis Sohn had operated on the assumption that if the United States and the Soviet Union could agree on disarmament, the Russians could persuade Peking. The growing Sino-Soviet split altered this reasoning, as did Clark's increasing disenchantment with official American policy toward Communist China. Thus, when Clark's good friend and doctor, Paul Dudley White, received an invitation to visit China from an eminent Chinese heart specialist he had met in Moscow, Clark decided to seek the advice of the most prominent American expert on China. He called Edgar Snow long-distance in Geneva. Snow was not at home, but an increasingly friendly correspondence followed. Clark wanted to know the best way to get around passport and visa difficulties. Snow gave him advice. Snow wrote letters to Chinese leaders, Mao Tse-tung included. He talked with Chinese officials in Switzerland. Clark and White worked through Averell Harriman, then assistant secretary of state for the Far East, and Harriman agreed to waive passport regulations if the Peking government would issue an official visa. Negotiations continued for two years; then in January 1965 the United States began the full-scale bombing of North Vietnam, and any chance that American citizens might travel in China was lost. It took six more years before ping pong balls broke the diplomatic logjam. Appropriately enough, the first American medical delegation to visit the People's Republic of China in 1971 was headed by Dr. White and Dr. E. Grey Dimond, and it was Edgar Snow who helped make the arrangements. Clark's daughter Mary made the trip and distributed copies of *World Peace through World Law*.

Another "typical" friend throughout the years was the young associate who would serve as Clark's eyes, ears, and legs during important public activities. Lloyd Derby, a young associate in the Root, Clark firm, played this role during the Plattsburg movement, always taking the train to Washington, buttonholing generals and senators, keeping track of votes. Alphonse Laporte performed a similar function for the National Economy League, as did Cloyd Laporte during the court fight. The elder Laporte still recalls with relish the telegram he sent to "G.C." in July 1937 when Senator Robinson died of a heart attack, thus ending Roosevelt's attempt to pass a bill. "FINISH TRIP," he wired Clark, then halfway through a North Cape cruise with his family. "COURT-PACKING KILLED FOR THIS SESSION." Howard Petersen, William Stewart, and Franklin Canfield were three young lawyers who did yeoman work for the National Emergency Committee in 1940. Petersen, who subsequently became an assistant secretary of war during the Truman administration, grew particularly close to Clark, even to the point of asking him to be godfather to his son, a duty which Clark, a Unitarian, assumed with grave dignity. Much later, when Petersen's son died under tragic circumstances after a long and suffering hospitalization,

Clark insisted on paying part of the medical expenses, as if to show Petersen that he grieved as much as the real father. Clark, for his part, came to respect Petersen as much as he did any younger colleague, and he always consulted him on important issues, notwithstanding the younger man's skepticism about disarmament and world government.

The pattern with younger colleagues continued. Portly Ernest "Doc" Bell, a jovial young attorney from Keene, New Hampshire, took over as Clark's factotum in the campaign for a national service law during World War II. Since Clark was under doctor's orders not to travel much during these years, Bell carried messages to James Wadsworth, Secretary Stimson, and President Roosevelt. Bell also served after World War II as counsel to Clark's citizens' committee to preserve Mount Monadnock. During the protracted litigation over the Arnold Arboretum, it was such younger lawyers as Tom Rankin and Endicott "Chub" Peabody who did most of the organizational spadework, while older lawyers like Joseph Welch, "Mike" Farley, and Robert Dodge also contributed their legal talents. Sam Spencer was another young friend of this period. Recruited by Clark from the Harvard history department to help with his memoirs, Spencer quickly found himself involved in Clark's peace activities, particularly in 1948 when Clark thought World War III a distinct possibility unless the Truman administration made greater efforts to negotiate with Russia. Even closer to Clark at this time were Alan Cranston and Cord Meyer, two young war veterans whose commitment to world government equaled his own. A few years later, during the McCarthy period, Meyer drifted away from the federalist movement and joined the CIA. Clark was disappointed, but their mutual respect never cooled. And Cranston, who became a United States senator from California after Clark's death, has suggested that he learned very well the central lesson of Grenville Clark's life, namely, that one can accomplish a great deal by avoiding personal credit and working through others.

Clark had a special fondness for Douglas Arant. After DeLancey Jay died in 1941, Clark probably regarded the courtly Alabama lawyer as his closest friend. They first became acquainted in 1937, when Arant, some twenty years younger than Clark, took an active part in the court fight. Clark was so impressed with his abilities that he put Arant's name first when selecting the American Bar Association Bill of Rights Committee in 1938. Arant succeeded Clark as chairman of that committee two years later. The Alabaman's influence with important Southern congressmen proved helpful in 1940 during the selective service campaign, as Arant spent countless hours in Clark's suite at the Hotel Carlton drafting amendments, making phone calls, planning strategy. Arant also served during the war as chairman of the Citizens' Committee for a National War Service Act. Although he became a world federalist and attended the two Dublin Conferences, Arant always felt disappointment that his Birmingham law practice prevented him from working more closely with Clark after 1945. Even so, they kept in constant touch through correspondence, numerous long-distance phone calls, and occasional visits. Not too long before Clark's death, Arant attempted one last collaboration—that of arranging an interview between Clark and President Johnson. He had once done some legal work for Mrs. Johnson in the 1930s, earning money which eventually went into her Austin radio station, and President Johnson always referred to Arant as "Lady Bird's lawyer." Clark, always hopeful that he could convince any reasonable person if given the chance, encouraged Arant's effort, as well as another by Senator Joe Clark, to arrange an audience. Unfortunately, the meeting never took place. Although one doubts that Clark could have affected the Vietnam war, it would provide a significant historical footnote to know what the author of *World Peace through World Law* might have said to Lyndon Johnson.

Louis Lusky was another young favorite. Having joined the Root, Clark firm in the 1930s after clerking for Justice Stone, Lusky proved indispensable to Clark and "Zech" Chafee in 1938 when they drew up the first briefs for the ABA committee in the Hague case. Indeed, Lusky became Clark's chief authority on civil rights. Much later, after establishing a successful practice in Louisville, where he argued the celebrated case of "Shuffling Sam" Thompson before the supreme court, he served as Clark's legal eyes and ears in the Uphaus case and on "watching briefs" during the Freedom Ride litigations in Alabama and Mississippi. Lusky stirred the older man's conscience with his reports from the South. They planned a book together, to be tentatively titled "Unequal

Justice under Law," and had Clark lived longer, the book might have ranked next to *World Peace through World Law* as a legal blueprint. In a letter written not too long before his death, Clark described a dream to Lusky, how he was running a long race but soon ran out of wind and had to stagger toward the finish line, only to find that Lusky had won the race. Perhaps this was his way of passing the torch to another generation.

Two younger men to whom he passed the torch were Robert Reno and Harry Hollins. Reno, a quiet Concord lawyer who graduated from that "other" law school (as he liked to joke to Mr. Clark), Yale, took on the duties of Clark's research associate in the early 1950s, forming part of the triumvirate (along with Ruth Wight and Louis Sohn) that produced *World Peace through World Law*. Reno also was co-counsel in the Uphaus case, and because of his proximity to Dublin he became attorney for the Clark family as well. Clark had complete trust in Reno, even to the point of telling friends that they had identical views, and so Reno became more than the older man's eyes and legs and sometimes acted as an alter ego. Hollins, who had married Betsy Jay, the daughter of his oldest friend, became the repository of Clark's hopes concerning world peace. Always an optimist about the ability of humans to find ways to survive, Clark nonetheless recognized the gap between his goal of world peace under world law and the existing system of national rivalries. Perhaps a crisis, like Cuba in 1962, would show statesmen that radical change was both possible and necessary. Maybe the bombs would have to fall. The only sensible course was to begin a program of education, to do as much as possible to bridge the chasm between the real and the ideal. Hence, Harry Hollins and the World Law Fund, which Hollins describes in his essay. Despite the tendency of historians and political scientists to view institutional change as slow and incremental, one might suggest that the revolution in communications and technology, the growing expense of armaments, and the current ecological crisis have converged to make radical change possible. Clark used to tell scoffers that no one had heard of airplanes when he was a boy. Why not think about peace and how to achieve world order?

One cannot leave out Louis Sohn, whose essay needs no great elaboration. A generation younger than Clark, the Polish refugee first met his future collaborator in 1944 at a time when Clark was making his crucial transition from war to peace. Sohn brought erudition and indefatigable energy to their joint effort. Even if Sohn was reluctant to call "Mr. Clark" by his first name, they made an excellent team, and it is fitting that a third edition of the introduction to *World Peace through World Law* should appear in 1973.

A word remains as to why Clark abandoned his "anonymous" role late in life and consented to be nominated for the Nobel Peace Prize, an honor (contrary to popular belief) that cannot occur without considerable effort at self-advertisement. Close associates like William Sheehan and Einar Rørstad did most of the proselytizing, but Clark found himself writing self-laudatory letters, the likes of which he had never written before. Why? The answer is again in character—he believed that the Nobel Prize would give greater recognition to the goals in *World Peace through World Law*. It was not for self-glorification, he would say to his friends, nor did he really think the Nobel Committee would select him, but maybe, just maybe, such an effort would further the cause. Surely he was correct. Had he won the Prize, then his example of a private citizen doing public work might have inspired others, just as Martin Luther King's award gave greater impetus to individuals who practiced civil disobedience in the face of public injustice.

No, Grenville Clark need not have been ashamed of seeking the fame and honor of the Nobel Prize. Nor should his friends have any doubts about paying him tribute in this volume. He was a "statesman incognito" whose example should be known to more than those who were his friends.

PART II

Portraits

MEMORIES OF GRENVILLE CLARK

Joseph S. Clark

The branch of the enormous Clark family to which Grenville Clark and I, his younger fifth cousin, belonged was founded by William Clark, who came to this country from England around 1648. William Clark was married and had had three children in New England before he traveled to Northampton, Massachusetts, where he had been offered twelve acres of free land if he would help protect the inhabitants of Northampton from the forays of the Indians.

William Clark had one horse, on which he seated his wife; their two small children rode in panniers on either side of the saddle. William and his son, a youngster of perhaps twelve, walked in front through the wilderness which then lay between the settlements on the eastern coast of Massachusetts and the frontier around Northampton.

Incidentally, and not altogether irrelevant to my story, the twelve acres are now a part of the Smith College campus. Some years ago I went there to lecture to the students and spent the night with President Thomas Mendenhall. I told him of my interest in William Clark, and my intention to go down to the local library shortly after breakfast in order to see what I could find out about him.

President Mendenhall then said to me: "You have just eaten breakfast on part of the twelve acres given to William Clark by

the town of Northampton and subsequently acquired by Smith
College; and what's more, I am your cousin Tom."

William had additional progeny and they, in turn, were very
prolific. Such names as Bohann, Enoch, and many such Old
Testament names predominate in their offspring. Finally, about
1830 there were three Clark brothers who left Northampton.
One of them went to Boston, another to New York, and the third
to Philadelphia. They each formed banking firms and all corresponded and did business with each other for many years to
come.

The Clark name was first to run out in Boston. One of the
distaff side married into the Grew family, hence Joseph Clark
Grew, distinguished statesman and diplomat during a substantial
period earlier in this century. There also is a family of Burnhams
in Boston who are related to the Clarks.

The second branch of the family, from which Grenny descended,
moved to New York. In 1845, the firm of E. W. Clark, Dodge
and Company was organized and established at 60 Wall Street
in New York City, later known as Clark, Dodge and Company,
and members of the Clark family have been with the firm through
the years until its recent absorption by Kidder Peabody and Company in 1974. Before the Civil War the firm, of which the original branch is still located in Philadelphia, had branches in St.
Louis, New Orleans, Boston, Burlington, Iowa, and Springfield,
Illinois. Grenny did not follow in the steps of his father, Louis
Crawford Clark, partner of the firm in his lifetime, however, but
took to the law as his discipline rather than commercial banking.

The third branch of the family, of which I am one, settled in
Philadelphia, where Enoch White Clark formed the original
branch of this family investment banking firm under the name
of E. Walter Clark and Company, in 1837. Jay Cooke, later
known as "the financier of the Civil War," was at one point an
office boy in this firm. It has been alleged the E. W. Clark and
Company substantially financed the Mexican War for the federal
government, and there is some historical evidence to support this
story.

My father, Joseph Sill Clark, was the son of Edward White
Clark, whose father was in turn Enoch White Clark. My father,
like Grenny, took to the law rather than to the family banking

business. Father was a good deal older than Grenny, having graduated from Harvard in the Class of 1883, whereas Grenny was in the Class of 1903. Wherefore, our family relationships are still often confused and the phrase "once removed" necessary to describe them.

The New York, Boston, and Philadelphia Clarks maintained a pleasant acquaintanceship throughout the years without any very real intimacy, although George C. Clark, who was Grenny's uncle, and his wife, Cousin Hattie, were quite close to my father, Joseph S., and his wife, Kate Avery Richardson, by reason of both families spending their summers in Southampton, Long Island, where the Philadelphia Clarks had first gone in 1896. I am sure that in this way my family came to know Grenny, although there was still no very close relationship between the families.

We now move forward to the early 1930s, when E. W. Clark and Company, who were represented by my father as their lawyer, became involved in a controversy with the Chase National Bank over an issue of stock called General Theatres Equipment, Inc. The Chase Bank had formed a syndicate. Marketing of the securities was a complete failure due first to the depression, and, secondly, to a great many misrepresentations for which E. W. Clark and Company blamed the Chase Bank in connection with the status of the General Theatres Equipment, Inc. The venture involved a typical variety of corporate financing engaged in during the late twenties and continued on into the early thirties based on the theory that prosperity would continue forever and that the equipment utilized in movie theaters all over the country would be a valuable source of profit indefinitely.

E. W. Clark and Company, headed by my uncle Clarence and my first cousins, Sewell and Sydney, concluded that they had a cause of action against the Chase Bank for misrepresentation. In order to press this claim it was necessary to have a New York lawyer to supplement the efforts of my father, his partners, and myself. I was then myself a quite young lawyer, having but recently graduated from the Law School in 1926, and still with the family firm before I left it to join contemporaries in another law firm.

We traveled to New York on several occasions to confer with Grenny on the matter. I was taken along for the ride at first but later was to do a good deal of the "spade work" which followed in connection with the preparation of our pleadings against the Chase Bank. Grenny looked kindly on me, and a friendship began which lasted through the years down to the time of his death.

My initial impression of him did not change much throughout the years. He was tall, with a friendly face which nevertheless could become very stern when a point at issue developed. His outstanding physical characteristics were his jutting jaw and the birthmark on the left of his forehead. He had a strong athletic build and close-cropped hair which was very dark brown at the time I first knew him. He was unfailingly courteous. He had a ready wit but was slow to speak and gave a general impression of granite ability and sincerity.

He was never a man of quick mind, rather a plodder than a brilliant inspirational lawyer. Nevertheless, his thinking was always sound. He came to conclusions slowly but, once having reached them, stuck to them with a great tenacity.

He assigned a young man from his law firm, Root, Clark, Buckner, Howland and Ballantine, to assist in the preparation of the very involved and technical complaint which was the basis of our cause of action. This was a competent and able younger lawyer of about my age, and we worked closely together on the job of preparation, which was gone over with infinite pains after we submitted the first draft by both my father and Grenny. I remember being impressed with the fact that Grenny had the complaint printed in galley proof at an early date. We went over the galleys marking out this and inserting that until finally, after months of work and research, its form and content satisfied Grenny and my father.

I had assumed that once the complaint was prepared and the court in which we would file suit was determined, we would go right ahead. However, Grenny had other ideas. He said that he wanted to go to Winthrop Aldrich, a friend of his who was the president of the Chase Bank, and put the proposition to him that his bank had done a grave injustice to E. W. Clark and Company and that he should not be put to the test of suit but should rather make a reasonable settlement on a voluntary basis. We Philadelphia Clarks were very much in favor of Grenny's suggestion because we knew that a long, drawn-out law suit would be of a doubtful result and would certainly end in our incurring very heavy expense even though, in the end, we might receive a substantial recovery.

Grenny set up an appointment with Winthrop Aldrich in the latter's office. I shall never forget his account of the interview, which none of the rest of us attended.

He said, "I sat down across the table from Winthrop and looked him in the eye. 'Winthrop,' I said, 'you and your bank have gravely wronged my clients. I have here a printed complaint in form to be filed tomorrow if necessary in Federal Court in New York.' " He then described how he outlined the basis of the complaint and said, "I think you should, as one gentleman to another, make a settlement of this matter without forcing my clients to go into court, for you and your bank have done them a grave injustice. Will you read the complaint yourself and I will come back at a later date to discuss the matter with you further?"

We were all much impressed with the thought of this man of iron walking into the office of one who was probably the most powerful banker in New York at that time to propose this ultimatum and attack the ethics of the bank.

I do not remember whether there were more meetings between Mr. Aldrich and Grenny but before much time elapsed, the claim of E. W. Clark and Company was satisfactorily settled and payment came from the Chase Bank to the Clark firm of several hundred thousand dollars. My admiration for Grenny as negotiator and lawyer in this instance was absolutely unbounded. It is not too much to say that he became one of my heroes at this early point in my own legal career.

A good many years went by then before I again saw Grenny. I knew, of course, of his work in connection with the founding of the United Nations, the treatises he had written on how to achieve world peace after World War II, and the very active part he took in the foundation of United World Federalists. I was quite remote from this at the time, and it was not until after I was elected to the U.S. Senate from Pennsylvania in the fall of 1956 that Grenny and I again came to be in touch over world peace issues.

I cannot remember precise incidents of the renewal of our old–young man's friendship, but fairly early in my service in the

Senate Grenny interested me in the cause of world peace through world law. Largely through his suggestion I prepared a Planning for Peace resolution which I offered in the U.S. Senate. Grenny helped a great deal with the preparation of the text, which outlined procedures for the United States to follow in order to take a position on behalf of our country in support of world peace through world law. We had several sessions in New York and also in Dublin, New Hampshire, at which we meticulously worked out the wording of this resolution.

When it was in satisfactory form, I circulated it among my colleagues in the Senate for co-sponsorship, obtaining the names of senators who were willing and prepared to be co-authors of the resolution. At one point we secured as many as 25 of the 100 senators in support of the resolution, including John F. Kennedy, then a senator from Massachusetts.

The resolution drew heavily upon *World Peace through World Law*, which was published by Grenny and Professor Louis B. Sohn of the Harvard Law School in 1958. The resolution, however, found no favor with the Foreign Relations Committee, of which I was not then a member. I was unable to persuade the chairman, J. William Fulbright, to hold hearings on it. And so, as a result, it lay dormant within the committee, although reintroduced every two years when a new Congress came along.

Finally, when I became a member of the Foreign Relations Committee, I was able to persuade the members to hold two days of hearings on the resolution. Despite these hearings, the committee never reported out the resolution. There was a great deal of skepticism, particularly among conservative members of the committee of both parties toward the whole concept of general and complete disarmament and the rule of enforceable world law which, of necessity, would have to accompany it. I believe I was considered a good deal of an impractical and starry-eyed idealist for taking the concept seriously.

In 1960, however, when John Foster Dulles was no longer secretary of state and Christian Herter was in that office, he announced that the fixed policy of the United States was to support general and complete disarmament under enforceable world law. I do not know the precise part Grenny played in this decision of Herter's; I do know they were acquainted with each other.

In 1960, John F. Kennedy, who had been a co-sponsor of the Planning for Peace resolution, was elected president of the United States. Unfortunately for our cause, he appointed Dean Rusk as his secretary of state. Rusk had not the slightest interest in either general and complete disarmament or the international institutions which must accompany it to assure that the world law which disarmament would require would be enforceable.

However, Kennedy did appoint John J. McCloy, Grenny's close friend, as his disarmament adviser. And Hubert Humphrey with a group of others in the Senate pushed through the Arms Control and Disarmament Agency Act, which Kennedy, under McCloy's tutelage, had been persuaded to offer to the Congress.

Arthur H. Dean was our representative at that time at the Disarmament Conference in Geneva. McCloy, Dean, and Grenny were all active in attempting to influence Kennedy toward the cause of world peace through world law. Rusk was, at best, neutral and, at worst, adverse. The Joint Chiefs of Staff were naturally in a position of animosity toward anything aiming at an end to the arms race, motivated, no doubt sincerely, by the feeling that "You can't trust the Russians."

I, too, had been working to persuade Kennedy to make some pronouncement which would advance further the Herter statement on general and complete disarmament, the same which, incidentally, Eisenhower, as far as I knew, had never overtly affirmed. However, Eisenhower did on one occasion make the statement that world peace was impossible without world law, carrying with it no doubt the implication that the world law would have to be enforceable. Arthur M. Schlesinger, Jr., who was then in an advisory capacity in the Kennedy White House, was also of considerable help.

Although I do not know just what part Grenny played in all this, it may have been a substantial one. Grenny's views on how world peace through world law could be advanced into the realm of practicality had always been through leadership from the White House. When later he became disabused of the view that either the United States or the Soviet Union would take a strong lead in this regard, he was to turn his thoughts to what other head of state might take it on.

I am positive, however, that in the early sixties, Grenny was exercising his strong influence on both Dean and McCloy to press Kennedy for a declaration of support for world peace through world law by the United States, and that for a time he came to feel a degree of optimism.

I had hoped that when Kennedy came to Independence Hall in Philadelphia on the Fourth of July in 1961 he would make such a statement. I was disappointed, as he did not even refer to the subject. However, he used the occasion to proclaim a declaration of interdependence of all of the nations and a need to put an end to the squabbling between nations in this ominous age of nuclear weapons.

In Kennedy's speeches at the United Nations in 1961, at American University in June of 1963, and again at the United Nations in September of 1963, just before his assassination, his words suggested that Kennedy might have become a convert to the Grenville Clark approach toward achieving world peace. These three speeches (and, I suppose, the interdependence speech, as well) were to me the "high water mark" in this country of the efforts to achieve a limited form of world government, the necessity for which Kennedy perhaps saw would need to be a part of general and complete disarmament. His untimely death put an end to these hopes, which Kennedy's successors have not revived.

During this period and also after the assassination of Kennedy, I saw a good deal of Grenny. I remember one very grand white tie dinner which I attended in New York where there were present many very prominent people, and for the first time I met Grenny's younger daughter, Louisa Spencer, and her husband and other members of the New York branch of the family. This was, however, primarily a social occasion. At other times, sometimes alone and once with my wife, I visited Grenny and Fanny Clark at their Dublin house, and of the wide variety of subjects covered, we had a number of very helpful sessions dealing with the problems of world peace. Again, I remember in particular one night spent in the guest house at Dublin while Fanny was still alive and the delightful dinner and evening the four of us had together.

Later, I would meet with Grenny alone; perhaps, we would have dinner at the Dublin Inn. He was then alone and not well but bravely contending with his lymphatic and throat condition.

He had been told he would have to go very light on alcohol. He could enjoy a cocktail before dinner although this was never a regular ritual with him. On this occasion he said to me he was going to ignore the advice of his physician, and so we had two good cocktails before a delicious meal and good conversation. Afterward, he told me he had felt no ill effects. I hope he was right.

On another occasion he had asked that I come to visit at the Dublin house and to stay over for lunch on the following day. Grenny had as his guests Dr. and Mrs. Paul Dudley White and also two charming young Russians with whom he was interested in talking about world peace. I had been speaking at Harvard University the evening before, and Grenny sent a car to Cambridge to bring me to Dublin in time to spend the night. The next morning was a little difficult with the young Russian guests because their English was rather weak, and so Grenny suggested I take them for a walk on the trails through the woods behind his house. It was the fall of the year, and the change of leaf was absolutely magnificent. I managed quite well with our limited ability to communicate with these very fine young men and I was happy to be able to spend some time with them.

Grenny's second wife, Mary (they were not then affianced), was also at this luncheon. I do not remember much of the conversation except that it was a very happy and gay time.

Later that day, before I left, Grenny told me that one of Fanny's last instructions to him before she died was that he must marry again. She wisely understood and foresaw that his need for solace and companionship would be great after their magnificent marriage of more than fifty years. He then went on to tell me he was thinking of getting married again, emphasizing that which Fanny had said, and asked me what I thought about it. I strongly urged him to get married and said I thought I knew whom he had in mind. He expressed complete surprise when I named Mary Brush James, who had been widowed some years before by William James, the painter. This had really been a guess on my part, but I thought I had noticed from their relations with each other on that day that there was something more between them than mere long-standing friendship.

Grenville Clark was born in New York City in 1882. He died on

January 12, 1967, at Dublin, New Hampshire. He was the architect of the, as yet, unbuilt structure of a world at peace under law. When President James B. Conant of Harvard awarded Grenville Clark an honorary degree some years ago, he referred to him as a "private citizen with the highest sense of duty. Stubborn defender of the rights of man." He was a man of character in the old New England sense of that word.

Grenville Clark was an Establishment man as that phrase is used today by many who do not like the Establishment. He was, however, a rebel within the Establishment, always ready to deviate from its tenets when he thought it wrong. Victorian, Edwardian, he was nonetheless to the day of his death an intensely modern man. His New England conscience impelled him into areas where few would have thought he would have ventured. A Harvard College graduate of the Class of 1903, a member of Phi Beta Kappa, Harvard Law School graduate with the Class of 1906, he was a friend and contemporary of Franklin Delano Roosevelt. In fact, he knew most of the great men of his time, going back to an interesting experience as a lad with Theodore Roosevelt on the occasion of President McKinley having been shot in Buffalo. Grenville Clark was with Vice President Roosevelt when the word came to him.

A Wall Street lawyer, he formed shortly after graduating from law school, the firm of Root, Clark and Bird, Root being Elihu Root, Jr., whose distinguished father served as counsel to the young firm. He was a big man, rugged, tough, wise, and gentle, with a great gift for friendship. He had incredible personal charm, largely through his simplicity. Again, his mind was sound, if not quick, penetrating and deliberate. Possessed of imagination and foresight, he was slow to decision; but when he came to it, he held to his ideas and acted on them.

A loyal son of Harvard, he served with distinction as a fellow of Harvard University, one of the small self-perpetuating oligarchy, the Harvard Corporation, which owns and governs the university. Upon the resignation of Abbott Lawrence Lowell before James B. Conant was selected to be president of Harvard, though he might have exerted himself and secured the position, he had his own candidate and I think preferred, not for the first time, the un-official role.

A few months before his death Grenny was interviewed by Richard D. Heffner for *McCall's* magazine. The end of the interview is worthy of repetition.

Clark: "But when I ask myself why I have spent many years of work and considerable money in the effort to prevent future wars, I feel that my dominant reason is a sense of shame at the incapacity of the human race to summon enough intelligence and will to solve this problem, when the knowledge and means to solve it are at hand. And since this failure offends me so deeply, I feel the necessity to attempt to educate enough people as to the ways and means to achieve world order that the result can actually be achieved in our time."

Interviewer: "Now as to the future: What hopes and plans have you?"

Clark: "I want very much to continue my work for peace. Specifically, I want to continue my advocacy of disarmament under a system of world law in the field of war prevention, convinced, as I am, that this is the only solution. And I want also to continue my work in the cause of justice and opportunity for the Negro. In the May issue of *McCall's* I read the answer of Pablo Casals to a similar question, and one thing in it fits my case perfectly. With almost no change, I can adopt it. Casals said that he wanted 'to follow to the end of my possibilities and potentialities.' My own hope is to write and talk and labor as best I can for all the ideas I most value. I hope to have a few more years of active work and to use them well."

Those few more years were not granted to him.

Alfred Lord Tennyson, who died when Grenville Clark was ten years old, taking some courage from Leonardo da Vinci's efforts to invent the airplane, described in "Locksley Hall" a war between

> * * * airy navies grappling in the central blue * * *
> Till the war drum throbbed no longer; and the
>   battle flags were furled

In the Parliament of man, the Federation of the world.
There the common sense of most shall hold a fretful
     realm in awe.
And the kindly earth shall slumber, lapt in universal law.

But Tennyson wrote another poem, "Ulysses," which in many ways to me exemplifies the magnificent character of Grenville Clark. In conclusion I quote:

> How dull it is to pause, to make an end,
> To rust unburnished, not to shine in use!
> As though to breathe were life. Life piled on life
> Were all too little, and of one to me
> Little remains. * * *

Then, speaking to his mariners, who had toiled and wrought and thought with him throughout the years of his many travels, he said, urging them to one more voyage before they die:

> Push off, and sitting well in order smite
> The sounding furrows; for my purpose holds
> To sail beyond the sunset, and the baths
> Of all the western stars, until I die. * * *
> Though much is taken, much abides; and though
> We are not now that strength which in old days
> Moved earth and heaven; that which we are, we are;
> One equal temper of heroic hearts,
> Made weak by time and fate, but strong in will
> To strive, to seek, to find, and not to yield.

Grenville Clark died with his mission unaccomplished, as many great men have done before him. To those after him I can commend no task more worthy than to pick up the torch he left behind. "Go ye and do likewise."

GRENVILLE CLARK:

As Seen from a Co-author's Perspective

Louis B. Sohn

On a spring day in 1944, a prominent New York lawyer, Grenville Clark, came into the Harvard office of Manley O. Hudson, then judge of the International Court of Justice. He said in a firm voice: "Manley, I decided to devote the rest of my life to world peace. We need a strong international organization to replace the League of Nations. I hope that you can help me to write a book on the subject." Judge Hudson pleaded lack of time, but pointed to me sitting on the other side of the table behind a tottering pile of books and noted: "This young man knows everything on the subject. He just helped me to prepare a book on *The International Law of the Future* which contains proposals for a new world organization. But I warn you that he is a radical, he wants to abolish the equality of states in favor of weighted voting." Mr. Clark replied that this was exactly what he wanted; he did not believe in equality of states either.

We went out of the office in order not to disturb Judge Hudson and settled in my little room in the basement of Langdell Hall, where I could show Mr. Clark all the books on weighted voting which I had collected in preparation for an article in the *American Political Science Review*. He was rather surprised, as he thought that the idea was a brand new one.

He showed me a short pamphlet he wrote in 1939 under the title *A Memorandum with Regard to a New Effort to Organize Peace Containing a Proposal for a "Federation of Free Peoples."* It was an adaptation of the Constitution of the United States and was similar to the "Union Now" proposals of Clarence Streit. I looked through it and, with some trepidation, I pointed out that in the United States we might be used to this approach but that other nations might prefer to build around international rather than national precedents. We had our first debate, which was about to end rather inconclusively, when I found the argument to persuade Mr. Clark. "We cannot start with just a small group of privileged nations, discriminating against the rest of the world." He thought a minute and replied with conviction: "No, I cannot stand discrimination. I have always fought against it in this country; I cannot promote it internationally. Our organization must be universal." This was our first joint decision, and he defended it vigorously at the Dublin, New Hampshire, meeting of the federalist groups in 1945, where his opposition forced a rupture in the federalist movement with the supporters of a more restricted "Union Now."

We worked together on a few short documents between 1945 and 1949. Starting in 1950, however, our plans became more ambitious. Mr. Clark decided then that nothing less than a comprehensive plan for a new world order would suffice, and I agreed to help him with it. The first result was a book entitled *A Plan for Peace*, which was published by Harper Brothers in 1950. Chapter Three contained our first proposals for general disarmament and charter revision. But this was only an outline and we started working hard in 1951 to fill in the details. In July 1953, we completed a revision of the charter, article by article, with a detailed commentary explaining the reasons for each change. This document was privately printed in July 1953, under the title *Peace through Disarmament and Charter Revision: Detailed Proposals for Revision of the United Nations Charter*. It was distributed in a large number of copies (more than 3000) throughout the world, and we received a tremendous amount of comments from many countries. A *Digest* prepared by Robert H. Reno, of Concord, New Hampshire, who became one of our most important advisers, brought our proposals to the attention of an even wider public.

The demand for this more popular version was amazingly strong for several years, and this document served as the basis for many discussion groups throughout the country, some of which sent us elaborate comments.

We were not satisfied, however, with the revision of the charter, and decided to draft detailed proposals on other aspects of world order. In February 1956, we completed a *Supplement to Peace through Disarmament and Charter Revision*, dealing exhaustively with disarmament and the United Nations Peace Force, and in outline form with the courts of the United Nations, a United Nations revenue system, privileges and immunities of the United Nations, and a "Bill of Rights" to protect individuals against abuse of power by the strengthened world authority. We waited again for comments, and we were not disappointed. At least two thousand persons commented on the 1953 and 1956 proposals; they included distinguished statesmen, lawyers, and scholars of many nations, but also many average citizens who offered some of the most searching questions and suggestions.

Having digested this mass of letters, we completed a revision of our manuscript and the Harvard University Press published it in 1958 under the title *World Peace through World Law*. A second edition was printed in 1960, with some minor changes, taking account of comments received and new developments (such as the need for provisions concerning outer space).

Soon thereafter Mr. Clark started worrying about the refusal of the United Nations to hold the Charter Review Conference provided for in Article 109, paragraph 3, of the charter. Mr. Clark was responsible for suggesting this provision in the first place. At the time of the San Francisco Conference he felt that the charter then adopted was not likely to be satisfactory and he wanted to make sure that there would be an adequate chance to revise it ten years later. His barrage of letters resulted in the insertion in the charter of a provision to that effect. But when the time arrived to hold the conference (for which our draft of 1953 could serve as a preparatory document), the General Assembly decided to postpone it to a more "appropriate time" and appointed a committee "to consider the question of fixing a time and place for the Conference." The committee never found the circumstances sufficiently auspicious and the conference was never held. Mr. Clark decided, therefore, that some other avenue must be found. We thought we spied an opening in the McCloy-Zorin "Joint Statement of Agreed Principles for Disarmament Negotiations," of September 20, 1961, which combined "general and complete disarmament" with "effective arrangements for the maintenance of peace," including a United Nations Force strong enough to suppress "any threat or use of arms in violation of the purposes and principles of the United Nations." We were further encouraged by the draft of a "Treaty on General and Complete Disarmament in a Peaceful World," which was presented by the United States to the eighteen-nation Disarmament Committee at Geneva on April 18, 1962. This treaty contained not only disarmament provisions similar to those in our previous drafts, but also a number of "measures to strengthen arrangements for keeping the peace" which, though they were in a rather rudimentary form, seemed to cover the same ground as our proposals.

After many long debates, and in the face of opposition from several of our close advisers, we decided to try an alternative route to our goal and we prepared a *Draft of a Proposed Treaty Establishing a World Disarmament and World Development Organization* (first draft, May 1962; second draft, May 1965). It was based on the idea that the charter did not preclude the acceptance by member states of more far-reaching obligations than those embodied in the charter itself. In particular, member states could agree to supplement the peace-keeping machinery of the United Nations through a treaty creating a new world security organization closely tied to the United Nations. This was done in several regional security arrangements; it could clearly be done on a global scale as well. The new draft did not differ in substance from our original proposals for charter revision, but it had to solve the additional problem of the relationship of the new organization to the United Nations. The provisions of the draft treaty for world economic development were also stronger than those in our previous proposals. This was primarily due to the fact that Mr. Clark took a trip around the world and was appalled by the conditions in India and various countries of the southern hemisphere; he decided that radical steps must be taken to deal with world poverty and that adequate funds were needed for that purpose.

Finally, in 1966 Mr. Clark decided that our two plans should be merged and synchronized to the maximum possible extent. This proved, however, more complicated than we originally thought and we had to be satisfied for the moment with a mechanical combination. The two plans were thus printed together by the Harvard University Press in a volume entitled *World Peace through World Law: Two Alternative Plans* (3rd ed., enl., 1966). Our plans for a more thorough revision were unfortunately frustrated by Mr. Clark's untimely death.

Looking back at our joint effort, the fact that stands out most in my mind is the amount of work that went into each successive draft. We spent at least one month every summer working on the text, and during the school year I commuted to Dublin for a few days every two or three weeks. Each day we worked together some four hours, leaving the rest of the time for separate work on portions of the draft. Usually we would discuss a problem for a while, then we would call our patient secretary, Mrs. Ruth Wight, and Mr. Clark would dictate to her the agreed text. Quite often in dictating the precise language we would discover some new difficulty and we would start arguing about it. After a while Mrs. Wight would decide that this question would not be solved quickly and would sneak out to type whatever had been dictated to her earlier. But her freedom did not last very long, and she would be summoned to take down a few additional sentences. After a few minutes a debate would again erupt and the whole performance would be repeated. Slowly the text would take shape and a few paragraphs would be finished.

Some battles, however, were never terminated, and an issue would raise anew its ugly head. For instance, Mr. Clark was deadly opposed to the idea of a bicameral legislature, but now and then a persuasive letter would arrive reminding us of the experience of all federal unions and the need to provide for the representation of states as well as peoples. We would discuss over and over again the arguments for and against the bicameral solution, and Mr. Clark would finally reject the idea. A few months later, however, we would go through the same story once more, discovering a few new angles but ending with the same result. At one time Mr. Clark did change his mind and after a letter from Max Habicht, of Switzerland, agreed to draft a provision for a second chamber of the General Assembly. But the draft got more and more complicated, and finally Mr. Clark rose in disgust, started stomping around the room, and exclaimed: "It is just not going to work. The two chambers will argue forever while the world will fall to pieces. We must have an efficient Assembly. The second house will only stand in the way." Out of the window it went for a while but, of course, it returned a few months later. Finally, when we had to draft the World Disarmament and World Development Treaty, a two-chamber system was in fact proposed, as the United Nations had to be given the right to stop certain activities of the new organization. Mr. Clark remained rather unhappy about it, but he was so certain of the need for a new start that he swallowed the bitter pill of bicameralism in order to have a better chance of reaching the great goal.

Mr. Clark was a superb draftsman. Nevertheless, he was forever trying to improve a text. He hated deadlines and resented the need to stop changing a draft in order to get the copy to the printer. He would sometimes revise a galley or even a page proof completely and the poor printer would have to start all over again. Quite often I did not envy Mrs. Wight when she had to go and pacify the printer to ensure that he would finish the book on time. But the result of this tinkering with the text was usually beneficial; the text would gain clarity and the thought would come through not only for an expert but even for an untutored layman. I shall never forget the experience with the headwaiter of a hotel in Minneapolis who, after a federalist dinner at which Norman Cousins extolled the importance of our book and at which I summarized our ideas, asked for a copy of the book and took it home to read. When he returned it the next day, he said: "I was told that this was a hard book to read, and the federalist lady at the literature table from whom I borrowed it said that she did not have the courage to start on it. I took the plunge and began at the beginning. I read through the night and I did not find anything too difficult for me. Everything was clearly explained, step by step, and everything fitted perfectly together." I hope that the lady who lent him the book then decided to read the book herself and that she had a similar experience.

One has to admit that the book is big and contains many details. But Mr. Clark insisted on clarifying every obscure point, on explaining the connections between various ideas and institutions, and on doing it in as plain and simple language as possible. We divided our work; I would prepare drafts on some sections, he would prepare the others. I was very proud if a sentence of mine passed through unscathed. Ordinarily, he would rewrite practically every sentence and improve it in the process. Sometimes, of course, an important idea was sacrificed on the altar of clarity. If I fought for it, he would find a way to accommodate me, and we would end with both a clear sentence and a better expression of my original thought. Of course, from time to time—though much less frequently—the shoe was on the other foot. Mr. Clark might dictate a beautiful, well-sounding sentence, and I might start probing it for its too-well-hidden meaning. After a vigorous defense, Mr. Clark would admit that the sentence did not add much to the explanation of a particular idea and would reluctantly agree to delete it. Sometimes, however, when he thought that I was not paying attention, he would try to smuggle his sentence back into the text, and would act like a little boy with his hand in a cookie jar when I caught him. Mrs. Wight would get a good laugh on such an occasion and would scold him: "I told you that we cut that out the other day, and you did not believe me." He would graciously admit his mistake then, and this was usually a good occasion for me to try to get one of my own ideas incorporated in the draft before he recovered from his embarrassment. The chance to get something new past his eagle eye was not great, but sometimes it worked for a while. Of course, unerringly in the next reading he would look with puzzlement at this particular piece and exclaim that we really did not discuss it fully and would demolish it or rewrite it in his own fashion. My little triumphs were often short-lived.

In later years, when I learned his style and method of approach, and when he became more accustomed to me and trusted me more implicitly, my share of the work increased and the number of his changes decreased. Finally, he allowed Mrs. Wight and me to read the proof by ourselves and make the necessary corrections without consulting him about every point. We knew then that we had an even greater responsibility and we argued frequently what he would do if he had to change it himself. Sometimes we would make the wrong decision and Mr. Clark would discover it in the printed text. He would change it in the next edition, but he would always double check to see whether we really had done it.

While Mr. Clark was very proud that our book was translated into many languages, he was always worrying that the translator might distort the meaning of our text. I only had the chance of seeing the proof of the French translation which was superbly done by the leader of the French federalists, Mr. Francis Gérard. Despite his special competence and deep knowledge of the field, we soon discovered that our text was sufficiently ambiguous in some places to cause a misleading translation. This was certainly a blow to our egos, as we had to admit that the fault was in large measure ours and not the translator's. I suppose we could have benefited equally from checking the other translations.

Over a period of some fifteen years I spent a large proportion of my time working with Grenville Clark. I learned much, not only about legal draftsmanship, but also about the substance of international relations and about the problems of the government and of the military forces. Mr. Clark's unique experience as adviser to the secretaries of state and war, his leading role in preparing the United States for two World Wars, gave him an insight into many problems which could not be easily matched. He embraced wholeheartedly the idea of world government, of world order based on law and justice; he had great compassion for those suffering at home and abroad because of their economic situation or discrimination. He had strong opinions on every subject and could defend them vigorously. He easily dominated every meeting in which he participated. At the same time, when we worked in his office on our difficult assignment, he always found time for an anecdote illuminating the problem under discussion, and his kindness to all of us was unbounded. He was a hard taskmaster, but it was nevertheless a pleasure to work with him, to share his thoughts, and to help him in reaching the goal he set for himself and for all of us. Though he is gone, those who felt close to him cannot just stop. The job is still here and he certainly expected us to continue. And so we shall.

GRENVILLE CLARK

Samuel R. Spencer, Jr.

In the spring of 1947, while still a graduate student at Harvard, I received a short note from Grenville Clark asking me to come to the Hotel Vendome to discuss the possibility of working with him. The fact that I had never heard of Grenville Clark despite his many distinctions says something about him. Few men of his time were more actively or consistently engaged in some form of service to society, but he always chose, almost stubbornly, to work as a private citizen rather than as a recognized public servant.

I do not believe that he ever really wanted public office, either as an elected official or as an appointee. Above all he cherished his independence, so much so that he could not have accepted the pragmatic compromises necessary to being elected, or the submergence of individual position necessary to a bureaucratic team effort. When he did agree, for once, to join Henry L. Stimson's staff at the War Department just prior to Pearl Harbor, he refused the nominal dollar-a-year salary and threw legal advisers into a tizzy trying to decide whether Clark could be shown "top secret" documents without taking a formal oath of office. Illness forced him to leave Washington in early 1942, and he returned to his preferred role of private citizen performing public service.

The one exception might have been an appointment to the Supreme Court of the United States, which would have left him the freedom of spirit and mind so essential to him. His mental acuity and high competence, his gift for analysis, and his sensi-

53

tivity to social needs would have made him a great justice. Whether Franklin Roosevelt would have appointed him I do not know, but the elements were there. Clark and Roosevelt had known each other since boyhood, had attended Harvard Law School together, and had served as young law clerks in the same firm. Clark had supported Roosevelt in 1932 and 1936. But characteristically, he threw away any chance he might have had when he organized a committee to oppose the president's plan for packing the Court in 1937.

During my two years of active association with him, I came to understand how typical his organization of that committee was. When we met at the Vendome in 1947, he had already retired from active participation in the Root, Clark firm. Because of a heart condition, his doctors had advised him that he must give up his strenuous activities of past years, and had suggested that he take it easy and write his memoirs. Dutifully, he was looking for a young graduate student in history to help with the project. I have forgotten the exact sequence of events, but it did not take me long to decide that I wanted the job.

We worked together at the Clark summer home, a comfortable, rambling red brick house at Dublin, New Hampshire, overlooking Dublin Lake just to the north. To the south, the property falls gently for a few hundred yards and then rises onto the slopes of Mount Monadnock, which presides tranquilly over the entire region and the small towns of Dublin, Peterborough, Rindge, and Jaffrey surrounding its base. I well remember the first day I reported for work after the term at Harvard had ended. Mr. Clark had set up an office in the barn, with work space for me and his long-time secretary, Miss Genevieve Maloney, who came back and forth at intervals from New York. Over the years he had collected reams of papers having to do with many past activities—so much so that the office could not hold all the required file cabinets. A part of them were in another section of the barn. We spent the day talking about the various enterprises in which he had been involved. At some point he concluded that I should begin my research by sifting out and organizing for him material having to do with the campaign to pass the Selective Service Act of 1940.

It was then late afternoon. He asked me if I would like to go for a swim. I replied that I would, but that I would have to go get my bathing suit. "You won't need any bathing suit," he replied. I followed him as he strode past the house, across the road, and into the woods surrounding the lake. When we came out to the water's edge at the point of the small wooded peninsula, he shucked off his clothes and struck out into the cold water. I followed suit, of course. This was a graphic first indication of something I soon came to realize fully: that despite good intentions of following doctors' orders, Grenville Clark could never have retired to a sedentary, inactive existence. At that point he still had ahead of him twenty years of active involvement in some of the most important work of his life.

As it turned out, it was I who wrote the memoirs—as far as they went—not Grenville Clark. The effort to write and push through Congress a peace-time draft act in the face of opposition from a politically conscious president and, curiously enough, from the chief of staff, was a story in itself. I set about to reconstruct it, from the beginning of the effort in the spring of 1940 to final passage of the bill at the end of the summer. Mr. Clark read my drafts with interest, but he never got around to doing more. A year later, during my second summer in Dublin, it had become quite apparent that he was far too busy in things of the present to deal seriously with past history. This he finally admitted to himself and to me. I asked him then if I might use the material as the basis for my doctoral dissertation. The result, the story of Grenville Clark and the Selective Training and Service Act of 1940, is on file at Widener Library.

In view of his later activities, especially those having to do with his effort for world peace through world law, Mr. Clark's leading role in such ventures as the Plattsburg movement and the campaign for a peacetime draft may seem paradoxical. It did to some of his associates. One of them was a man who had worked closely with him in the effort for the Selective Service Act. "I was all for Grenny when we were working together in 1940," he said to me, "but I can't go along with him on this One World stuff." The explanation is perfectly logical. It lies, first of all, in Grenville Clark's great flexibility. He could be neither categorized nor pigeonholed. It lies also in his extraordinary perception and breadth of vision. Different times in the affairs of men call for different remedies. To help marshal the resources of the United

States and the Free World against Hitler had been the need of 1940. The greater, long-range need of the world beyond the wars was and is for a system of government that will put the good of all peoples above narrow national interests.

Every major effort in which Clark involved himself through his long lifetime was based on one conviction which he repeated to me time and again. The wording varied occasionally, but the essence of it remained the same. The people will save their country, he liked to say, if their government does its job only moderately well. This is not to say that he was hostile to or contemptuous of government. But he had little faith that government, with its built-in handicaps of bureaucracy and slowness of movement, could come through in a time of real crisis. At such a time, the citizenry itself had to do the job. Many realized in 1915 and 1916 that the United States was drifting ever closer to the maelstrom of the war in Europe; a few saw that its military forces, and especially its officer corps, were completely inadequate to participation in a major conflict. It was not the government, but Grenville Clark and a group of other determined young men who organized the Plattsburg movement and produced a nucleus of officers to lead the national army raised by the draft in 1917. When the government was about to go astray, as Grenville Clark conceived it in 1937, he and his committee helped block the president's plan to subvert the Constitution and pack the Supreme Court. When, in 1940, France was conquered and Britain was reeling from the effects of Dunkirk and the Blitz, it would have seemed only natural that the government itself should have sponsored a Selective Service Act. Not so. It was an election year, and President Roosevelt rightly sensed the strength of isolationism and the public's fear of involvement. Here again came Clark and his citizens' committee to act when government itself would not act. Because they did, we had an army in time, but barely so. Later, when all governments were too bound by fear and tradition to surrender national interests for the good of the whole, Clark and other private citizens carried the banner for limited world government as the best hope for peace. There were other causes too, such as the legal defense fund of the NAACP and the Bill of Rights Committee of the American Bar Association. All of them illustrated his belief that enlightened citizens cannot and must not depend solely upon government to save society.

Once when I had been away for the weekend, I came back to find the usually uncluttered driveway and yard of the house at Dublin filled with cars. I doubted that they were there for a party; the Clarks lived simply, and rarely if ever entertained large groups. It turned out to be another of Mr. Clark's committees—the Committee for the Preservation of Mount Monadnock. The burgeoning radio industry wanted to erect a large tower on top of the old mountain as a relay for radio signals. Officialdom was about to approve it. But neither the state nor the radio industry knew with whom they had to reckon. Mr. Clark and the citizens of the Monadnock region were not about to let their mountain be disfigured. The tower was never built.

Mr. Clark was Dublin's first citizen. Appropriately, his telephone number was number 1. Long distance operators, when I had occasion to call him from other areas, took this number in disbelief. But as a telephone user he deserved it. By the time I knew him, the telephone was his contact with the active world. His range of friends was great. It included many distinguished persons —Conant of Harvard and Dodds of Princeton, Frankfurter of the Supreme Court, John McCloy, and a host of others. But with all of his own wisdom and knowledge, he had the great capacity of wanting to listen to and learn from all kinds of people. As he did with others, he would call me from time to time over the years after I left Dublin in the fall of 1948. Sometimes he wanted to check on a detail about which I knew; sometimes he wanted a bit of information; at other times he just wanted to talk. I remember one particular occasion in the early fall of 1960. The talk was mostly about politics, and he wanted to be sure that I was going to vote for young Senator Kennedy. A man of vigor and style himself, he responded to the same qualities in Kennedy.

As I think about Grenville Clark, his independence keeps coming to the fore as his most salient characteristic. As an illustration of it, I like best the story he used to enjoy telling about himself. During his student days at Harvard he was a member of the Porcellian Club, one of the most exclusive of the exclusives. No outsiders, no guests of any kind, were allowed within the sacred confines of the Porcellian clubrooms. Defying tradition, Grenville Clark braved the frowns of his fellows by taking a nonmember to the club on one occasion. Many years later, he was in Cambridge with his friend Henry L. Stimson, who was at that time an officer in the president's cabinet. As an alumnus, he invited Mr. Stimson to go to the Porcellian with him. The next day, he received from the secretary of the club a reprimand which began, "Inasmuch as you have persisted in breaking the rules by bringing nonmembers to the Porcellian Club . . ."

Then, as he was all his life, Grenville Clark was his own man. He did what he believed necessary and right to do. In doing so, he served the people and causes that were important to him—his family, Harvard University, his country, the whole of mankind. And he served them extraordinarily well.

TRIBUTE TO GRENVILLE CLARK

W. Averell Harriman

———◆———

Lawyer by profession, Grenville Clark, as private citizen, profoundly influenced national and world affairs. On numerous occasions and for considerable periods of time, he put aside his own work to devote his time and resources to the defense of freedom-loving peoples against tyranny. His passion for anonymity was unique. His achievements even now—after fifty years—are known to only a relatively small group.

Of these achievements, those listed below seem to be most directly related to "the promotion of mutual friendship and respect, peaceful intercourse, justice and fraternity among nations."

1) Early in 1915 Grenville Clark came to the conclusion that the United States would have to come to the aid of the Allied forces in Europe. (At that time sentiment in America was strongly against preparation for such action.) Realizing America's lack of trained officers, Clark formed a group which proposed to the War Department that military training be offered to business and professional men, in order to have ready a pool of officer candidates if and when America would be required to enter the war. The War Department agreed, only on condition that Clark would assume the task of finding volunteers who would, at their own expense, report for training at an army post in Plattsburg, New York. Clark then began an intensive campaign to recruit and train volunteers, under which 29,000 officers and 130,000 technicians were readied. A French military historian said for the United

States to have raised so quickly an armed force of two million men was not remarkable, but to have produced the officers to command them was "a military miracle." It was in large measure a personal contribution by Grenville Clark to Allied victory. In 1921 Clark was awarded the Distinguished Service Medal.

2) His later efforts to help prepare America to join the Allies in defeating the Axis powers, I believe, contributed to the shortening of World War II by many months. In 1940, although the U.S. government had already begun industrial mobilization, there were no plans for mobilizing fighting men. Opposition to conscription was powerful. Both the president and the army were opposed to it. Grenville Clark drafted what has come to be known as the Selective Service Act and began campaigning for its passage in the U.S. Congress. In the spring of 1940 it was generally believed that Clark's proposed legislation would not obtain as much as one vote in three in the U.S. Senate. Although the bill had little administration support until its enactment, it passed the Senate in August by almost two to one and became law in September. General Pershing and others have said that "had it not been for Grenville Clark we would not have had any training act until Pearl Harbor."

Early in 1944, when it became clear that the Allied forces would prevail, Secretary of War Henry L. Stimson urged Clark to devote his efforts to "stopping World War III."

Grenville Clark next turned his towering legal talents to the problem of establishing the rule of law—instead of the rule of war—as the means of settling disputes between nations. (As early as 1939 Clark had drafted a tentative constitution for an international federation.) Thus, when Stimson urged that he think of ways to "stop World War III," Clark expanded his proposals, and in 1944 published, in the *Indiana Law Review*, his draft for an effective world organization.

To succeed, it would have to have those powers "directly and plainly related to the maintenance of the peace," including: a world legislature with a carefully worked-out system of proportional representation; an executive council chosen by and responsible to the legislature; a world police force composed of volunteers (by quota, to prevent any country or bloc of countries from exerting undue influence); international courts and other tribunals to deal with all disputes between nations; and a reliable world revenue system with funds collected through each country's tax machinery. Radical as those ideas seemed, Clark did not believe that they were a fraction as perilous as a nuclear arms race.

4) Following the Dumbarton Oaks Conference which kept national sovereignty sacrosanct, Grenville Clark once again took action. He arranged for the convening of a group of influential Americans in the fall of 1945 at Dublin, New Hampshire. Headed by Justice Owen J. Roberts and attended by editors, educators, lawyers, and other public figures, the conference issued a public statement to the effect that practical provisions must be put into the United Nations Charter to make it sufficiently democratic and effective. It called for a yielding of national sovereignty, a representative assembly, and an executive without veto.

5) Grenville Clark then devoted a twelve-year project to study and rewrite the United Nations Charter. Published in 1958, *World Peace through World Law* was an expansion of Clark's original plan, and included precise and detailed proposals of how the United Nations could be modified and strengthened to maintain the peace. Translated in full or abridged form into twelve languages, including Russian and Chinese, the book has been characterized by scholars and lawyers as "the greatest contribution of the American profession of law to world peace."

6) In 1959 Grenville Clark was awarded the Gold Medal by the American Bar Association, an association of 95,000 American lawyers, with the following words:

> Since World War II he has devoted his time and resources to the study of possible formulas for world peace and disarmament, seeking to preserve mankind from the destruction of war. His conclusions are embodied in his pioneering book with Professor Sohn, *World Peace through World Law*. It is not necessary to agree with all of his conclusions to recognize in this monumental work a major contribution to world literature on this subject and a basis for discussion and exploration of the problem incident to the acceptance and enforcement of the Rule of Law between nations.

7) Shortly after the election of President John F. Kennedy, Grenville Clark, in a communication to the new president, recommended that he go before the United Nations and commit America to the goal of "universal and complete disarmament" coupled

with United Nations revisions, which would include the machinery for inspection and enforcement. President Kennedy, almost immediately upon taking office, appointed John J. McCloy, who had admired Grenville Clark's mind and energies ever since their association at Plattsburg prior to World War I, as his special adviser on disarmament. John McCloy characterized Grenville Clark's proposals for world order as "the only light I can see at the end of the tunnel." In September of 1961 the McCloy-Zorin agreement calling for "general and complete disarmament" was issued shortly before President Kennedy's historic address at the United Nations in which he summoned the world to a "peace race" based upon total national disarmament.

8) In the remaining years until his death in 1967, Grenville Clark served as the prime mover of The World Law Fund, which promoted the inclusion of the study of world order in the curricula of almost all universities and colleges in America and a number of other countries. In the course of this activity, the fund has printed and distributed thousands of publications.

9) In the fall of 1965, Grenville Clark convened a second Dublin Conference—twenty years after the original meeting. Another vigorous statement was issued by participants in that conference.

For all of the above work and the motivation behind it, Grenville Clark, in my opinion, deserves the designation "world patriot." I knew him personally for more than fifty years. He had a unique warmth of interest and understanding of other people. For my part he always gave me a feeling that he was interested in matters that concerned me and gave me considerate encouragement whenever I sought his advice. I wish he were still with us.

A TRIBUTE TO GRENVILLE CLARK

John J. McCloy

All who had heard of Grenville Clark knew that he was a great patriot and a man of extraordinary perception and energy, but those who really followed the life of this man sensed that he was something more. Now and then a figure comes along who possesses these attributes to such a marked degree that, set apart from his fellow men, he becomes a leader and a factor in history. A certain isolation forms about such men, somewhat as any great prophet becomes isolated. They also induce a sense of awe. I am frank to admit that I had always been somewhat awed by Grenville Clark. In terms of his range of mind and effectiveness in achieving what he set out to accomplish, I am not certain I ever knew his equal. He was one of the most liberal-minded men I ever knew, and yet his singleness of purpose when he set out to marshal the forces needed to accomplish his objectives was about as liberal as a railroad train plunging through a tunnel. Whenever I saw him, I thought of Hawthorne's Great Stone Face which from high up discerns things unseen or ignored by all of us who merely travel the valleys. But this is not the complete image either, for it is too static and there was nothing immobile about Grenville Clark.

For all his calm farsightedness, Grenville Clark always possessed this indomitable urge to advance the progress of man toward the light, and obstacles have only served to stimulate him.

I think of the contribution he made in preparing this country for its participation in World War I. But for him and men like "Sec" Root, Ted Roosevelt, Jr., and Archie Thacher, for all of Woodrow Wilson's desire to make the world safe for democracy by force of arms in World War I, there would have been no trained field and company officers to direct the American forces when they went overseas; but for Clark and those associated with him at that time—but for his vision displayed two years before we entered that war, General Pershing's insistence in 1918 on an integrated American army, rather than a mere cadre of American manpower to be fed into Allied units, would not have had much meaning. Though the country as a whole may have forgotten it, there are still some of us today who followed Clark to Plattsburg and can testify firsthand to the enormous contribution this man and those with whom he then was closely associated made to the effectiveness of the American military effort.

More of us can recall his perseverance and his heroic part in obtaining the passage of the Selective Service Act in World War II. And here it was his own personal effort rather than that of any group which was responsible for the result. His extraordinary personal drive, ingenuity, and persuasiveness almost made that a one-man operation.

We frequently use the word "patriot" rather loosely but I know of no one who was entitled to bear the title "patriot" more justly than he if the measure of patriotism is enlightened devotion to one's country and whole-souled application of one's energies to its welfare.

These military achievements are a part of history, but in his later years and on the basis of a long life given to weighing the forces that move about the world, he saw as clearly as the dawn that in a nuclear world mankind could no longer survive if it continued to resort to war as a method of settling international disputes. With remorseless logic and reasoning, he confronted mankind with the alternatives to the destruction which the presence of nuclear weapons compels. No one has studied as fully and as penetratingly as he the forms which our society should follow if the values of our civilization are to be preserved from nuclear destruction.

His conceptions had always been bold and clear cut, but I would say that never before had they been as bold, and as carefully articulated, as he presented them in the cause of peace. He had stood in the center of two great crises which his country faced and which shook the world. Then he faced with the same vigor and acumen that marked his earlier roles the crisis with which the whole world is now confronted. Whether his analysis provides the solution may be a matter of debate and some controversy, but none can deny that the issues we face embody the very hope of mankind itself. The world is in vital need of a solution, and in the face of such a need there is small wonder that Grenville Clark set himself the task of supplying it.

PART III

Legal Friendships

GRENVILLE CLARK:

A Lifelong Friend

John M. Korner

My association and lifelong friendship with Grenville Clark started in 1912, when the law firm of Root, Clark and Bird opened with offices in a three-room suite on the tenth floor of 31 Nassau Street, New York.

The three partners—Elihu Root, Jr., Grenville Clark, and Francis W. Bird, Jr.—were classmates at Harvard Law School and had, I suppose, formed their law partnership shortly before their graduation.

All three were scions of illustrious fathers and forebears. Elihu Root, Jr., was the son of a distinguished statesman and lawyer, with long service as secretary of war and secretary of state. Grenville Clark's father was senior partner in the banking firm of Clark, Dodge and Co., New York, and his grandfather, LeGrand B. Cannon, was closely identified with the civic and business growth of the city of New York in the early nineteenth century. Francis W. Bird, Jr., was the son of a former governor of the Commonwealth of Massachusetts.

In 1912 there were only four employees at Root, Clark and Bird—Alfred C. Intemann, a young lawyer, was the principal law clerk and acted as office manager. Miss E. Bessey performed all the stenographic and typing work for the partners, also holding the notarial seal. Edward F. Quinn was the junior law clerk. And I performed all the duties which willing boys were expected to do in those days—filling inkwells; answering the telephone switch-board; studying typing and shorthand to assist the legal secretary; occasionally answering court calendars; as well as aiding in process serving.

Between 1912 and 1917, the firm expanded considerably. Several young attorneys, Mansfield Ferry, Lloyd Derby, and Robert P. Patterson, were added to the legal staff.

Around 1914 Francis W. Bird, Jr., disassociated himself from the firm and returned to Massachusetts to devote himself to politics. Shortly thereafter, two young attorneys, Emory R. Buckner and Silas W. Howland, who had known Grenville Clark and Elihu Root, Jr., in law school, dissolved the firm of Buckner and Howland, with offices at 28–30 Nassau Street, and became associated into the firm of Root, Clark, Buckner and Howland. This firm later added Arthur A. Ballantine and remained in practice for many years, with many of the foremost corporations and individuals in the business world as its clients.

During the critical period prior to World War I, both Grenville Clark and Elihu Root, Jr., had the wisdom and foresight to see the inevitable involvement of our country in this conflagration. They were deeply disturbed with our lack of preparedness for war as well as an almost totally untrained and unprepared officer training and recruitment program.

Almost single-handedly Grenville Clark and Elihu Root, Jr., threw their talents and enormous energy into successfully forming the Plattsburg Training Camp, which caught on, and was truly the forerunner of what is today known as R.O.T.C. Thousands of young men attended this training camp and later trained as officers when we entered World War I.

When war was declared in 1917, the young law firm sent its two senior partners, several junior attorneys, and its junior assistant into the military service. Major Elihu Root, Jr., served with distinction as a combat infantry officer and battalion major, with the American Expeditionary Forces in France. Lieutenant Colonel Grenville Clark, AGO, served in a very vital and sensitive post in Washington, D.C. Robert P. Patterson also served in France as a combat captain of infantry—and in later years himself became secretary of war. John M. Korner enlisted in the field artillery, serving in France as a warrant officer and later on the personal staff of General John J. Pershing until his discharge from military service in July 1920, as first lieutenant.

Regretfully, my association with Grenville Clark's law firm and the many gifted men on their staff did not continue after World War I, although my personal relationship and valuable friendship with both Grenville Clark and Elihu Root, Jr., lasted throughout almost a half century until their deaths.

After discharge from the U.S. Army in 1920 I became associated with a firm engaged in international cable and radio communications, with headquarters in New York, known then as All America Cables, Inc. (now a subsidiary of ITT). In 1934 I accepted assignment to the foreign staff of this company and my family and I served in Panama, Colombia, Argentina, and Cuba thereafter for almost twenty years.

During our sojourn in Latin America in this period, it was our great pleasure to greet Mr. and Mrs. Grenville Clark in two Latin American countries when they went down on separate cruises.

The first was 1940. Ominous rumblings were heard from far-off Japan. We were living on the Panama Canal Zone and were aware of its vulnerable location. In previous years we had been able to visit the Panama Canal Locks freely. Now, there were guards whose presence gave a sense of urgency to the news.

It was with joy, however, that we received a letter from Grenville Clark and his wife saying that they expected to be in Cristobal, C.Z. (which is on the Atlantic side of the Canal), when the cruise ship they were on touched at this port. They would like to see us and could it be arranged? We replied at once that we would call for them at the quay as soon as their ship docked. In those days there was no road across the isthmus. This meant that we could not use our own car, and so we went by train from Balboa (on the Pacific side where we resided) to Cristobal. Upon our arrival, we hired a car and driver for the day, and went on for a happy reunion with Mr. and Mrs. Clark. When asked where they wanted to go they pointed to their binoculars and indicated that they would like, if possible, to see one of the U.S. military installations and to combine that with some bird watching—one of their favorite pastimes. As we drove along the road to one of the forts, the trusty binoculars were used more than once to spot a tropical bird along the way. Upon reaching Fort Davis, a smartly turned-out sentry stepped out, asked our business there, and when told we had distinguished visitors from Washington, he saluted; then politely asked whether we had any cameras or binoculars. Both sets were cheerfully handed over to be checked, then the following ensued:

SENTRY: "Do you have any other binoculars?"

WE: "No, only those two."

SENTRY, reaching over to flip open the dashboard glove compartment of our recently hired car *and* discovering a small set of binoculars, said sternly:

"EVERYBODY OUT OF THE CAR!!"

In great embarrassment we stood by while every inch of the car was searched—floor boards pulled up, seat backs pulled forward, mud guards inspected, and rear trunk ransacked. At long last we were allowed once again to re-enter the car and the driver was ordered to proceed along the main road only.

As we settled back in our seats, in his mild quiet way Mr. Clark said: "In Washington my office is just down the hall from Secretary Stimson's. I shall certainly tell him that he has at least *one* young man who is guarding the Panama Canal with great care."

In the late 1940s we were living in Havana. Once again Mr. and Mrs. Clark wrote us that they would like to see us when the *Mauretania* made its call at Havana. We arranged a small dinner party at the American Club for that evening in their honor. During our drive in the afternoon Mr. Clark mentioned that John W. Davis was also aboard the ship and they had been together much of the time. We inquired whether Mr. Davis would care to join us for dinner. Mr. Davis would! That evening, Mr. Clark was seated at the right of the hostess, and Mr. Davis, who had been nominee for president of the United States in 1924, sat at her left.

The law offices of Root, Clark and Bird had as one of its clients Andrew Carnegie, the philanthropist, and Mr. Carnegie's signature was needed on a document involving a huge sum of money. I was dispatched to deliver this document to Mr. Carnegie personally at his residence on Fifth Avenue that evening after dinner. Mr. Clark made it clear to me that I was to bring the document back to the law office that evening. Upon entering the Carnegie residence, the butler referred me to a very pleasant and dignified gentleman (who I later learned was Mr. Bertram, the private secretary) who advised me he would take the document in to Mr. Carnegie. My instructions, to my mind, did not envisage relinquishing the document to anyone, repeat anyone, other than Mr. Carnegie and I steadfastly held my ground. Whereupon I was ushered into the library and handed the document to Mr. Carnegie, whose picture I had seen a number of times. I respectfully requested his signature and after referring it to Mr. Bertram, who was present in the room, he asked if it was correct and when assured, he signed it and handed it back to me with a twinkle in his eye, stating, "It is verra important to carry out orders, m-lad!!"

On another early occasion, in an old decrepit loft building on the Lower West Side of New York, Mr. Clark and I waited all one night, watching for a slippery individual who was involved in bankruptcy proceedings in which Root, Clark, Buckner and Howland were involved legally, to turn up at the loft with a truck, as Mr. Clark suspected, to remove some assets. We were finally rewarded around dawn the next morning, when a truck arrived at the loft and the principal and his driver entered the loft. We remained motionless until the first hand truck of goods was leaving the premises. Mr. Clark ran down one flight of stairs and I the rear stairs to prevent their escape. Mr. Clark had a summons already on the man before he knew what had happened and he and the driver fled in panic in the truck. He was later indicted and convicted of criminal fraud.

GRENVILLE CLARK

Henry Mayer

———————————◆•◆———————————

Our paths first crossed in 1913, when I was employed at the age
of seventeen by the law firm of Root, Clark, Buckner and Howland as a super-duper office boy while going to law school at night.

It was my job to run the copy press and the switchboard, to
serve and file papers, to search records, and occasionally to take
home one of the young daughters of my employers if she stayed
late at a party in the city.

While the firm was small, consisting of the four partners and a
managing attorney, as well as a subtenant to help them pay the
rent, I had a ball. I got into the whole spectrum of litigation and
corporate work either as a briefcase carrier or a draftsman of
simpler types of legal papers. The office grew to enormous proportions in the eight years I was with them. When I left, there
were fifty lawyers occupying two floors of an office building and as
many secretaries and stenographers. I was the first one to leave the
firm. To commemorate the occasion, I was given an engrossed
and extravagantly worded set of resolutions together with a few
of the firm's clients for whom I had been doing work exclusively
and, most important of all, the warm embrace of wonderful well-
wishers and fine friends who ceremoniously met in the firm's vast
library to bid me a fond farewell.

Grenville Clark inspired this moving and human touch which
capped a relationship I have treasured ever since. I always felt indebted to him for having accelerated my annual bonus one year

so that I could help my folks to buy a private home in Harlem to house our family of ten.

I have a vivid recollection of sharing with him a highly publicized and somewhat sensational experience.

The struggling law firm in its formative years prior to World War I took over from another law firm, Bowers and Sands, the collection of deficiency judgments obtained in foreclosure proceedings. Hardly a profitable venture since few were ever collected. Yet as Emory Buckner used to say: "Let's take it. We don't know what next month will bring."

One of these judgments involved a man by the name of Hoadley and his wife. Hoadley was a speculator in transit stocks and had made and lost several fortunes.

It was my job to go after the Hoadleys as persistently as Adam Clayton Powell was later pursued by the lawyer for Mrs. Jones, whom Powell libeled. So I got an order to examine the Hoadleys and served it on them. They failed to show. I then got an order to punish them for contempt of court. When they failed to appear, I got a warrant for their arrest. Then the chase began. The Hoadleys had a town house which included a tunnel enabling them to escape from their creditors and find refuge on their yacht, which was anchored in the Hudson.

One day I got a tip that they were in the Hotel Netherland (now the Sherry-Netherland) at Fifty-ninth Street and Fifth Avenue. I immediately alerted a deputy sheriff to meet me at the hotel. When we got there, Mrs. Hoadley, wearing a white opera cape, started for her chauffeured car. I nudged the deputy sheriff but he was scared to execute the warrant. I directed him (I think imperiously in spite of my youth) to arrest her. When he still held back, I literally pushed him into her arms and announced she was under arrest. When she began to create a scene, I suggested we all return to the Hoadley suite in the hotel. We did so. When I found Hoadley there, I told him he was under arrest too. At first he tried to bluster his way out of his predicament. Then he went to the phone.

In short order, William J. Flynn, then head of the U.S. Secret Service and a friend of Hoadley's, appeared. He was followed by Hoadley's lawyer, Bainbridge Colby, who later became secretary of state under Woodrow Wilson. Colby, who was drunk, became a little drunker when Hoadley, a good sport, ordered rounds of drinks to be brought up to the suite.

The deputy sheriff, who was scared, brought the sheriff's then counsel Olvany over pronto. Olvany later became a supreme court judge and head of Tammany Hall.

I was overwhelmed by all this talent so I sent for Grenville Clark, who showed his imperturbability by sitting down, opening a newspaper, and calmly announcing that he would give the Hoadleys one hour to raise the $10,000 they had to pay or go to jail. Colby said he was going to rejoin Judge Cohalan at the Metropolitan Club and have the judge vacate the warrant of arrest. Mr. Clark told him to go ahead and be damned.

Though Colby was in his cups, he still had sense enough to realize he had met his match and he had Hoadley send Pliney Fisk, the banker, out to raise the necessary amount in cash at three o'clock in the morning. When the cash arrived, Mr. Clark reached out and took it. That started a donnybrook. Olvany said the money belonged to the sheriff (he was right). Mr. Clark said: "Nothing doing." When Olvany persisted, Mr. Clark said he would like to speak to me in the hallway. When we got outside, he handed me ten thousand-dollar bills and said: "Run like hell, Henry." And run I did, down ten flights of steps and a couple of miles to my home. I was not going to risk losing a fortune like that (it sure was huge to me) in any subway. I stuck it under my pillow and slept not a wink that night.

The next day when Mr. Clark and I reported to the office, Mr. Buckner, with his instinct for public relations, called an immediate press conference. I was permitted to revel in the telling of all the lurid details: the search for Hoadley, the town house, the tunnel for escape beneath it, the yacht in the Hudson, and the final dénouement at the Hotel Netherland with the illustrious cast of characters who came to Hoadley's assistance and, finally, my race home with the fortune. The newspapers ate it up. The *American* (since folded up by Hearst) had a two-page spread in its Sunday edition with pictures of the town house, the yacht, the hotel, the Hoadleys, Flynn, the head of the U.S. Secret Service, Colby, Fisk, the banker—even the ten thouasnd-dollar bills.

It was my first experience with public relations and I've been balmy about it ever since.

One last characteristic story and I will be through with my eulogy of this great American. My son, Martin, was writing the biography of Emory R. Buckner, Mr. Clark's glamorous and illustrious partner who died in 1941 and in his relatively short life left a record of similar accomplishments. My son called Mr. Clark from Boston and suggested meeting him the next day at his home in Dublin, New Hampshire. Mr. Clark said he was leaving that night for London and suggested that my son fly over and meet him at the Park Lane Hotel. He added that he would pay my son's expenses since he was subjecting him to the inconvenience of following him abroad. Martin said that would not be necessary since he was flying to Geneva, Switzerland, at the expense of the Twentieth Century Fund in connection with a project he was working on for that organization. He met Mr. Clark in London and found him full of enthusiasm. He was planning to see Prime Minister Harold Wilson, then fly to Russia to meet Kosygin and his partner in crime, Brezhnev, in Moscow. Then he expected to fly to Peking and visit with Mao, the Chinese leader—all in the interests of world peace. And he was then eighty-three years old— an amazing man and a truly great American and citizen of the world.

Yes—

"Lives of great men all remind us
We can make our lives sublime
And departing leave behind us
Footprints on the sands of time."

G.C.

Cloyd Laporte

—————◆—————

When I came down from Harvard Law School in February 1920, to seek a job with the young firm of Root, Clark, Buckner and Howland in the old building at 31 Nassau Street, I first saw Emory R. Buckner, who took me around the office to meet the other partners—all founders of a small firm which was to grow to immense size and great prestige.

I shook hands with Grenville Clark and had a brief talk with him, in which he told me something about the firm's practice. He impressed me as a serious, thoughtful man. When I came to the office in the summer, I was assigned to work with him, and for several years I was primarily his law clerk, although from time to time I did tasks for each of the other partners.

Clark did not work fast, but steadily and thoroughly. He had a tenacity in striving toward the goal which he desired to achieve for his client, which I have never seen equaled in any other lawyer in the more than fifty years of my own practice. Thus, in a tangled situation involving a building at Forty-second Street and Fifth Avenue which our client, Hart Schaffner and Marx of Chicago wished to acquire for one of its New York outlets, practically everybody, including the principals, their Chicago lawyers, and an architect who was itching to go to work on the necessary physical changes, had given up hope. But G.C. hung on, and the seemingly endless complications, which involved an existing lease and a re-calcitrant estate, were ironed out and the deal was closed to the satisfaction of all parties. The architect confided to me that he had despaired long before, and that it was only G.C.'s persistence that had brought about a solution. I am sure that this was the view of all the negotiators.

Grenville Clark as a practicing lawyer can, I think, best be described as a "generalist." He took on a variety of cases and matters —corporation matters, litigations involving contracts, wills and estates, and miscellaneous controversies. The fact that an area of practice was new to him did not deter him from taking on an assignment in the unfamiliar field. He always handled such matters with his customary thoroughness and persistence, achieving the best results which were attainable under the circumstances of the case or matter. An outstanding example of his versatility was his work in the field of railroad reorganization and also of railroad rates. He made himself an expert in these subjects and acquired special influence with the Interstate Commerce Commission because of the soundness of his views.

While Clark did not adopt one of the usual specialties, such as tax, real property, wills and estates, corporate finance, or litigation to the exclusion of the others, he operated with success in all of them. He might have been called a perfectionist. The close personal attention which he gave to solving the problems of his clients brought him almost unfailing success, but it also caused him great personal strain during his years of active practice.

His method of familiarizing himself with the facts and issues in a case already pending in the office, which he took on for trial, or in a pending matter which called for analysis, planning, and negotiation, may be illustrated by the case of *Bibb Manufacturing Company* v. *Pope*, which Clark took on for trial from Emory Buckner, who was unable to try it because of other maturing commitments, Buckner being the trial partner of the young firm.

I had prepared some preliminary memoranda of law and was now Clark's assistant in the preparation for trial. At Clark's request, I brought all the files in the case into his room. Clark got down on his knees on the floor of his office and removed each paper from the file, read it, and laid it on the floor, to be joined by other papers dealing with the same general aspect of the case. Leo Gottlieb, my classmate, also in Root, Clark, passed our open door and was highly amused at the spectacle of two lawyers, the senior and his law clerk, on their knees on the floor, fumbling with various documents and memoranda. Before the papers were stockpiled in appropriate segments, Grenville Clark had read each one and had already acquired a firm grasp of the facts and issues. The papers, thus sorted, were reverently returned to the files for future consultations.

The actual trial occupied about three days before Judge Augustus N. Hand (then a federal district judge) and a jury, after which we moved for a directed verdict on the ground that the facts were all in writing, to be gleaned from various telegrams, letters, and memoranda exchanged by the parties, with no relevant external evidence. To be sure, the defendant's counsel had put the president of their client on the stand, and he had been allowed to testify regarding the meaning of the written messages sent by his company, using the first person, as "I meant," and so forth. On cross-examination, Clark asked this witness whether he could swear that he wrote any of those messages himself. The reply was negative, whereupon Clark remarked, "But you are perfectly willing to swear to what you meant in those letters and telegrams."

We delivered a memorandum, on which I had worked, supporting our contention that the case had to be decided by the Court, with the jury merely accepting the judge's direction. Judge Hand agreed, and dismissed the jury pursuant to a stipulation of counsel that the verdict would be entered thereafter, as directed by the Court, without requiring the jury to be present. Hand apologized to the jury for having kept them in court for the three days of the trial without permitting them to decide the case. Of course, he put the blame on the law, which required him to make the decision.

Then G.C. and I, assisted also by my colleague Alec Royce, went to work to prepare a careful brief and also a revision of Clark's notes, which he had used in his oral argument, because Judge Hand had expressed a desire to see them. These and all exhibits were put in apple-pie order; the process was an eye opener to Royce and me, so careful was G.C. not only to have all the papers *be* right, but also *look* right, be logically arranged, and readily readable. To Royce it was the last straw when, the job finished, G.C. handed the folder to Royce and asked him to take it up to the Federal Court House and deliver it directly to the judge in his chambers, rather than have it go through the clerk's office. He would not entrust an ordinary messenger with it, but sent it up by a *Harvard Law Review* man, who for the moment felt that that ministerial assignment was rather infra dig. (Of course, copies went to opposing counsel.)

But the result! After a few days, the decision came down directing a verdict in favor of the plaintiff, our client, for the full *ad damnum*, plus interest, a total of about $100,000—in the real money of the twenties. The verdict was unanimously upheld on appeal.

A most unusual case, in which I worked with G.C. in preparing the brief, involved an attack by a justice of the New York supreme court (the court of first instance in this state) on the jurisdiction of the appellate division, in which the state constitution lodged the power of assigning the justices to the various parts. Justice John Ford asserted that this power was to be exercised mechanically or mathematically, so that each justice would have an equal time with all the others in the various parts and terms. He proved beyond doubt that he had been assigned almost exclusively to the trial of negligence actions and excluded from the equity parts where receiverships and other patronage were dispensed. This policy was deliberate and represented a careful appraisal of Judge Ford's competence. He instituted an action in the second department for an injunction requiring the appellate division in the first department to assign him to his "fair share of all the work of the Court."

The judicial defendants asked Senator Root to undertake their defense. G.C., with minor help from me, prepared the brief. When he delivered it to the senator, the latter looked it over and remarked laconically that he thought he could "work something out." Actually, the brief in final form was almost exactly as written by G.C. Senator Root's argument and the brief prevailed in all three courts.

Our fee came in the form of a dinner at the Manhattan Club, given to Senator Root and all of the founding partners of the firm (plus me, because I had worked on the case). Emory Buckner, I believe, did not attend because prohibition was then in effect and Buckner was U.S. Attorney. But the liquor was legal, as well as varied, and indeed complete, because it was preprohibition liquor from the club's own cellars, delivered without transportation or sale.

One could, by researching our old files, accumulate a number of similar instances of the thoroughness and persistence of Clark's work as a practicing lawyer. In fact, once he had taken on a situation, G.C. lavished on it all his tenacity and effort, without regard as to whether the *res* was sufficient to justify financially such expenditure of effort, or would result in a loss to the firm and to him as a partner.

G.C. was deep rather than facile—both in thought and expression. He once told me that the "only" way to write anything well was to do it with a pencil and a pad of paper; this in an age still holding sway, when a lawyer almost always rang for a stenographer and started dictating. The former method indeed does bring better results, the latter having only the virtue of being quicker.

Emory Buckner once said that the reason G.C. did not make the *Law Review* was that he "could not operate on a three-hour basis," referring to the practice at Harvard of making the grade for an entire course depend on the blue book of a three-hour examination. G.C. needed more time for thought, leading to a better and deeper product. With his inner urge for perfection, a trait which entails close personal attention, G.C. was not a good delegator; indeed, the strains of his hard personal work led to a breakdown, which took him out of the practice for a year and a half in his late thirties. But he made a complete recovery, and went on to the great achievements of his life.

G.C. also had a quiet sense of humor. It came out, not in the telling of anecdotes, but in passing remarks about situations. Humor being intangible and my memory weak, I cannot recount instances, but I do recall laughing to myself at some of his remarks, even after I was home at the day's end.

I have known many public-spirited lawyers in my more than fifty years at the bar, but I have never known one who had that spirit so intensely and deeply, and who was so far-seeing into the problems, not only of the present, but also of the future, and withal so practiced in devising both short- and far-ranging solutions. I was privileged to work with him on some of them while he was in the office.

The first of his projects in which I functioned at all—in a most minor way—was his work in bringing about a reawakening to the great principles embodied in the Bill of Rights to the federal Constitution, particularly those relating to freedom of speech, press, and assembly, provided in the First Amendment. He prepared a memorandum on the subject, in which he said that the people had "lost the feel" of those great rights. He sent me to Washington to interview some senators in order to get their reactions to his plan for bringing them again to the attention of the country. I received good receptions from the several senators with whom I conferred, and sensed that they were especially impressed by his telling phrase regarding the loss by the people of "the feel" of the Bill of Rights. Senator Nye of North Dakota was among those who were keenly interested.

As a newspaper reader I had formed an unfavorable opinion of Senator Nye because of his efforts to show that our participation in what is now called the First World War was due to machinations of arms manufacturers who wished to expand their markets —an idea which was dropped when Germany again attacked in the more comprehensive Second World War. But I found that Nye was really public spirited, although wrong-headed at times. In fact, I came away convinced that members of Congress were not the irresponsible political beings then pictured in the press but, in large part at least, really wanted to do what they thought was best for the country.

G.C. followed up on this subject by getting the American Bar Association to set up a Bill of Rights Committee. G.C. himself was the obivous choice for chairman of that committee, and he headed it for some years. He obtained a grant from the Carnegie Foundation to establish a periodical which he named *The Bill of Rights Review*. He edited and published it for several years. It did its job; the "feel" of those rights was restored, and the U.S. Supreme Court vindicated them in its opinions.

One of the most significant cases came up from New Jersey, where Boss Hague was preventing the use of parks and other public places by groups which he considered "subversive," or at least radical. G.C. obtained authority from the American Bar Association to prepare and file a brief on its behalf, as *amicus curiae*. It was that brief which brought about the decision that Hague's restrictive ordinances were unconstitutional. These activities of G.C. I knew about, but did not have a part in them.

I did have some part in another activity of his: the fight against what came to be called Franklin Roosevelt's court-packing plan. It will be recalled that the Supreme Court at that time had a truly conservative cast. In the name of "liberty of contract" it had stricken such social legislation as laws restricting child labor; it had also required a six per cent return on investment in railroads and other utilities, but the Fourteenth Amendment, which had been designed to secure full civil rights to the former slaves, had never been applied in their behalf.

Several statutes passed by the Roosevelt Congresses, such as the Agricultural Adjustment Act, had been held unconstitutional, usually by five-to-four majorities. The last straw came with the Court's similarly divided decision in the *Schecter* (or "sick-chicken") case, voiding the National Industrial Recovery Act—the so-called N.R.A., whose symbol, widely used in propaganda, was a painting of a big "Blue Eagle." Actually, this decision was not an unpopular one, and in fact it relieved the administration of a problem, because by that time the act was generally recognized to be a failure. But it was made a *casus belli* by FDR, who sounded a call to arms against the Supreme Court. The president's scheme was to add judges to the Court so that, by appointing the right men, the existing majority on the Court could be swamped and its philosophy reversed.

Lawyers throughout the country were aghast at this effort to make the Court subservient to the other branches of government. The president was taking advantage of a loophole in the Constitution consisting of its failure to specify the number of judges who were to constitute the Supreme Court. Bryce, in his masterly treatise "The American Commonwealth," had pointed out this omission years earlier. If this plan to increase the number of judges and pack the Court were permitted to succeed, a dangerous precedent would be set, for use whenever a president and Congress became dissatisfied with a decision or decisions of the Supreme Court.

Nearly all lawyers saw the danger and were against the plan. But few did more than pass resolutions against it. G.C. was of a different mold. He believed in action, and immediately went to work. He organized a Citizens' Committee to oppose the attempt of his college mate FDR to seize control of the Court, with membership eventually in forty-two states. C. C. Burlingham, a former president of the Association of the Bar of the City of New York and of the Harvard Club of New York City, who lived to be over 100 years of age, was a co-chairman of the committee, but the work and guidance fell upon G.C. He called on me to do the secretarial work.

Again G.C. sent me to Washington to interview senators in collecting information and views on how to make the committee's work effective. The senators with whom I spoke—including Edward Burke of Nebraska, Walter George of Georgia, Tom Connally of Texas, Burton K. Wheeler of Montana, and Arthur Vandenberg of Michigan—welcomed me, as the representative of the committee, with open arms. Vandenberg made the most important contribution. He wrote me a letter suggesting that the most effective contribution we could make to the fight would be to confine our membership to persons who had voted for FDR in both of his elections, 1932 and 1936, thus confronting him with the opposition of his own supporters. This advice, which proved the absence of partisan motives on his part, was accepted, and I was required to write letters to some members, kicking them off the committee. These included me, except that I did not write myself a letter, because in 1936 I had made what I have long considered the most ridiculous vote of my life: pulling down the lever for Landon. My name no longer appeared as secretary of a member, but I continued to do the secretarial work.

Neither Burlingham nor G.C. had to resign, which is sure proof that they had both voted for FDR, at least the first two times.

The battle raged through the early months of 1937, with newspaper and radio publicity. G.C. arranged a dinner meeting of the committee in Washington, with several senators present as guests, including Connally and Wheeler. Wheeler, who later received much credit for the defeat of the scheme, was at that time in a blue funk and indicated that he thought it was impossible to win. He was bucked up at the meeting, particularly by the more optimistic statements of G.C., reinforced by G.C.'s obvious determination to carry on the fight to the end.

The fight was successful. It happened that I was able to make some contribution from a different angle. Colonel Henry L. Stimson, as president of the Association of the Bar of the City of New York, appointed me chairman of the association's Committee on Federal Legislation; this was at the suggestion of C. C. Burlingham, G.C.'s co-chairman of his Citizens' Committee. The battle in the Senate was moving to its climax. In order to seem to respond to the widespread criticism of the original court-packing plan, a few changes were made in the scheme; instead of permitting the president to make a considerable number of new appointments to the Supreme Court immediately and all at one time, he was to spread them over two calendar years. This change would only postpone completion of the packing to the following January. It was a fraud, but it fooled some people, including three opposition senators. In order to allow almost no time for consideration of this amendment, it was proposed just as the Fourth of July weekend was coming up, with the Judiciary Committee's vote due immediately thereafter. Our bar association committee, however, had been following these moves closely, and we already had our report in proof form.

At that juncture, the hand of Providence intervened with the sudden death of Senator Robinson of Arkansas, who was carrying the ball for FDR. Since the battle continued to rage in Congress and in the country, FDR in a "Dear Alben" letter to the new majority leader, Senator Alben W. Barkley, chided the senators for "playing politics" while the body of the deceased leader was still unburied—lying in state in the rotunda of the Capitol. In my political naïveté, I felt that we should withhold our report until after the funeral.

But it happened that a member of our bar committee, Professor Noel Dowling of Columbia Law School, was in Washington to confer with Senator Burke of Nebraska on another matter; Senator Burke was leading the opposition to the entire court-packing scheme. Dowling had a copy of our report with him and showed it to Burke. Burke approved the report, which analyzed the revised plan and showed that it still carried the substantive evils of the original bill. He said in effect, "This whole matter will be decided on the funeral train to Little Rock." He wanted enough copies by the next morning. Dowling got me on the phone at my apartment, where I was relaxing in a friendly poker game. I immediately telephoned the printer, and Burke got the report. It was released to the press and printed in full on the front page of the *New York Times*. I was never informed as to what Burke did with the report, or whether it had any effect, but shortly thereafter the entire matter was definitely shelved by the Senate.

During the last week or two, G.C. had been on a trip to Russia. I received a cable from him asking for a cable report on the progress of the fight of, as I recall, about fifty words. I was indeed glad to be able to wire him that our efforts had been crowned with success by an overwhelming vote in the Senate.

While vacancies occurring naturally did give FDR the opportunity to appoint new judges of his selection, this was very different from establishing a precedent for court packing through additional judges. There is still that hole in the Constitution which does not specify the number of justices, but the idea of permitting the president and Congress to use it to seize control of the third branch of the government received a telling blow in the rejection by Congress of this effort, now of evil memory.

GRENVILLE CLARK:

Legal Preceptor

Henry J. Friendly

———◆•◆———

I was fortunate in my legal preceptors. Professor Frankfurter took a special interest in me during my years at the Harvard Law School. Thanks to him, I became law clerk to Mr. Justice Brandeis. After that memorable year I was apprenticed, in the fall of 1928, to Grenville Clark.

The differences among these three great lawyers need not be labored. But there were similarities as well. All three moved easily in great affairs, although Brandeis and Frankfurter had been obliged to struggle to win places that were Clark's almost for the asking. All believed in the high importance of facts; these must be faced squarely, never ignored or distorted. All regarded being a citizen of the United States as a supreme privilege and considered, in consequence, that public duty transcended any private interest. All were men of courage—willing to stand up and fight for their convictions, however unpopular these were and whatever the cost in bitterness of opposition or loss of friends. Clark, like Brandeis, had somewhat the quality of a Roman senator; it is easy to think of him demanding the destruction of Carthage or denouncing Catiline.

My apprenticeship came about this way: G.C. had recently returned to 31 Nassau Street after an extended absence because of nervous exhaustion and overwork. The firm—more particularly its manager, Emory Buckner—thought the breakdown had been due to Clark's failure to follow Buckner's principle of "organizing" a job with a sufficient force of young lawyers, and that the failure might have derived from Clark's fear of imposing unduly on a youngster already heavily committed to other tasks. The remedy was to make a junior available to Clark and no one else.

The theory may have been good, but the results were not. Although G.C. professed high regard for my help, his demands took only half my time. While making his rounds one morning, Buckner found me engaged in a second or third reading of the *New York Times*. He said I did not look very busy. I readily agreed, explained the cause, and expressed my dissatisfaction that a lawyer I so greatly admired could find so little for me to do. Buckner laughed, said he had not really expected the experiment to work, undertook to remove the restriction on my availability, and indicated I would not lack assignments. He was right. One of these turned out to be a very minor job for a rather small client of Mr. Root, Pan American Airways. Thus began thirty years as an "expert" on aviation law; thus also is the role of accident in human affairs.

Although I naturally thought G.C. had erred in not making greater use of my talents, I can now understand why he did not. Much as he liked Buckner and was liked in return, I doubt that he truly accepted Buckner's thesis that the client had engaged the firm; he thought his clients had hired him. Like Brandeis, he was the old-fashioned lawyer who took pleasure in doing his own work; he found real joy in writing out a contract, letter, or brief, either in full or in outline, on a yellow pad on which the script always wandered dangerously away from the left-hand margin. Once the material got into proof, he could equal Frankfurter or Brandeis in his willingness to mangle it. While I may not have been fully aware at the time, these tastes were my own. Although being a member of two large law firms and general counsel of a great corporation required me to learn how to utilize teams of lawyers, one of the joys of the bench has been the opportunity again to do my own work, aided only by one or two bright young men to whom only rarely do I confine the task of drafting the ultimate product.

Despite my liberation to accept calls from other partners, there were several years when I worked a good deal for G.C. Our cases mainly concerned railroads, for which my training under Professor Frankfurter and Justice Brandeis served me well. Our most important assignment stemmed from a retainer G.C. had received from a group of insurance companies and savings banks which were concerned over their investments in bonds of the western trunk lines. They feared that proceedings under the Hoch-Smith Resolution of 1925 might lead to serious rate reductions on agricultural products whereas, in their view, increases were required. We worked closely with the railroad lawyers, yet maintained an independent stance. It must be hard for young lawyers today to comprehend an era when the ICC was spoken of simply as "the Commission" and an argument before that body was treated almost as seriously as one before the Supreme Court. I doubt that anyone, Brandeis included, ever made better argument before "the Commission" than G.C did in these cases. What was impressive, beyond his command of the facts, was his moral force. Commissioners might disagree with him and did, but they could not fail to respect his complete sincerity.

Subject only to the limitation I have outlined, G.C. was a great chief—welcoming suggestions, appreciative of aid, considerate of other aspects of one's life, loyal in the last degree, putting his junior forward at every opportunity. I am certain it was due to him that, as a relatively young lawyer, I was retained to make the overall financial presentation for the country's railroads in Ex parte No. 123, "the Fifteen Per Cent Case, 1937." Once you were his friend, there was literally nothing he would not do. You had only to ask; indeed, he liked even better to help without being asked, and without his activity being known.

As the years went on, I had less and less opportunity to work for G.C. More than two years were happily spent as chief assistant to a promising junior partner, John M. Harlan, in the fascinating Wendel estate litigation. No sooner was that over than I was plunged into the Paramount insolvency proceedings, where the massiveness of the problems required that young lawyers be given a degree of individual responsibility beyond their normal lot. The once-little airline, which spanned the Pacific in 1934 and was to fly the Atlantic five years later, came to demand more of my attention, especially after it and others became objects of inquiry by

Senator Hugo L. Black, and this led to passage of the Civil Aeronautics Act of 1938 and many proceedings thereunder. Meanwhile G.C. was giving more and more time to his duties as a Fellow of Harvard University and to public service.

It is a great joy that another happy accident enabled me to be with G.C. during what was perhaps his greatest contribution to our country—the enactment of the Selective Service Act of 1940, a feat accomplished by him and a few associates with nothing more than benevolent neutrality from his friend in the White House. Chance willed that I too should be spending much of the summer of 1940 in Washington on matters relating to the national defense. This was a contract, highly classified at the time, whereby Pan American Airways would construct air bases for the United States in countries in the Caribbean and South America unwilling to allow our government to do this on its own. These bases, initially conceived as necessary for the United States to defend the hump of South America against Hitler, later proved enormously useful for the ferrying of aircraft, men, and supplies to Africa, and for countering German submarines in the Caribbean and South Atlantic. Drafting the contract with the judge advocate general of the army, working out the financial details in a manner best designed to preserve the secrecy desired by President Roosevelt, and obtaining necessary clearances from various departments proved to be a laborious task. It was a welcome relief to walk across the street from my billet at the Statler to G.C.'s suite at the Carlton during a summer evening and find him, as of old, with a yellow pad on his knee, this time engaged in drafting the statute, preparing a committee report, or writing Senator X or Representative Y. I cannot recall that I was of any aid except as a sounding board, but it was good to be around.

I last saw G.C. at the funeral of our dear friend Mr. Justice Frankfurter, in early 1965. He seemed much as when I had first met him nearly forty years before—erect of bearing, quick of eye, correct of mien, happy in his new marriage. We promised to see each other again soon; to my regret we never did. But his memory lives in all whom he touched. I count his tutelage and friendship among the highest blessings of my life. When the chips are down, one thinks of Grenville Clark and wonders what he would have done.

GRENVILLE CLARK:

Some Stories and Personal Recollections

Lyman M. Tondel, Jr.

In the spring of 1935 I had the good fortune to obtain a summer clerkship with Root, Clark, Buckner and Ballantine. All four of the partners were then among the best-known lawyers in the country. Elihu Root, Jr., was widely esteemed for his skills in many fields—military, educational, financial, business, aviation, art, and even sailing, as well as law. He was then involved in the Rock Island litigation in which he was ultimately to persuade the United States Supreme Court of the constitutionality of the railroad reorganization provisions of the Bankruptcy Act. Emory Buckner had gained renown as U.S. attorney for the Southern District of New York in the troubled days of prohibition, and as a great, understanding, and ever-helpful friend of young law graduates. He was generally regarded as one of the great litigators of his time. Arthur Ballantine had helped steer the nation through the banking crisis as undersecretary of the treasury under President Hoover and as a holdover, without title, in the first few months of the Roosevelt administration. His reputation as a business and tax lawyer was pre-eminent.

I did not know much about Grenville Clark but quickly learned that he, with "Sec" Root, Delancey Jay, and others, had organized the Plattsburg movement for the training of officers in World

War I and had been a personal friend and adviser of Franklin
Roosevelt for many years. I also learned that the firm's representation of the Bank of Manhattan was largely due to him; that he
and Mr. Root had organized the Fiduciary Trust Company; and
that he and Mr. Root were primarily responsible for the firm's
representation of the trustees in bankruptcy of Paramount Pictures, which was one of the monumental reorganization projects
of the thirties, involving almost 500 corporations. But I had no
real idea of the measure of the man.

The way I met him would alone have made me remember him.
Rather early that first summer I was sitting by myself in the library at Root, Clark before the office opened—a lonesome "eager
beaver" from the Pacific Northwest. Suddenly and unexpectedly
a very large hand at the end of a very long arm presented itself in
front of my face and a voice from behind said, "My name's Clark."
If ever a man looked the part of a patrician, it was Grenville
Clark—born to wealth, education in the finest schools, welcomed
in high society, intellectually profound and open-minded, and,
when convinced, stubborn. He was an extraordinary man physically, standing about six feet, with broad shoulders, impressive
jaw, a light in his eyes, and a well-controlled, ready tongue.

I went to Root, Clark permanently in the fall of 1936 and before long I became aware of other qualities in Mr. Clark not quite
so evident at first sight. We had annual Gridiron Club–type din-
ners, the theme of which was to make good fun of each other.
Between the original lines recited on those occasions, however,
lay germs of truth, and I quickly learned:

> "There are many who think Grennie
> is the club man's maximum.
> But the highbrows lift their eyebrows
> when he snaps his chewing gum."

Every year for many years by popular demand, because the story
got more outrageous with each telling, Mr. Clark would be asked
to tell a rather earthy mule story about one of his alleged experiences in the Okanogan Valley of the state of Washington, where
he had spent some time as a young man. He knew how to enjoy
good fun.

Another rumored episode proved Mr. Clark could have poise

under any circumstances. One summer night when he was alone
at his house at 216 East Seventy-second Street, the doorbell rang.
There was a telegram to sign for. He had been about to get into
bed and was wearing no slippers and a nightshirt. As he signed
for the telegram he was unaware he had allowed the door behind
him to snap shut. Mr. Clark had no key, and so he found himself
in the small vestibule where he was not about to spend the night.
He unsuccessfully explored the front of the house to see if he
could gain entry, and then walked to the curb to hail a taxi. The
first few cabs were wary of what they saw, but at last a taxi
stopped and its astonished driver asked, "Where to?" Mr. Clark
directed he be taken to the Knickerbocker Club. Arrived at the
Club, he asked the doorman to pay the fare, and almost but not
quite succeeded in dashing through the entrance hall to the
elevator unseen by any members.

In 1931, Mr. Clark was elected a member of the seven-man Corporation which runs Harvard University. At a Root, Clark dinner
these lines were added to the Clark poem:

> "All Porcellian's
> sainted hellions,
> stuffed the ballot box
> for Clark.
> Now he's lost on
> trains for Boston,
> Just a Harvard hierarch."

He made such an impression on the Corporation at Harvard that
when a new president was to be chosen to succeed President
Lowell, he and James Bryant Conant each had three votes when
Mr. Clark cast the deciding vote for Conant. At least this is the
story told by Ernest Henderson, his neighbor in his beloved Dublin, New Hampshire.

Then came World War II and Mr. Clark's efforts to secure
selective service, and many other activities that others knew more
about than I. One incident sticks in my mind. The year must have
been 1941, prior to Pearl Harbor. I happened to be in the midwest
on business and was startled and delighted to be paged for what I
believe was the first time in my life in an Indianapolis hotel. I
was even more impressed with myself when I answered the phone

and the voice said, "This is the mayor of Indianapolis. I understand you are from Mr. Clark's office. He is arriving here in a
little while and we would like to know when and where he is arriving so that we may have an escort for him." I did not realize
that Mr. Clark was received by escorts when he visited cities. I
told the mayor that I did not know Mr. Clark's plans but would
be glad to call the office and inquire. I called his secretary, Genevieve Maloney, and I shall never forget her response: "I don't
know when he's arriving but I suppose he'll come in on an upper
berth as usual." I reported to the mayor only that I could not
learn Mr. Clark's plans.

After lunch that day, however, I picked up a paper with a
streamer headline: "FDR'S CLOSEST ADVISER IN CITY." I
knew that Secretary Frank Knox was in the city, and while I had
not realized that he was FDR's closest adviser, I assumed the
paper was referring to Knox. Great was my surprise, however,
when I read the story and found that it was Mr. Clark to whom
the paper was referring. Whether that newspaper knew what it
was talking about or not I shall never know, but I can guess.

Mr. Clark never really returned to Root, Clark, Buckner and
Ballantine. He had already started to work on what he called "a
plan for peace." And especially after the horrors of World War
II he had determined to do what he could in the rest of his life-
time to lay the basis for permanent world peace. At the memorial
service for him shortly after his death in 1967, the Reverend Dr.
Harrington said that he had regarded Mr. Clark as an archmilita-
rist for several decades because of his work in connection with the
Plattsburg movement, selective service, the declaration of World
War II, and his service as Secretary Stimson's aide, and that he,
Dr. Harrington, was astonished to discover when he met Mr.
Clark that the "militarist" was as surely a man of peace as ever
lived.

The fact was, as Dr. Harrington recognized, that Mr. Clark
"damned consistency." If he saw this country on the verge of a
war which it must win, he threw all his energies into whatever
seemed needed to win the war and to make conditions as tolerable
as possible to those who must fight. But if the opportunity even
remotely presented itself he wanted to work for peace.

In the postwar years he also (not surprisingly) became one of the leading protectors of civil rights and an ever-vigilant advocate of what he thought was right. It was Mr. Clark who somehow found half a million dollars to establish the NAACP solidly in its legal defense program. When blacks in the south could not get bail, it was Mr. Clark who raised more money and led the fight for bail bonds. Even when he thought his beloved Harvard had betrayed a trust in the Arnold Arboretum controversy, he left the Corporation forever and fought it in the courts.

After Mr. Clark had been without a Wall Street address for seven years (1946–1953), he and Mr. Root became counsel to what is now Cleary, Gottlieb, Steen and Hamilton. Mr. Clark was enthusiastic. He gave a dinner at the Knickerbocker Club for the members of the firm and was obviously delighted at his new association even though it was largely a continuation of his old one. But the fates were against his spending much time at the firm. He suffered an ailment which made him particularly susceptible to virus and for many years he was cautioned against coming into crowded areas. The first Mrs. Clark, Fanny Dwight, a perfectly lovely and remarkable person, was adamant against his entering New York City. So for many years, Mr. Clark confined his visits to very, very few occasions. He kept his house in East Williston on Long Island during this period but most of his time was spent in Dublin working on his plan for peace, which in due course became his world-renowned joint work with Professor Louis Sohn of Harvard entitled *World Peace through World Law*. In its preparation he made, or renewed, contacts with leaders from all around the world, such as Nehru and Lord Attlee.

Grenville Clark has now gone to his fathers. He never held political office. He was never well known to the public at large. He was accustomed to abuse for his outspoken beliefs. He was independent to a degree that no public man can ever be. He was fortunate in having the conveniences and assets of inherited wealth, but I doubt that its absence really would have substantially affected his approach to life. There have been few senators and perhaps only some presidents in this century who have had as great an influence on the course of events as Mr. Clark. He took his means of impressing the people where he found them. He used the powers of conviction with a small circle of influential friends; he pamphleteered; he worked through bar associations;

and as time wore on he used his towering reputation. He accomplished great things.

And what of his life as a lawyer? First of all in the first thirty years of adult life he was a fine lawyer in a variety of fields. He attracted important clients, he handled small as well as large matters with infinite skill and he earned a great reputation among his fellow members of the bar. He ultimately received the American Bar Association Medal. However, he never forgot that part of being a lawyer is being a professional man in the best sense of the world. He never forgot his obligations to the public. He utilized the opportunities that the freedom of being a professional man afforded him to embark on his many great endeavors.

There are many pedestrian, brilliant, money-saving, successful craftsmen in the law. There are rich lawyers. There are famous lawyers. But even some of the attributes that Grenville Clark exemplified can make of a lawyer a mighty person.

GRENVILLE CLARK

Lloyd K. Garrison

When I graduated from the Harvard Law School in 1922 I was lucky enough to obtain a job with the much-sought-after firm of Root, Clark, Buckner and Howland. There were then about forty lawyers in the office, including the four very able partners.

I was not at first assigned to work with Grenny Clark. My association with him in the office was accidental. We both happened to be friends of the two Hands, Augustus and Learned, who were then on the U.S. District Court bench. One of them, I can't remember which, in 1924 assigned Grenny to a bankruptcy matter of some importance, as a result of which he gained some acquaintance with that field of law and presently became chairman of the Bankruptcy Committee of the Association of the Bar of the City of New York. Meanwhile, the Hands had each appointed me to some small receiverships which the indulgent firm allowed me to handle. The upshot was that Grenny persuaded his Bankruptcy Committee to appoint me as secretary. So Grenny and I would go to meetings together and at the end of the year he let me draft the report for the committee. Through this collaboration we became good friends.

He was an excellent chairman. By letting the other fellows talk he never seemed to be running the show but he always managed to steer it in the direction he wished. He had clear and simple objectives—nothing fancy or erudite but practical and down to earth. He was patient, humorous, and always gave his committee members the feeling that he was enjoying each of them as human beings even more than the work of the committee. They responded in kind and would have done anything he asked. Watching him at work, I could see that he was a natural-born leader of men, and I always thought he would have made a superb general.

He was slow and methodical in his legal craftsmanship. I never saw him hurried or impatient. He had great powers of concentration and, unlike his partners, he preferred to work on one thing at a time, staying with it regardless of the hours it might cost him.

I remember once going to his house in the late afternoon with a document he had to look over before the next morning. It was shortly before a dinner party which he and Mrs. Clark were giving. He was already dressed in his tuxedo and received me in the living room. To my surprise I noticed that on his starched shirt front, the stiff kind men wore in those days, some water had been spilled, perhaps from a cocktail shaker whose top had flown off or from a vase of flowers which he might have upset.

He did not, however, exhibit any self-consciousness about his appearance. He evidently had concluded that if he had gone to change his shirt he would be hurried, and it was not in his nature to be hurried. First things first. So we sat down together at a desk and he read the document very carefully. Then with a little smile, as if to say "I think you will be satisfied with what I am going to do," he picked up a pen—not a fountain pen but the old-fashioned kind with a changeable point—dipped it in a bottle of ink, and wrote a few corrections along the margin of the document, to be inserted at particular spots. I can still see his hand going up and down and along very slowly and precisely and I can still hear the scratch of the somewhat rusty pen as the words took shape. I observed later at the office that he seemed to prefer pen and ink to pencil or to a fountain pen, perhaps because this old-fashioned method was best suited to the even pace of his thoughts.

After a little talk our work was finished and as I stood to go the first guests arrived. The timing was perfect, and I am sure that he continued to be quite unconcerned about the state of his shirt.

Many years later, toward the end of his life when he was living in Dublin, Mrs. Garrison and I spent a weekend with him and

Mrs. Clark. There were just the four of us and Mrs. Clark did the cooking, which she was good at and seemed to enjoy. He was by then immersed in his plan for amending the charter of the United Nations so as to provide for a true world government. This was to be achieved not at one stroke but by a series of steps in the course of which, as national armaments were reduced each year in accordance with agreed-upon quotas, an international force under the United Nations would be built up which would ultimately be capable of enforcing decisions in international disputes.

What particularly struck me at the time was the way he had gone about the job and his long view of the future. He combined to the highest degree in this, as in his other undertakings, pragmatism with inventiveness. The train of his thought, as we talked about it during that weekend, might be summarized roughly as follows. We must start with the situation as we find it, and build on what we have. The United Nations is a going concern, and instead of scrapping it and starting afresh we should strive to perfect it. It has no real power and therefore there is no world law. But without world law there cannot be peace. We must therefore revise the structure of the United Nations so that it can attain the necessary power, with institutions and proceedings appropriate to a system of law. The way to get on with this business is to draw up specific charter amendments for people to consider. Otherwise, there will be nothing but talk and drift. Someone must make a beginning. With superb self-confidence, but without egotism, he had decided to undertake this task. The man who had been the father of the draft in World War II, now in a time of peace was bending all his energies toward the prevention of future wars.

He had no illusions that his plan as written would be adopted. He was serene, however, in the conviction that the existence of a plan, however imperfect, would be an indispensable starting point. It would have to be followed by vigorous efforts to promote its consideration on a worldwide basis. Without the setting in motion of this process the race against time might not be won.

So he was in correspondence about his plan with leading men in different countries. He showed me some of this correspondence, and I was impressed on the one hand by his modesty and on the other by the strength of his commitment and his will. He was no Utopian. He sought nothing for himself. He was a hard-headed lawyer going about a job that someone had to do, and the only difference between this and previous tasks was that this was over-whelmingly the most important and the most urgent for the main-tenance of civilization.

While absorbed in the cause of world peace, he never lost sight of the importance of upholding the rule of law in domestic affairs. He took a continuing interest in the NAACP Legal Defense and Educational Fund, Inc., and in the series of law suits which the Fund brought to enforce the constitutional rights of Negroes. He contributed with spectacular generosity to this work and made his gifts on an annual matching basis which produced other large gifts. Mrs. Garrison and I went to a large Fund dinner where he was the principal speaker. He spoke simply and modestly, without notes and without oratorical flourishes, but with immense effect. He drew everyone to him and received a standing ovation at the end. It was touching to see the warmth of affection and the depth of respect which all those present felt for him.

I remember a letter he wrote during this period to the *New York Times* in praise of the young volunteers who were going south, at great personal risk, to join Negroes in demonstrations for the vindication of their rights, and to help them in law suits. At the time he wrote the letter these young people were being criticized for going too fast and hurting their own cause. But he defended them vigorously, and referred to them as the "elite" of our times. So he joined hands with a new generation in support of the Bill of Rights and the rule of law, to which he had devoted so much of his own life.

I shall always think of him as a worthy successor to the eight-eenth-century patriots who wrote the Declaration of Indepen-dence, established the Constitution, and fought ceaselessly for freedom and for a just and peaceful ordering of human affairs.

A VERMONT LAWYER'S VIEW

John M. Dinse

Shortly after I began the practice of law in Burlington, Vermont, I became aware of the fact that Grenville Clark, a distinguished lawyer and statesman, not only had a Vermont background, but also that he still maintained his contact with the state. His brother, Julian, lived in the family home in Burlington and also had a sizable farm north of Burlington near the Canadian border.

For years the firm which I had joined had represented Clark family interests. One of the favorite stories around the office had to do with a request by Grenville Clark to withdraw as co-trustee of one of the family trusts being administered locally. Since it was a rather sizable trust, the probate judge was amazed that Mr. Clark would forego the privilege (and fees) connected with such a trusteeship. When questioned about this by the judge, Mr. Clark reportedly allowed that he was agreeable to foregoing this job and the fees since he was rather busy and had "done rather well at the law."

I was aware that he was a senior partner in a distinguished New York law firm and had "done rather well at the law" when my senior partner one day informed me that Mr. Clark was in Vermont and needed some legal advice and I had been selected to perform the task. It was with some apprehension that I undertook this task, rather like a lowly parishioner being asked to counsel the pope on matters spiritual. I found Mr. Clark at a boarding house in Highgate, Vermont, where he frequently stayed while duck hunting at some marshes in which the family held part ownership. I was vaguely aware of these duck marshes, and I knew they lay between the Clark family farm and a federal government wildlife refuge. I was later to learn more of these marshes since his brother, Julian, prior to his death, had made an agreement with the government to acquire part of the marshes. After Julian's death, his brother, Grenville, held the U.S. government at bay for a considerable time before they acquired possession, for the apparent purpose of extending his period of enjoyment of the marshes.

In any event, on the appointed day I traveled to Highgate to meet Grenville Clark for the first time. This imposing gentleman was even more so dressed in the rugged garments of a duck hunter as I met him in the modest living room of the boarding house.

The legal problem which he presented to me turned out to be rather fascinating. He wished to purchase hunting rights in an adjoining marsh and wanted to know the nature of these rights and how they could be bought, sold, and transferred. As we discussed the problem he carefully pointed out that whatever the response he wished to have it on one page, clearly stated. I agreed and ultimately did as he requested, although I found the problem sufficiently interesting to send him also a brief several pages long for which he later thanked me most graciously.

As we sat and discussed his problem, we were interrupted by the arrival of the driver for his brother, Julian. Julian, also an avid hunter, had been crippled by polio and required assistance wherever he went. The driver informed Grenville that his brother wished to see him outside immediately. Outside we found Julian Clark in his station wagon along with one or two other family retainers who excitedly told his brother that a large flight of Canadian geese had just landed in one of their nearby fields. Without delay we proceeded a short distance to the Clark farm.

When we arrived the field was literally covered with huge geese, and the Clark brothers were obviously transfixed by what they saw. It was a bitter fall day, and I was ill prepared for the occasion in my gray flannel suit and city shoes. There is some question in my mind whether it was more interesting to watch the geese or the Clarks, as each seemed to be looking over the other.

Finally, after what seemed to me a terribly long time, the driver was requested to put the birds up so that they could be observed in flight. This he did, and they were truly a magnificent sight against the leaden sky.

Only after the last of the geese disappeared from sight did Grenville Clark remember his shivering young legal adviser, at which time we returned to the boarding house to resume our conference. I have always been grateful that our relationship, which lasted for many years thereafter, started out in this manner. While I had every reason to be awe-stricken in the presence of Grenville Clark, I knew from the beginning that one who delighted in the objects of nature as he obviously did, was someone to be respected, but not to be feared. I am sure this was the message he wanted to convey.

A VIEW FROM TEXAS

James P. Hart

My year with Root, Clark began in October 1928. Livingston Hall, then with the firm, had been largely influential in my decision to go there. In those days third-year law school men, in Harvard as elsewhere, went around asking for jobs. I knew that I was lucky that Root, Clark would take me, because from what I had heard and what I saw when I visited them on my job-seeking tour, I felt that the action was there.

Root, Clark's offices at 31 Nassau were overflowing. Later that year they expanded into the adjoining building and even the young recruits then had separate offices, but I started with two officemates. One, Henry J. Friendly, I had seen at Harvard Law School, where he had been editor of the *Law Review* during my second year and where he was known as the man who had made the highest grades since Louis Brandeis. Friendly had just completed a year of clerking for Justice Brandeis when he joined Root, Clark. My other officemate was John A. Wilson (now of Shearman and Sterling), who had taken his law degree at Oxford. Being so closely associated with these two men was a privilege, although at times it became a little confusing when all three of us began dictating (to live secretaries, not to machines) at the same time. Every now and then we would pause in our work and relax and just talk. Wilson would almost always entertain Friendly and me with selections from his great store of memorized quotations. Judging from his eloquence in those sessions, I can readily understand his success as a trial lawyer.

My assignment was to the probate division. The line of authority above me was to Mr. Loyal Leale, Mr. Alfred Intemann, and, at the top, Mr. Grenville Clark. There was a general feeling of cordial, mutual respect throughout the office, from the senior partners to the youngest clerk. My contacts with the senior partners were not numerous, but they were all pleasant. Mr. Root once summoned me to his office to explain a memorandum I had written, and he pleased me mightily by accepting it as I had written it. Mr. Clark then was the same as I have always remembered him—a broad-visioned lawyer, a commanding figure in any group, friendly but very determined, a true Yankee who won the esteem and admiration of this Texan.

Toward the end of my year in New York, my wife and I decided that, after all, we wanted to raise our family in Texas, where we were born and reared, notwithstanding the attractions of New York for both of us, including particularly Root, Clark. Except for a glimpse of him at an American Bar Association meeting in San Francisco in the 1930s, it was a number of years after we moved back to Austin before I saw Mr. Clark again, when he visited his daughter and her family. In informal social surroundings, Mr. Clark was as gracious as he had been impressive in handling technical legal conferences. Later he engaged me to help clear up some rather complicated problems relating to an investment he had made in West Texas oil properties. He honored me by asking me to participate in the work of the Second Dublin Conference in 1965, and it was there that I last saw him.

Looking back over the years, one remembers personally a few men of outstanding character and influence on others. Mr. Grenville Clark was one of those men in my life.

PART IV

Civil Rights

GRENVILLE CLARK, 1882–1967

Louis Lusky

———————◆———————

I knew Mr. Grenville Clark for the last twenty-eight years of his life and followed his work with great and increasing admiration. In October 1938, I was employed as a junior associate by the New York law firm of Root, Clark, Buckner and Ballantine, in which he was a senior partner. That firm was one of the great Wall Street legal establishments; and I expected to find that its efforts were committed exclusively to the service of large corporate interests and to defense of the vested rights of wealthy individuals. I quickly learned, however, that—due largely to the public service ideals of Mr. Clark—its perspective was far broader.

Soon after my arrival, for instance, Mr. Clark invited me to work with him in the preparation of briefs *amicus curiae* for the newly established Bill of Rights Committee of the American Bar Association. At that time the association—which was and is the most influential spokesman for the American bar—was much more conservative in its outlook than it is today, and had done little to participate in the tremendous social changes of the day. In particular, it had failed to speak effectively in defense of our constitutionally guaranteed freedoms of speech, press, assembly, and religion, which are more directly important to the dissenter and the disinherited than to the wealthy conformist. But in 1938, as a result of an address by Mr. Clark in which he urged that protection of civil liberties is a high duty of the American lawyer, the association established a Bill of Rights Committee and made Mr. Clark its first chairman.

It was my privilege, as a very young attorney (my work with Mr. Clark's firm was my first experience as a practicing lawyer), to assist Mr. Clark in writing the first two of the great briefs filed by his committee. Both of them dealt with difficult issues of fundamental importance, on which the existing law was doubtful. In both, the committee's position was ultimately accepted by the Supreme Court. The cases are succinctly described as follows by Irving Dilliard in "Grenville Clark: Public Citizen" (*The American Scholar* 33, no. 1 [Winter 1963–64]: 5–6):

> The committee went into action . . . in two eminent civil liberties cases. First it strongly opposed Mayor Frank Hague in his arbitrary and unconstitutional deportation of Norman Thomas from Jersey City where the Socialist leader was prevented from addressing a public meeting. In the Hague case the committee was resoundingly on the winning side. Then, after a year of study of the compulsory flag salute issue, the committee filed a brief, prepared by Clark and * Chafee, in opposition to the claims of the Minersville (Pa.) School District that it could, first, compel children to salute the flag as a condition to staying in school, and, second, that if pupils did not join in the compulsory flag salute the School Board had the authority to suspend them.
>
> Two children in the school, Lillian Gobitis, aged twelve, and her brother William, aged ten, refused to take part in the daily salute. Their parents taught them that according to their religion (Jehovah's Witnesses) to salute the flag was to "bow down before a graven image." The committee's brief argued that to insist on the flag salute in those circumstances amounted to an unconstitutional infringement of religious liberty. Here the committee in June, 1940, lost 8 to 1—temporarily. The majority opinion written by classmate Frankfurter, then a new Justice, was soon seriously weakened in the 5 to 4 handbills case also arising from the activities of the Jehovah's Witnesses. In less than three years, the 8 to 1 decision in *Minersville School District* v. *Gobitis* was reversed by the Supreme Court in the 6 to 3 decision in *West Virginia State Board of Education* v. *Barnette*. The brief of Clark and Chafee and the Bill of Rights Committee of the American Bar Association had become the law of the land.

* Zechariah

After World War II I left New York and returned to Louisville, Kentucky, my home town, to practice law. But I continued to follow Mr. Clark's work, and—to my great pleasure—he kept in touch with me. Over the years he continued to demonstrate his devotion to the cause of the basic individual rights and freedoms. Time and again he wrote me words of encouragement and support with respect to unpopular civil liberties cases on which I was working in Louisville; and I have little doubt that he did the same thing for others of the many young lawyers whose early careers he helped to guide. One of them, incidentally, later sat on the Supreme Court of the United States (John M. Harlan) and another on the United States Court of Appeals for the Second Circuit in New York (Henry J. Friendly).

In 1960 my association with Mr. Clark again became more direct. He retained me to serve as attorney for Dr. Willard Uphaus, a pacifist who was imprisoned in New Hampshire because of his continued refusal to name the hundreds of people who had visited his summer camp, known as "World Fellowship," in an official investigation which Dr. Uphaus thought was intended for the sole purpose of exposing those people to ostracism and obloquy because of their lawful but unpopular views. The U.S. Supreme Court, in a 5 to 4 decision, had held that Dr. Uphaus could be imprisoned for the rest of his life unless he abandoned his conscientious objections and disclosed the names. Dr. Uphaus, a theologian of strong convictions, had remained firm—and so had the New Hampshire authorities.

At his own expense, Mr. Clark retained me to request reconsideration of the matter by the Supreme Court of the United States. In a 6 to 3 decision, the Court adhered to its previous views. But shortly thereafter—as a direct result, I think, of Mr. Clark's efforts—the New Hampshire authorities relented and liberated Dr. Uphaus.

In the spring of 1961 Mr. Clark called upon me again in a civil liberties matter. He retained my services, once more at his own expense, as an observer in the so-called Freedom Ride cases in Montgomery, Alabama, and Jackson, Mississippi, where Negroes were prosecuted for asserting their constitutional right to equal treatment in interstate travel. And in October of that year, with no publicity at all, he advanced $20,000 of his own money to help meet the exorbitant demands for bail that threatened to lead many of those Negroes to give up their fight for acquittal—a fight they won years later, in the U.S. Supreme Court.

Because Mr. Clark's efforts to bring about the establishment of world peace through world law are already well known, I have thought it appropriate here to emphasize his work in the field of civil liberties, for it may be less familiar. In closing, however, I do wish to add a word about Mr. Clark's direct contribution to the peace effort. *World Peace through World Law*, the book he wrote with Professor Louis B. Sohn of Harvard Law School, stands unrivaled as the best starting point for any serious discussion of the peace problem. Recently *Political Science Quartely* published an article I wrote, "Four Problems in Lawmaking for Peace," in which I suggested the need for further study of some of the issues dealt with in the Clark and Sohn book. I must confess to some personal distress, because of the necessity of saying some basically critical things about the book. But Mr. Clark, to whom I showed the manuscript, gave his warm approval and encouragement to its publication.

I think he was the greatest American lawyer of his time.

ONE MAN'S CONCEPTION

OF GRENVILLE CLARK

Francis E. Rivers

One of Emerson's essays, "Uses of Great Men," contains the sentence: "The search after the great is the dream of youth, and the most serious occupation of manhood." My few associations with Grenville Clark made me feel that I had succeeded in that most serious occupation; and had found a great man.

My first reason for having this feeling is: he exemplifies for me a paradigm of the creative leader of great movements. I believe that in all the movements in which he played a prominent part, he would be deemed the Great Initiator, the Organizer, the one who was both the Idea and the Will. This seemed to be his life-style, for example: to recognize that the sinking of the *Lusitania* would eventually lead the country into war, and then to begin necessary preparations for getting and training officers indispensable for leading an efficient national army of the United States of America.

The same type of action appeared in all of his subsequent ventures: from the Plattsburg camps to his 1960 proposal to aid the Negroes' fight for full, equal citizenship by means of the Grenville Clark Plan. His organizing and leading the successful fight against the packing of the Supreme Court, his sponsorship of the Selective Service Act, and his important influence on assembling world leaders to help in the creation of world law as a means to world peace were all products and examples of this Great Initiative.

To describe him as the "Plumed Knight" or the "Happy Warrior" may be unfitting, but to me he always has seemed to be the man who:

> "Plays in the many games of life
> That one, Where what he most doth value
> Must be won."

It was fortunate that he inherited the freedom which is indispensable for one being the Great Initiator of movements: economic security which enabled him to take the courageous position on every important issue, without any need for indulging in distortions or compromises in order to serve a pressing economic need, or without any thought for advancing careerist ambitions. How many lawyers could, or would have taken effective lead in starting a movement against the court-packing bill of his friend the president of the United States? And how many could have still retained that friendship, so that three years later he could be instrumental in having that president accept Henry L. Stimson as his secretary of war?

At the same time, however, so adverse an effect did Mr. Clark's brilliant success with the Plattsburg movement have upon my own fortunes, and the things nearest to me, that it was not until much later in life that circumstances permitted me to become objective about him and appreciate fully his greatness.

His plan for creating the Plattsburg Officers' Training Camp was initiated while I was in New Haven, Connecticut, a graduate of Yale College (Phi Beta Kappa), and had completed my first year at Harvard Law School. Hence, I felt that I was suitable material for admission as an officer candidate at Plattsburg or any other officers' training camp. Upon making application, and being called in for an interview by the commanding officer of that area, I was told that I was rejected upon the ground that I was a Negro, and that none of these camps would accept any Negroes for training as army officers. My subsequent experiences were: I was admitted to the racially segregated officers' training camp at Fort Des Moines, Iowa, where I completed the four-month course. The persons comprising the Des Moines camp were: 1) a few white commissioned officers in charge of all the training; 2) a number of Negro noncommissioned officers, regular army, who directed all the training of all officer candidates; 3) the Negro trainees, most of whom had just graduated from various colleges, particularly those in New England.

At the termination of the Fort Des Moines Training Camp all the noncommissioned regular army Negro candidates were commissioned as captains or majors, while all of the civilian Negro candidates were limited to ranks of first or second lieutenant and assigned to serve under the former noncommissioned Negro officers. It was bad enough that this subordination was imposed for the duration on college-trained Negroes to serve under enlisted men from the regular army (even though such rule was not followed in the divisions where white soldiers were assigned), but the war department also exhibited a callous disregard for normal sensitivities when the certificates of commission showed clearly that the word "captain" had been erased and replaced by "first lieutenant."

All these Negro officers and soldiers were then placed in two racially segregated divisions and sent to Europe in the winter of 1917–1918, where most of these Negro men experienced humiliating treatment and frustrating activity, such as assignment to labor battalions or other duties far from active combat areas. The result was a false legacy from the Argonne Forest that the Negro soldier fights better under a white officer.

The thinking, imagination, professional skill, tactful activity, and resolution exhibited by Mr. Clark in achieving the Selective Service Act in 1940 was unprecedented and perhaps will never be matched by any single private citizen again. There was, however, nothing included in that act to bar Negro soldiers from again being required to fight under segregated conditions, even though such fighting was aimed at destroying the racial intolerance practiced by Hitler's Germany. It is difficult for an admirer of Mr. Clark not to feel somewhat disappointed that in constructing this Selected Service Act, he did not challenge in any way the rigid tradition of racial segregation in our armed forces.

However, in view of Mr. Clark's habit of putting "first things first" we can believe that he put "winning the war" above everything else, and he had, as did Mr. Stimson, "a mistrust of the use

of the army as an agency of social reform." In any event, so far
as I know, Mr. Clark's record prior to 1960 contains little evidence
whether he revered the guarantees owed to the Negro under the
"Equal Protection Clause," as much as he did the First Amendment freedoms owed to every citizen, where the record was most
clear.

Convincing evidence of his devotion to *civil liberties* was shown
in his courageous and able handling of the battle over these First
Amendment rights in the famous cases of Gobitis, Uphaus, and
Norman Thomas. It was shown further in the distinguished work
he did in the 1930s with the *Bill of Rights Review*, which stated
as its objective the maintenance of both the *letter and spirit of
the law of civil liberties*. (The rights of Equal Protection of the
Law under the Fourteenth Amendment were still being inter-
preted loosely as being covered under civil liberties.) Hence it is,
that one accustomed to putting Mr. Clark's career in such per-
spectives would be most agreeably surprised, if not shocked, upon
learning that Mr. Clark had written the views concerning the
problem of Negro rights as appeared in his important May 2,
1960, letter to Dr. Allan Knight Chalmers.

The logical explanation is that he had believed in a single interpretation of the Constitution and Bill of Rights all along. He
felt strongly that the maintenance of a caste system in America
for more than twenty million people was repugnant to, and inconsistent with, the existence of the United States of America as a
constitutional democracy, and the achievement of any world peace
through world law.

In this letter to Dr. Chalmers (then president of the NAACP
Legal Defense and Educational Fund, Inc.) he spoke of having
been influenced by a recent reading of Allen Nevins's two volumes,
The Emergence of Lincoln, covering the years 1857–1861. He believed that instructive parallels existed between those years and
what had occurred following the Supreme Court's 1954 decision
on school segregation. Perhaps his highly developed sense of history was by itself the main influence on him. However, his letter
coincided with the famous *massive resistance*, attempts by Negroes
to free themselves from caste discrimination by means of sit-ins,
freedom rides, and ignoring color lines. This counterresistance by
black Americans, aided by many whites, resulted in a multiplicity

of arrests, unlimited brutality and homicides, long confinement before trial, as well as harsh prison sentences. I know that this state of affairs disturbed Mr. Clark tremendously. He worked unceasingly at great expense to provide bail and court representation for as many of these defendants as he could.

It is possible that the whole climate of revolution during these years instilled in Mr. Clark the thought that making the Fourteenth Amendment mean what it says for Negroes as well as whites was an idea whose time had come.

I like to believe that the resolute purposes and skillful fights in the courts waged by the Legal Defense Fund and the many able lawyers it recruited from all groups contributed to Mr. Clark's decision to make his fight for equal civil rights of an importance almost matching, if not equal to, that of his fight for world peace through world law.

Another observation is the following: this marks the first time that anyone had presented a carefully thought-out analysis of the various elements of the whole problem—its unlimited cost, the need for developing the continuing money-raising organization, fixing the minimum of contribution at a realistic and demanding level, and himself setting an inspiring example by pledging to give a large sum annually for a number of years.

Certainly the letter is an example of Mr. Clark following his own injunction which is quoted in Mr. Dilliard's article in *American Scholar:* "For I wish that our thinking shall not be crippled by timidity or undue regard for tradition but shall be imaginative and creative as the problem is vast and new. I further wish that we may resist any temptation to avoid the hardest problems." One has to feel that Mr. Clark in composing the letter, and in all actions he took to assist this fight for equal rights, performed with the same techniques and high standards as were present in his convening of the Dublin Conference in 1945 out of which came the Dublin Declaration.

To see Mr. Clark working later, when he projected how he would implement the promises of his 1960 letter in his Last Will, was an inspiring example in concentration: it was a cold bleak day in the country; his wife was upstairs suffering with a terminal illness; but from when Mr. Clark started, to when he finished, his attention never left the problem and he missed no detail.

Dr. Donald S. Harrington of the Community Church of New York, when speaking at the memorial held for Mr. Clark at his church on January 22, 1967, mentioned the fact that in May of 1964 he made an additional anonymous personal contribution of more than half a million dollars to the NAACP Legal Defense and Educational Fund. Officers and directors of the Legal Defense Fund have cited this distinguished gift not only because of its munificence but also because it meant that Mr. Clark, in his final testamentary disposition, had shown respect for the eternal fight for equal rights to human dignity, as he had done for the eternal fight to secure world peace through world law.

Felix Frankfurter once told an anecdote about Mr. Clark at Harvard Law School which, without perhaps meaning it, gave a prophetic illustration of what would be Mr. Clark's personality and his continuing struggles of a lifetime.

> Grenville Clark, a great citizen, and I were in the same class. He was one of these deep, but slow minds. He was always a little behind the most active minds in the class. Joey Beale (Harvard professor, Conflict of Laws) would get off these funny theories of his. Some of us who were more agile than Grennie—not deeper, but more agile; they're very different things—would give Joey Beale a run for his money. After a while everybody would know where everybody was and we would quit. Beale one day got off a most preposterous theory, trying to reconcile the irreconcilable. The hunt was on. After a while the hunt stopped, but Grennie Clark was still reflecting on this when everybody was through with it. He intervened and said: "But Mr. Beale, the rule that you've formulated is very difficult to apply." Beale almost jumped across the table and beat him with one of his outrageous bits of casuistic repartee: "Mr. Clark, I haven't advertised this as a cinch course."

It is fair to say, however, that whatever may have been Mr. Clark's type of mind, it was always one of America's most valuable and creative properties, at least from the time of the Plattsburg movement to the time of his death. Nothing could convey better the most notable characteristics of Mr. Clark than his statement: *"But Mr. Beale, the rule that you've formulated is very difficult to apply."*

It illustrates that even then (1906, at twenty-four years of age) he searched for theories which could be applied; that he was resolute in his search for reality, for testing whether he had found it; and was concerned with finding the truth; and not concerned with proving his mind equal to, or more brilliant than, his fellow students.

It shows a man concerned with finding ways to translate an idea into a form most suited for constructing a new reality. This was particularly true of his effort to find methods which would finance a fight of endless duration so that the *modus vivendi* of all Negroes and whites, in the army as well as in civilian life, be equal status and mutual enjoyment instead of segregation.

And so we can believe that during a lifetime of seeking to find and formulate rules which can be applied, Mr. Clark, in keeping with the injunction he gave at the bar convention where he received the Gold Medal, resisted any temptation to take the easy way. Moreover, as one of his last charges, he undertook perhaps the hardest problem of America: raising the capital needed to forge a successful *modus vivendi* between whites and Negroes.

And so, in January 1967, at Dublin, New Hampshire, when I joined the audience in their singing in most spirited fashion "Onward Christian Soldiers," I felt Mr. Clark was there and still trying to urge us on to meet bigger challenges.

A MEMO ON GRENVILLE CLARK

Roger N. Baldwin

Although I had known Grenville Clark slightly at Harvard, where he was an impressive upperclassman, and read and heard of him in subsequent years, it was not until he surprisingly came forth in the American Bar Association in 1938 as a champion of civil liberties that I had a measure of his stature as a courageous liberal.

The Union was then in two federal court cases testing the Bill of Rights, and Grenville Clark promptly got his new committee of the Bar Association to file *amicus* briefs, then an unheard-of procedure. Such was his prestige that he could swing it. I marveled at it then and told him so, expressing my doubts about continued Association support if he withdrew. But he was convinced he had started it on a useful course because it was right. He expected his moral judgment to be shared. It was not, and in a few years his successors had given up any effort. The Bill of Rights was too controversial to get lawyers to agree on its interpretations. Although I did not mention his effort to him after its failure, I am sure he must have recognized how personal it had been.

He joined the National Committee of the ACLU and remained a member until his death, never, so far as I recollect, raising any question about the many controversial positions the Union took. His defense of academic freedom at Harvard as a member of the Corporation served as an eloquent expression of principles we all shared.

In later years Grenville Clark and I became associated with the

United Nations efforts to build a world order of law. I worked through the human rights agencies, he through the wider fields of disarmament and international law. As the human rights agencies became blocked by the resistance of national sovereignty, I turned more to figuring how it could be broken down. I had read his proposals but I could not see the road from where we were to where he wanted to go. So twice I went to see him in Dublin, two successive summers when I was visiting nearby. I put my concerns to him. He answered that it was not his role to chart the course; he had set the goal, analyzed the problems, and detailed the proper arrangements. It was for others to find the way.

I was struck then, as I was later by his public speeches, with the force of his faith that what was right would prevail if enough people understood. His great talents as a lawyer combined with moral fire to make him a pioneer on the road to the goal of a world of law and peace.

GRENVILLE CLARK

Jack Greenberg

———◆———

I personally knew Grenville Clark only slightly, although he made a considerable impact on the Legal Defense Fund and helped stimulate its growth at a critical time in history. Before I became director-counsel in 1961, Mr. Clark had written to Allan Knight Chalmers proposing that we enlist financial support from the public on a sustained, predictable basis so that we could have the funds to bring cases over a number of years without fear of starting things we could not finish.

This led to the development of the Grenville Clark Plan, in which we enlisted financial support on that basis. The effect was substantial. What happened was that a number of contributors did pledge funds over a number of years. But many others who did not join the Grenville Clark Plan had their sights raised and, in fact, gave more and regularly. At the time of the great civil rights demonstrations, sit-ins, freedom marches, Mr. Clark became even more convinced about the rightness of his proposal and urged it strongly upon us and others whom he could influence.

I recall meeting with him several times, once in New Hampshire, once at his home on Long Island, and once at the Columbia University Club in New York City. I was amazed at his vigor and clarity of thought. He, a number of times, analogized the Grenville Clark Plan to planning for a major war, referring back to his experience in setting up the draft in World War I and World War II.

On one occasion I asked him what stimulated his interest in race relations and he referred to an incident in his childhood when he had to move to South Carolina for his health. There he saw black people being treated quite literally no better than dogs at the plantation where he stayed, and the episode so affected him that for the remainder of his life he was dedicated to racial equality. It would be simplistic to accept this as the only reason for his social views, but doubtless it contributed.

He arranged his estate in a way to assure the Legal Defense Fund a grant of $50,000 a year for ten years following his death. The money comes in now and is an important part of our financial resources.

He had the faith and vision and capacity to make large commitments and think in terms of the future of a nation (and even the world). That was to me his most striking quality. It is the sort of thing that characterized the founding fathers of this nation and which we will need in greater measure if we are to arrive at his goals of world peace and racial equality.

GRENVILLE CLARK AND

THE HARRY BRIDGES EPISODE

Charles E. Wyzanski, Jr.

I encountered Grenville Clark many times during his long life, and I admired him greatly. Even when we differed during the Arnold Arboretum controversy, he treated me gently and in the most gentlemanly manner.

There was one episode in Mr. Clark's career which is not well known and in which I had a direct personal involvement. It was in the late 1930s, and my involvement consisted of efforts on behalf of Secretary of Labor Frances Perkins to persuade Grenville Clark to accept appointment as a special hearing officer to determine whether Harry Bridges, the head of the West Coast Longshoremen's Union, was an alien who sought the overthrow of the United States by violence, and so was deportable under existing immigration laws.

Harry Bridges had been for several years an active radical leader of the longshoremen on the West Coast. He was also Australian-born. Steamship owners, patriotic societies like the Daughters of the American Revolution, the conservative press, and the vocal right-wing of Congress (led by Martin Dies of Texas) had a firm, volubly expressed conviction that Bridges was a dangerous alien whose residence in the United States should be terminated because he fell within the statutory provisions for deportation. Secretary Perkins, who detested Bridges personally (largely because his sexual activities did not comport with her puritanical standards), had never been persuaded that there was even a *prima facie* case against the Australian Bridges. With rectitude and high conscientious views of her duty as secretary of labor, she had consistently refused to issue a deportation warrant. She was fully prepared to suffer the political consequences. And these were not long in coming. A House committee was about to summon her for testimony regarding possible impeachment when I entered the drama. From Ropes, Gray, Boyden and Perkins (the Boston law firm in which I had become a partner after serving from 1933 to 1935 as her solicitor at the Department of Labor), I was asked to come to Washington to help her prepare her statement before the House committee and to give her general counsel. The statement having been prepared and delivered, I then advised her that the best course would be to issue a complaint against Bridges, and to call upon the labor leader to give testimony bearing upon his deportability—such evidence to be received and appraised by a special appointee, whose findings and conclusions she, as secretary of labor, would review. I proposed that she appoint Grenville Clark. Miss Perkins acceded to my suggestions and authorized me to approach him. Grenny, as soon as he returned from a holiday off the Georgia coast, received me at his Nassau Street New York office.

The story told, Grenny with characteristic thoroughness cross-examined me on all the details and discussed the legality, propriety, and wisdom of the proposed procedures. He saw the disadvantages to him personally if he became involved—but these were matters of no account to him. He recognized Secretary Perkins' high motives, her serious political plight, and the necessity of drastic action to serve the public interest. He accepted the assignment. I left.

A few days later, in discussions with his partners, Grenny was reminded that one of them was principal counsel for the American-Hawaiian Steamship Company, the chief antagonist of Bridges and a constant negotiator with the Longshoremen's Union. Grenny phoned me to return to New York. When I came, he pointed to the conflict of interest and we agreed that he could not serve as planned. Then we discussed who should be the appointee. It was our common conclusion that the best substitute should be the newly named dean of the Harvard Law School, James M. Landis, who had recently been a weekend guest of the Clarks'. And so it was. Jim Landis found Bridges nondeportable; Miss Perkins affirmed his findings. Congress then transferred administration of the immigration laws to the department of justice. Attorney General Robert Jackson issued a warrant for the arrest of Bridges. Francis Biddle in the interim succeeded Jackson as attorney general. The Justice Department ordered deportation, and, finally, just as the United States became involved in World War II, the deportation order was reversed by the Supreme Court of the United States. And, perhaps most ironically, Harry Bridges became one of the most fervent labor leaders in support of the wartime effort. The Longshoremen's Union did not strike during World War II.

It was an interesting episode, one in which Grenny played his usual inconspicuous (albeit important) role.

GRENVILLE CLARK
AND THE UPHAUS CASE
Robert H. Reno

———◆———

A mutual friend of Grenville Clark and myself once said, "It takes Mr. Clark forever to make up his mind, but I've never known him to be wrong." Both parts of that observation are bound to be a little inaccurate, but, in any event, it did not take him long to make up his mind about the imprisonment of Willard Uphaus in December 1959. Only three days after Uphaus was committed to the Merrimack County Jail, "there to remain for one year . . . or until he purges himself of contempt or until further order of this Court," Clark wrote to Wesley Powell, then governor of New Hampshire, urging Uphaus' immediate release from jail, and his efforts on Uphaus' behalf continued until he was finally set free almost a year later—two days before the original commitment of one year had expired.

Uphaus' case had generated considerable notoriety, both at home and abroad, in the late 1950s. The attorney general of New Hampshire, Louis C. Wyman, acting as a one-man legislative "committee" to investigate subversive activities, pursuant to authority granted to him by the New Hampshire legislature in 1953 and subsequently extended, undertook an investigation of World Fellowship, a summer camp near Conway, New Hampshire, of which Uphaus was director. In the course of that investigation the attorney general questioned Uphaus privately on at least two occasions. Uphaus answered without reservations all questions about his own affiliations and behavior and about the activities at the camp. On grounds of conscience, however, he refused to provide information about the names of the nonprofessional employees at the camp; to furnish correspondence between himself and speakers invited to the camp; and to identify the persons who had attended the camp in 1954 and 1955—approximately 300 during each year.

The only real dispute involved the names of the guests at the camp, and it was this issue which became the basis of Uphaus' confinement. As one local observer put it, "It's a shame to send an old man to jail because he won't give up his Christmas card list." Clark's response to that comment was that it "has some real Christmas and Christian spirit in it, of which we could do with a little more now."

On March 31, 1960, the New Hampshire supreme court upheld the lower court order confining Uphaus, and a few days later Clark shifted into high gear in a new effort to get Uphaus' case before the U.S. Supreme Court, at his own expense. (On a previous appeal that Court had upheld the constitutionality of the New Hampshire statute authorizing the investigation.) This move by Clark should have come as no surprise to those who knew him well or remembered his work with the Bill of Rights Committee of the American Bar Association in the late 1930s. I'm sure it did not surprise Louis Lusky, a former clerk of Mr. Justice Stone and an old friend of Clark's from the days of Lusky's service as a young lawyer in the Root, Clark firm. After a few telephone calls from Dublin to Louisville, Kentucky, where Lusky was then practicing, Lusky came to New Hampshire to talk with Clark about the possibility of getting the case to the U.S. Supreme Court once more—provided that Uphaus was willing and that appropriate arrangements could be made for Lusky to have full authority and responsibility for the appeal.

It was not as easy to perfect these arrangements as one might assume. Mr. Clark was the moving force in bringing about an agreement, and once that had been done, primarily by telephone, he, in his customary way, reduced it to writing, making sure that no possible point had been overlooked and that all interested persons were fully informed. From that point forward, although he had originally told Uphaus that he would not be able to participate in the effort himself, he was in almost daily communication, by telephone or letter, with Louis Lusky and me. His analysis of the legal niceties of the case was superb, and his direction of both strategy and tactics indicated why he was one of the great lawyers of the twentieth century.

The first move was a petition to the supreme court of New Hampshire for Uphaus' release on bail, pending the new appeal to the U.S. Supreme Court. The petition was argued before the New Hampshire court on June 8, and that same day Mr. Clark issued the following statement:

> I regard the jailing of Dr. Uphaus as a glaring injustice, which is a disgrace to New Hampshire and a discredit to our country. I also believe that his continued detention in jail because, for reasons of conscience, he will not disclose certain names is unconstitutional under our Federal Constitution; and I believe that the legal issues, some of them new, should be reconsidered by the Supreme Court of the United States. These are the reasons why I have assumed the legal expenses of the new proceedings. It is a privilege to help in the effort to remedy this shocking injustice.

In this, as in other situations, there was no doubt about Clark's position.

The New Hampshire supreme court denied Uphaus' petition for bail, as had been expected. This was followed immediately by a similar motion presented to Mr. Justice Frankfurter, the full court having recessed for the summer. It, too, was denied, and Mr. Justice Black then declined to act on the bail application, saying that the questions presented were so similar to those raised in the first Uphaus appeal, in which he dissented, that he did not wish to pass on the application and asked that it be presented to another justice. The bail motion was then presented to Mr. Justice Douglas.

In the meantime, the jurisdictional statement was prepared and filed with the Supreme Court. Two weeks later word was received that Mr. Justice Douglas had referred the bail motion to the entire Court and that it had been denied, with the chief justice, Mr. Justice Black, and Mr. Justice Douglas noting their opinion that it should be granted.

It was soon October 1960. The Court had reconvened. A brief had been filed in opposition to the attorney general's motion to dismiss the appeal. As Clark wrote to Lusky, "Everything possible has been done to get a reconsideration in Washington." Although he believed that the odds were heavy against the appeal being accepted, in typical Clark style he was already putting his mind to whether a new bail motion should be made if, by chance, the Court were to take jurisdiction of the case.

His thinking had gone even further. He wrote to Lusky: "I have my mind [on] planning very methodically and carefully as to what strategy and tactics to adopt, assuming as we should assume that Wyman pursues his persecution of Uphaus on and after December 14. . . . I think it would be well actually to write down a sort of battle plan to meet the two or three possible forms of attack which Wyman will presumably adopt. . . ."

The "possible forms of attack" were discussed in much detail, by letter and telephone, during the next few weeks, with Clark an active participant in all the deliberations. Finally, on November 14, the U.S. Supreme Court declined to hear the case. Uphaus, whose cheerful stoicism was a hallmark of this case, did not seem to be particularly surprised or overly disappointed. He did express concern about being finally released from jail on December 14, the expiration of his one-year sentence.

There was one bright side, however, to the denial of appeal: ordinarily there are no dissenting opinions upon denial of an appeal, but this time there were two. As Lusky wrote to Uphaus, "The fine dissenting opinions make it plain that your effort to obtain a further test of your rights was by no means an unreasonable one." Justice Black's dissent, in particular, stands as one of the most eloquent affirmations to individual liberties delivered in recent times.

Clark, after reading the Court's majority opinions, commented that "this court is just too weak on these issues, considering the trend of the times. 'Old man Hughes' would never let them get away with this."

On December 8, Attorney General Wyman, egged on by the Manchester *Union-Leader*, requested the New Hampshire superior court to keep Uphaus in jail after the expiration of the one-year sentence *indefinitely* if he did not purge himself of contempt by giving the names of his guests. This motion was denied. Whether the attorney general planned to subpoena Uphaus again as he left the jail on December 14 will probably never be known, for the judge who had sent Uphaus to jail released him on Sunday, December 12, with no advance notice, and he quietly left the state and the jurisdiction of both the attorney general and the New Hampshire courts.

Mr. Clark had summarized his feeling about the entire effort in a letter to Lusky on November 17:

> The outcome . . . is something of a disappointment, though not a shock. For the fact is that the cards were pretty well stacked against us from the beginning, having in mind the unfortunate combination of circumstances including: (a) the international tension growing more tense during our period of activity and (b) a bad Court for this sort of case. . . .
>
> With regard to a third appeal to the Supreme Court if the imprisonment is continued after December 14, my belief is that there should be such an appeal even if the continued imprisonment is based on the old statute. For I think that there would come a point, and very likely on that appeal, when even the present Court would turn around.

More than a decade after the last Uphaus appeal, certain things still stand out clearly in the recollection of one who was associated with it.

First and foremost was Mr. Clark's determination that a wrong should be righted and his willingness to mobilize and finance such an effort, regardless of the odds against him. Although "disappointed" with the outcome, he felt that "the effort we have made has been well worthwhile from my point of view."

But then I suppose the determination to right wrongs had always been true of the man, and the other memories of the Uphaus case which stick in my mind were also typical of Grenville Clark: careful analysis of the issues; a painstaking search for any point which might previously have been overlooked; full use of the telephone to confer with the best people available on any given point, regardless of where they were; attention to what most of us would have dismissed as insignificant detail; patience; determination; careful thought; more determination; never losing sight of the desired end; not being deterred by obstacles; courage; and at the end, asking no credit for himself.

GRENVILLE CLARK:

A Vignette

William Worthy

———————◆———————

Rarely does a person facing a possible five years in a federal peni-
tentiary in an unpopular political case open the morning mail to
find an unsolicited defense fund contribution from a prestigious
Wall Street lawyer with impeccable Establishment credentials.

A decade ago, this was my personal introduction to Grenville
Clark. In a transparent effort to discourage any reporting from
Cuba that deviated from the official line ("chaos" on the island;
the "imminent collapse" of Fidel Castro; a population yearning
to rebel against a "brutal tyranny" of Hitlerian proportions), I had
been indicted in April 1962 by a federal grand jury in Miami on
the novel and startling charge of returning to my native land from
Cuba "without bearing a valid passport." It so happened that five
years earlier I had gone to China in defiance of a similar State
Department travel ban, and John Foster Dulles had refused to re-
new my passport.

Those now of college age are largely unaware of the hysteria
that gripped this country early in the 1960s in the wake of the
Cuban revolution. It was a foregone conclusion that I would be
convicted and sentenced to prison in the U.S. District Court in
Miami—and I was. Attorneys who specialized in civil liberties
cases differed among themselves about my likely fate on appeal—
especially when the appeal had to be filed during the very month

of the Cuban missile crisis! Some lawyers felt that the Supreme Court would uphold the right to travel and the right to know, even in the face of the prevailing climate, perhaps by a five-to-four majority. Others were more pessimistic.

While the American press had largely supported my right to report from China, I received relatively little journalistic support in the Cuba prosecution, although the First Amendment principles were the same in both cases. The climate was such that few would risk being labeled "pro Castro," even on a straight civil liberties issue. *Retroactively*, once my conviction was unanimously reversed in 1964 and the law declared unconstitutional on its face, the *New York Times* and other influential publications decided that the State and Justice Departments had been wrong in initiating the prosecution.

Thus my surprise during 1962 to open an envelope with an unfamiliar New Hampshire postmark and to find inside a check and a supportive letter from Grenville Clark. After having read about my case in *Rights*, the organ of the National Emergency Civil Liberties Committee, he had then obtained my address from the director. That so distinguished a partner in what my mother would have called "a princely law firm" even read an NECLC publication—in a period when that organization was being attacked as a "Communist front" and worse—also surprised me initially. At the time I was unaware of Mr. Clark's regal indifference to what others might think of his determination to uphold personal liberty.

Almost two years elapsed before I actually met Grenville Clark. But in the meantime we came to know each other through correspondence and through lengthy long-distance calls. In 1963, a group of physician scholars who wished to visit China (nine years before Richard Nixon made such ideas respectable) approached Mr. Clark to seek his legal support. With an attention to detail that most attorneys would have relegated to an assistant or a secretary, he telephoned me several times for advice on the most fruitful ways of contacting the Chinese for visas. To him, the estrangement of the peoples of China and the United States was wholly undesirable. In the willingness of the academics to visit Peking he perceived an opportunity to diminish that alienation and also to undermine the still existing travel bans.

By 1964, Grenville Clark decided that he himself would also

like to visit China, and again he was in touch with me. Once more I saw the energy that he poured into anything he regarded important. Learning that I was soon leaving for the forbidden land of North Vietnam and that I hoped, while in Hanoi, to obtain a Chinese visa, he asked me to hand-deliver to the Chinese embassy a letter from him applying for entry into China.

That was when the two of us met, at his hotel in New York, for the one and only time. The start of the bombing of North Vietnam was only three months away. As a lawyer, Grenville Clark knew that in the war climate heating up in Washington I might well be prosecuted once again—this time for *leaving* the United States for a country officially out of bounds. He never said so, but I thought then and think now that his unsolicited $400 check for expenses toward the trip was his deliberate way of involving himself in my "illegality."

If the Johnson administration had chosen to indict me (and federal agents visited the travel agency that booked me to Hanoi), I believe that Grenville Clark would have stepped forward and publicly insisted that he too be prosecuted for having aided and abetted the journey. From the start, he was as opposed as I was to U.S. intervention in Vietnam. I surmised that, in that pivotal 1964–1965 period, even at the age of eighty-two, Grenville Clark would have welcomed the opportunity to put his monumental prestige on the line, as a "criminal" defendant in a federal trial, to help stop the war to strengthen the Bill of Rights at home.

In the light of Vietnam, many persons in the United States are beginning to re-examine the historical preludes to Mylai, from the brutalities of the slave trade, through the massacres of the Indians, to the "water-cure" tortures during our colonial wars in Cuba and the Philippines. By some political alchemy, in virtually all those great moral crises, this country has produced a Henry Thoreau, a Wendell Phillips, a Moorfield Storey, a Hugo Black, a Grenville Clark: towering figures, self-assured men driven by a sense of duty who have spoken truth to power.

The genius of these men—these "fundamentalists" in their fidelity to intellectual honesty and to personal freedom—is that they "raised a standard to which all honorable men may repair."

In the flush of youthful idealism, how easy it is to defend the right when many of one's peers also stand at the barricades. How much lonelier it is, at age sixty, seventy, eighty, when virtually none of those peers are still *engagé*. The Boston *Globe* editorialist was stating a general life principle, but he could have been pointing to the life of Grenville Clark when he wrote:

"To fight in confident expectation of victory is the proper valor of youth; the virtue of mature years is to fight equally in the face of strong prospect of frustration."

PART V

Educational

Friendships

MY FRIEND GRENVILLE CLARK

Harold W. Dodds

This is an unabashed, highly personal tribute to Private Citizen Clark, as he has been called by Irving Dilliard, by one who delighted in his friendship for more than thirty years. It will not deal with his professional life or his tours of duty, both formal and informal, in the public service, which others can cover better than I. One must also understand that Mrs. Clark played her part at every step in his career. Their two natures ideally supplemented each other in a deep and mutual loyalty.

Our friendship burst, as it were, from the blue. In the autumn of 1936 FDR was campaigning against Alf Landon for a second term. As one would expect, college faculty opinion polls were running in favor of the New Deal. Coincidentally, a natural controversy over teachers' loyalty oaths had raised the temperature of teachers and heresy hunters alike. Academic freedom, at best a unique sort of freedom difficult for many laymen to comprehend, was undergoing its periodic hostile scrutiny. Ultraconservative alumni, a small but vocal proportion of the whole, were declaring New Dealers unfit to teach youth and threatening to boycott Alma Mater's fund-raising efforts. Because of the depression, contributions were not plentiful, and so complaints from conservative alumni caused some nervousness among fund raisers.

A young and untested university president, I was casting about for a good opportunity to make my position clear to the Princeton faculty and the public generally when I read a strong statement by Grenville Clark, evoked by some alumni unrest that had surfaced at Harvard. The fall meeting of our Graduate Council provided the opportunity I was seeking. What could carry greater conviction, I reasoned, to a group of successful professional men and men of business and thence to our alumni at large, than an address by a highly respected partner of an eminent and conservative law firm, a Fellow of that select body, the President and Fellows of Harvard College, and one possessing such an impeccable social background? He cheerfully accepted our invitation, made the case for academic freedom cogently and convincingly, arguing that teachers should enjoy the full rights of free citizens and that academic freedom was an essential element of the whole bundle of freedoms guaranteed by the Bill of Rights. I endorsed his remarks without reservation and the matter of protesting alumni and faculty freedoms was closed.

Mrs. Clark came with her husband on their first visit to our home. It proved to be the prelude to many other get-togethers, some at Princeton, some at their Long Island home, and later at Outlet Farm in Dublin. For during their first visit of about twenty-four hours' duration some spark passed between the Clarks and the Doddses which worked to transform an acquaintanceship, begun in a service generously rendered and gratefully acknowledged, into what was for us a rare and happy friendship. Before long we had slipped unconsciously into a first-name basis, a relationship more carefully guarded then than today.

Soon I came to see that Mr. Clark's views regarding academic freedom were but a sample of his strong hostility to any effort to narrow the broad scope of the first ten amendments to the Constitution. Throughout his life he remained an energetic opponent of any attempt to erode their full meaning.

It was natural that as a well-informed Fellow of the Corporation at Harvard University, Mr. Clark should think of enlisting college students in his effort to keep intact the whole broad sweep of the first ten amendments. He was sharp in his criticism of the colleges for their failure to indoctrinate their students with an understanding that these amendments remain the true expression of America's idea of human values. To meet this neglect he proposed a special course of study to be required for all students, and a broader program for law schools, which would drive home with no "ifs, ands, or buts" the significance of our civil liberties. I felt that while there was truth in his indictment, its element of indoctrination would be counterproductive. Moreover, being aware of faculty hostility to the very word "indoctrination" and familiar with faculty reaction to the mere suspicion of external influences seeking to promote personal viewpoints, and anticipating student resistance to indoctrination in a campus environment which stresses thinking for oneself, I countered by proposing a milder course of action which avoided the taint of "indoctrination" but radical enough to command the attention of any college president. As it happened, we were not then to progress further with this effort, for hostilities in Europe intervened and the proposals we were considering gave way to crucial matters of war and peace.

Today I have to confess that he sensed more strongly than I the probability of a McCarthy era and how easily large elements of our population can be beguiled into approving, even cheering on, gross violations of basic constitutional principles.

The outbreak of hostilities in Europe in 1939 turned Mr. Clark's thoughts first to strengthening our defenses, for he knew in his bones that we would be drawn into the war sooner or later. At once he began to press for more officer training opportunities. As in World War I, when he masterminded the Plattsburg movement, he foresaw that the army's plans for obtaining emergency officer personnel would fall far short of wartime requirements. He also quickly aligned himself with those advocating universal selective service at a time when to argue for more officer-training facilities, even college R.O.T.C. programs, was considered war-mongering, unbecoming to an advocate of universal law as the way to lasting peace.

But war could not divert him from what was to become his chief concern throughout the rest of his life, the search for a system of world peace. He saw that even if we did not join our natural allies in a shooting war, America would be involved in the peacemaking process. Accordingly, he began to speculate on what the peace terms should be and how the peacemakers might be influenced toward universal disarmament under a supranational peace-keeping authority. In November 1939 the Clarks visited us at Princeton along with President and Mrs. Conant on the weekend of the Harvard football game. After dinner he read to the five of us the outline of a proposal for a *Union of Free Peoples* able to enforce peace through law which, refined and expanded, was published ten years later under the title *A Plan for Peace.* My wife's log records that we sat up late discussing it.

Although I endorsed wholeheartedly Mr. Clark's thesis that disarmament and world government are essential to real world peace, I could not escape the feeling that his outlook reflected too exclusively a legalistic concept of human relations, and I argued that there were certain obstacles along the way that deserved more attention than he was paying to them. He wrote me in 1952, "I have an idea that you think that I take this world affairs business too seriously and that I can accomplish more about them than I really can."

In reply I had to confess that I did not share his belief that fear engendered by nuclear bombs would suffice to drive nations to accept world government as their principal instrumentality for attaining national goals. Among the deeply seated obstacles to be overcome were lack of a common world faith in the Anglo-Saxon tradition of parliaments and courts, the continuing existence of an outworn concept of national sovereignty, and a corresponding trust in the nation-state as the proper source of law and protector of citizen interests. My hope, which is still far from fulfillment, was that the United Nations would develop its potential as an international service agency performing certain practical tasks, common to all states, better than each state could by acting individually. An early example was the Universal Postal Union, which has succeeded in making the whole world substantially one postal union. True, we are witnessing today the coming and going of new international organizations and committees, most striking in areas of finance and commerce, for solving crises beyond the capacity of a single country to resolve by itself, but they tend to be merely *ad hoc*, impermanent organizations floating outside the United Nations.

(It would be interesting to know just how Mr. Clark would analyze the possibility that today's rapidly growing multinational corporations will advance world peace, as claimed by some, or serve rather as promoters of discord and disruption. I think I can guess where he would end up—always optimistic.) My ready (perhaps too ready) analogy was the way king's justice in England came to prevail over feudal justice, namely, by providing a superior system of law better able to meet the need of an expanding economy.

Of course, all this was familiar ground to Mr. Clark. Later, I came to appreciate that to his everlasting credit no such considerations diverted him. The favorable reception of *World Peace through World Law*, and its translation into several languages brought him profound if quiet satisfaction. For Grenny his *magnum opus* was not an end but a new beginning. When the leaders of nations come to consider world law and order seriously, his masterpiece will be welcomed as a textbook and guide to policy. In the meantime it will continue as an educational force, keeping the ideal alive and suggesting how it might be put into effect.

It may well be that fear will prove a stronger deterrent to war today than at the time of the publication of *World Peace through World Law*. Peoples of the world are coming to realize the true extent of the devastation wrought in Indochina by means of new, more dreadful, and more indiscriminate instruments of destruction, not to mention less publicized but even deadlier wars in Africa and elsewhere. The Great Powers may be nearer to accepting the broad validity of Mr. Clark's formula than seemed possible as recently as twenty years ago. Moreover, the fear element today is buttressed by a growing realization among nation-states that many problems of commerce and industry are essentially world problems beyond the capacity of any single one or any balance-of-power system to resolve.

Nevertheless, however deeply I respected Mr. Clark's unswerving dedication to a great cause, the richest memories of my wife and myself converge on our visits to Outlet Farm. They were soul-refreshing occasions for us. The Clarks kept their friendships in repair. They were the perfect hosts.

What helped to make the times so memorable for us was a mutual fondness for good conversation, sober or lighthearted and generously laced with humor. Naturally we touched on current events and subjects such as universities, civil rights, and peace through law, but these did not engage our full attention by any means. Our visits were opportunities for relaxation devoid of any touch of boredom. I enjoyed his stories of personal experiences with the famous and the near famous, living and dead, which he spiced with character analyses flavored with a piquant wit such as I could not hope to match. I felt that such released time from his self-imposed daily quota of work was good for him; I knew it was for me.

For him Outlet Farm was a tonic for both mind and body as well as a tranquilizer for tense nerves. In the spring of 1957 he recorded this influence in a long handwritten letter which said, "Fanny and I have not been off the farm for three months except for a half dozen trips to Peterborough. It has been a new experience but very gratifying and nourishing to see Monadnock in a new winter mood every morning. . . . Our little mountain has an entirely different aspect in winter, much larger and more remote and impressive." Yet he never seemed out of touch with events. He used the long-distance telephone as freely as one might in a simpler era talk to a neighbor over a garden fence; his telephone bills must have been formidable.

Mrs. Clark was always keenly interested in her husband's career, intelligently knowledgeable regarding his work, and eager to see his plans succeed. My wife enjoyed her stories of life in Dublin, Boston, New York, and Washington. Her opinions regarding men and events were her own and they were both entertaining and enlightening. My wife and I admired her skillful management of the home, farm, and garden. The thickness of the cream she served at table remains a pleasant memory and an example of the pleasure she derived from small things as well as great.

The two wives had a common interest in horticulture, at which Mrs. Clark was an expert, and the management of their husbands. For her, looking after a wholly dedicated husband, inclined to make excessive demands on limited health reserves, was no easy or intermittent responsibility. For years he suffered an incurable ailment with grace and fortitude. It was characteristic of him that he found both humor and comfort in the refusal of his London specialist to predict how long he might live because at his age there were so many other diseases he might die from.

Cleveland Amory was right when, in his *Proper Bostonians*, he described Mr. Clark as a patrician. He moved easily among the great for he was at home with them, yet he moved with equal ease among the small for he felt at home with them also. He was a patrician in the best sense of the term. He met fully John Buchan's definition of an aristocrat: "one who gives more to the world than he takes from it." His forthcoming biography will deserve wide reading by young people; it will be an inspiration to them, a reassurance that one need not exhaust oneself in scrambles for public office and personal fame in order to serve well his day and age. Private Citizen Clark has shown that there are quiet but singularly effective ways to serve the public welfare.

CONSERVATION BY CONVERSATION

John S. Dickey

The fact that Grenville Clark was a large person in all ways was manifest to anyone who shared a duck blind with him. Physically it was a tight fit, but the conversation was capacious.

The Clark marsh is located in the Missisquoi River delta where that stream enters the northernmost end of Lake Champlain's one hundred plus miles of historic water. This hunting area has been in the Clark family for several generations although some years prior to my first visit to it a large portion had gone into the establishment of the Missisquoi National Wildlife Refuge. Mr. Clark's brother, Julian, was the principal owner of the family marsh at the time and it was supplemented by hunting rights in the Cranberry Creek region which had been reserved to the Clark family and a retired French-Canadian blacksmith for a period of twenty years, as I recall, when the properties were transferred from private ownership to the federal government. As it turned out, the extensions of the duration of these rights was destined to become a diversionary target for Grenny's inexhaustible mental energies, and during our last years together his "negotiations with the government" on this subject provided a semicomic relief for some of our more somber conversations and our spasmodic attention to the ostensible reason for our cheek-to-jowl presence, duck hunting.

Since these recollections are focused on G. Clark's conversations rather than our hunting, there is regretfully little opportunity here for saying very much about the ducks (blacks, mallards, and a few

146

teal), the dogs (Labradors), the guides (Vermonters), the decoys, the blinds, the place itself, and, of course, the weather, each of which, as any hunter knows, plays a key part in the elemental drama of duck hunting. It is pertinent to say, however, that while Grenny was enough of a shot to bag his four ducks on most days when the ducks were around and although he enjoyed a "good shoot," he definitely prized the place and the occasion more than he did the bag. Toward the end of our fifteen years of hunting together he would sometimes remark, without making too much of a point of it, that as the ducks got fewer and he got older he wasn't sure how many more he wanted to kill. Indeed, he may have become more ambivalent about the shooting than he admitted to himself, but the pull of the total experience was deeply rooted in him and never weakened.

My first effort to become personally acquainted with Mr. Clark appropriately enough grew out of our mutual interest in the Champlain-Missisquoi area and although the particular effort was abortive, it did provide us with an introduction to each other that both of us enjoyed. In the fall of 1951 I was on the sleeper from New York City to St. Albans, Vermont, to spend a few days at the camp on Lake Champlain which Mrs. Dickey and I had recently acquired. Just before we reached St. Albans I struck up a washroom conversation with a fellow traveler obviously dressed for a day of hunting who it turned out was being met by his friend Grenville Clark, Jr. In response to my expressed interest in meeting Mr. Clark, Sr., as one of our leading citizens, my traveling acquaintance, Ralph Hornblower, Jr., remarked that Mr. Clark, Sr., would probably be with the group at the station. As I passed the group in the station, I spotted a strong-faced older man in hunter's garb and, introducing myself, inquired whether he might not be Mr. Clark, Sr. Smiling quietly, he replied, "No, I am Mr. Clark's guide. He was not able to come." On hearing about the incident, Mr. Clark came over to our camp to introduce himself. But he never got over the very genuine pleasure of having John Tracy, the guide, mistaken for him. Occasionally after a period of silence in the blind he would look out over the marsh and simply say, "You know, one of the nicest things that has happened to me was your thinking that that was the way I ought to look. A man couldn't do better than to look like John Tracy."

On our first hunt together in October 1951 Grenny's conversation quickly focused on the subject which was to be the pivotal concern of his life until his death, namely the development of world peace through world law. He opened the discussion by asking how I, as one who had participated in the San Francisco United Nations Conference in 1945, felt about the United Nations as a peace-keeping agency. He was politely interested in my account of the United Nations founding and he agreed with an emphatic "certainly" with my view that U.S. leadership had been unduly timid and unresourceful in its approach to the veto provisions of the charter, particularly as they operated to freeze the amendment procedure. But then, as in each of our later conversations, it was not the past or the perplexities of contemporary problems that commanded his thoughts. He was a man seized of the future and, beyond the bare requirements of politeness, he made no pretense to the contrary.

Korea was a case in point. I attributed great importance to the fact that, however fortuitously, our resistance to that aggression was being carried on under the aegis of the United Nations. Grenny viewed it as all right but not very important. He wasn't particularly interested in the foreign policy problems involved; he surmised that our strong reaction to the North Korean attack was dominantly an anti-Soviet response rather than a fundamental concern for the collective security system and in any event he held the considered view that the existing U.N. organization could never be adequate to the task of keeping a just peace without fundamental changes in the direction of limited world government or world federalism. For him the thing that really mattered at that point was to come to grips in a hard-headed way with the intellectual problem of formulating concretely and as precisely as possible the terms of a charter that would be adequate to the tasks of world peace.

In between relatively infrequent flurries of action or the more frequent moments of enjoined silence and no movement as some wary blacks "looked us over" out of range, our talk came back time after time to the question of how to get done what needed to be done. As I look back over our discussions of the problems of how and when, it seems to me that Grenny based his indomitable faith in a rational outcome on three things:

First, there had to be a plan, a program for action that was adequate to the task. I remember the pleasure he took in recounting with graphic detail the story of a personal happening that demonstrated for him the indispensable need for a plan of action if people are to put their backs into doing something about a problem. It seems that in the days when "getting stuck in the mud" was more than a figure of speech, Mr. Clark and a lawyer friend got their car royally mired on a mud road. Their uninformed efforts to combat the mud resulted in two things: the car sank deeper, and, with no idea as to what to do about it, they concluded it was hopeless and gave up. Happily a more experienced man appeared who, after taking stock of the situation, proposed a plan of action around which the despairing lawyers rallied their efforts and, as they thought, miraculously freed their vehicle from its seemingly hopeless plight. It was such a plan of action that was needed if the intelligent but necessarily inexperienced people of the world were now to be effectively rallied to the tasks of creating a just and lawful international community.

Another thing that was necessary, he said, was for the situation to get worse—as, of course, it would. Over the years, especially after he and Professor Sohn got their plan formulated and published under the title *World Peace through World Law,* and as governments seemed to harden in their indifference to it or in their judgment of its impracticality for their purposes, Mr. Clark increasingly invoked the cold, but for him certain, comfort that things would begin to look up after they had gotten still worse.

But above all else, he kept saying, education will ultimately bring the people of the world to understand their stake in a lawful community. And if they understand it, he would say with closing-curtain finality, they'll get it.

Grenny's talk on all subjects revealed an abiding faith in the power of education. I don't recall our ever discussing the idea of progress, *per se*; he was not much given to pondering out loud about such generalities, at least in a duck blind, but neither did he ever waste time in doubting the power for good in human affairs of more and better education. Needless to say, his concept of education reached far beyond the classroom. He had a fastidious taste for good thinking, but he was not afraid of considered conviction as part of the educational process. He understood the problem and the danger of propagandizing, but his talk was often tinged with disdain when he spoke of the "aseptic objectivity" of educational institutions and particularly of the large foundations in the face of the world's need for greater understanding and swifter change than the classical processes of education could produce. Risk for risk he was disposed to take his chances with the harm of unwise conviction and untruthful propaganda in a free marketplace of ideas as compared with the revolutionary upheavals and reactionary suppressions of a world mired down in the status quo.

When it came to formal education, our talk rarely ranged very far beyond the two institutions with which we had been or were personally involved, Harvard and Dartmouth. Grenny's pride in his Harvard College and Harvard Law School connections needed and got little time in his talk; it was the more impressive because it could be taken for granted.

Likewise his service as a member of the Harvard Corporation was one of those things whose importance required no elaboration. I recall only two aspects of that service that he mentioned more than casually. The first related to his public espousal of the cause of academic freedom in the face of the strident anticommunism and various loyalty oath measures that came to the fore in the aftermath of World War II. He took the lead in the matter both because he believed this kind of freedom was fundamental to Harvard's welfare and because he believed that he as a member of the Corporation and a "Wall Street lawyer" was in a better position to answer Harvard's critics than was President Conant, who inevitably, because of his office, was himself a target. He never dwelt on it, but when he spoke of it you had no doubt that this activity had been the most satisfying experience he had in Harvard's service. It incidentally brought him acclaim throughout the larger academic community in a way that pleased him. Specifically, it led to his being invited by the then president of Princeton, Harold Dodds, to consult with the Princeton authorities on the general problem and out of this came a sustained and valued friendship with President Dodds.

The other Harvard item on the agenda of our conversations was, of course, the Arnold Arboretum controversy. I hope some other good came out of this long drawn-out, bitter dispute, but I personally can only bear witness that it contributed to the preservation of the black duck population. There was no other subject, not even that of world peace, that produced quite the preoccupied concern on Grenny's part that this one did. When he spoke of it neither of us paid much attention to the ducks until at some point he would abruptly rise to his feet, take a shot at a departing duck, and conclude that year's installment of the Arboretum story with the half-chuckled observation: "We haven't been paying attention to business, have we?"

This is not the place, if indeed there is a place, for telling that unhappy story which centered on the question of Harvard's right under the terms of a gift to transfer certain collections and activities from the Arboretum itself to Cambridge. Grenny at first hoped that the Harvard authorities would cooperate in seeking a judicial ruling on the action which he and the other members of the Corporation had approved, mistakenly as he later thought. Failing to persuade Harvard to his view, he led an adversary effort which ended in 1966 with a divided Massachusetts supreme court upholding the university's position.

The dispute divided friends from friends and there can be no question that the controversy eventually corroded Grenny's relationship to Harvard. I was sorry about that and as an outsider I tried unsuccessfully several times to be a peacemaker, but as a friend I was even more concerned about the time and energy he gave to the affair. He insisted that he was not letting it distract him from his more positive purposes, but Grenny was not one to take any cause lightly and if our duck-blind agenda was any gauge of things, it's probably not too much to say that if he had any albatross to contend with during this period it was the Arboretum controversy. Let it be said, however, that on this, as on other issues that commanded his concern, there was a minimum of personalities in his talk. He felt strongly about his causes, but he rarely reduced them to the level of persons; he preferred to think and talk about fundamentals.

Even though Grenny did not spend much time looking for personal devils as the causes of the world's problems, he was something of a connoisseur of persons. He was interested in the way people of his acquaintance took the world. He usually spoke of people in a concrete context, letting the particular happening testify to a man's quality of mind, character, size, or foibles. He en-

joyed relating how his grandfather's respect for Lincoln was mani-
fested by his insistence that he should always be referred to as
"*Mister* Lincoln"; he rated Elihu Root, Sr., Henry Stimson, and
John McCloy among the "first-raters" in American statecraft; he
was intrigued by Felix Frankfurter and enjoyed relating how they
had teamed up to get Henry Stimson appointed secretary of war in
World War II; he repeatedly cited FDR, usually with a chuckle,
as an example that some men can overcome anything—"even being
born rich"; he was drawn to Lord Attlee's spunk and forthright-
ness; he dismissed a certain newspaper publisher as being beneath
notice—"he was even a mean kid"; and there were a good many
prominent people who were "all right but not worth spending
much time on."

Grenny had serious health problems during these years, but he
was largely content to leave these worries to the doctors and his
wife; he was matter-of-fact but comfortably reticent about personal
affairs and for the most part they did not figure prominently in his
talk. He did speak his admiration for Dr. Paul Dudley White's
"good sense" and he relished the sage "reassurance" a London
specialist gave him about his lymphoma: "If you were a younger
man it would be serious, but at your age a lot of other things could
happen."

After "peace through world law," the cause closest to Grenville
Clark during this period was equal justice for the Negro in American society. Having committed myself to this cause in 1947 as a
member of President Truman's Committee on Civil Rights, the
subject, like that of international affairs, was inevitably a perennial
one for us.

Grenny's talk about racial affairs was much more focused on
problems and the contemporary scene than was the case with his
discussion of peace. Likewise the subject unleashed his capacity
for outrage as was rarely the case with the other things he talked
about. He had no patience whatsoever with the foot draggers, let
alone the convinced segregationists. On one occasion he spoke
about sending "a little money" to provide bail for the release of
"freedom riders" who were being held in jail in Mississippi. One
of the occasions when we both looked straight ahead out over the
marsh for some minutes was when he told me about a decision he
and his wife, Fanny, had taken during her last illness to put money

behind the defense fund of the NAACP. He had a lively, sustained interest in the A.B.C. (A Better Chance) program we pioneered at Dartmouth to help educationally disadvantaged youngsters, mainly Negroes, prepare for attendance at first-rate secondary schools and eventually college. He became so interested in it that he came to Hanover one summer to talk about the project and its possible relevance to the problem of getting more Negroes into our highly competitive professional schools, especially the law schools. He finished the visit off by taking dinner that evening with the A.B.C. boys, an experience he liked to recall as one of unusual pleasure for him.

Perhaps this is the point to say that such on-the-spot meetings with the disadvantaged were not a common thing for him. In this area of concern, as well as elsewhere, he was essentially a man who operated offstage and he had not the slightest taste for personal "showboating," whatever the cause. In the best sense his tastes were aristocratic. But when it came to his convictions, he placed his bets on "the people." I was impressed by his staunch support of the Supreme Court's "one man one vote" decision. Yes, he recognized the difficulties and he was sorry if it eventually put places such as Vermont at a disadvantage, but the principle was inescapable and he "rather thought" the good changes would outweigh the bad ones.

Invariably each year as we came back to the international scene and Grenny's prime concern, the development of adequate world law for keeping the peace, we discussed the outlook for Soviet cooperation. During the last several years of his life he became actively interested in trying to establish contact with the People's Republic of China, but all his approaches in this direction were abortive. Throughout these years Grenny remained a determined optimist concerning the eventual cooperation of the Soviets in some form of limited world government. I characterize his optimism as "determined" because it seemed to me to spring from his considered judgment of what was necessary rather than any Pollyannaism in his nature. When I pressed him on the question (I was never able to be as "determined" about it as he was), he would sometimes concede it might take a little longer than he reckoned. But more often he countered with the observation that much would depend on us, whether we could get over our systematic, stereotyped reactions of suspicion and antagonism to all things Communist. It would probably be too strong to say that he had confidence in the Soviet's readiness to consider his program seriously in the near future. But sorry as he was to have them plead the necessity for "wars of liberation" to him, he remained determined to the end not to assume that a negative response was indefinitely inevitable. Here again, and perhaps here in particular, he had confidence in the ultimate capacity of Russians for realism and in his basic faith that when things got bad enough, all civilized men would recognize and act on their need for peace through world law.

As Grenny's age and failing health brought closer the inevitable curtain on his duck-hunting days, he spoke on several occasions about his growing ambivalence about the future of duck hunting in general and of his interest in the marsh in particular. He had genuinely enjoyed the negotiations he had carried on with the federal authorities for a number of years to prolong the family's hunting privileges on the property conveyed earlier to the federal government for refuge purposes, and he was truly grateful for having been able to finish out his days in the marsh that meant so much to him. But as I indicated earlier, he now had serious doubts about there being much more of a future for duck hunting as he had known it. On our last trip together he said, "I've made up my mind that I'm really more concerned about preserving the marsh as it is and the ducks that use it than I am about hunting. I hope it's not just that I'm at the end of my hunting and I don't think it is. But I'm not sure and I'd like Grenny Jr. to have a chance at a little more of it if he wants it; I'm simply going to tell him that it will be up to him, but when he's finished with it, if it were my decision it would go to the refuge."

Our conversations had worked a modest measure of waterfowl conservation, but maybe things could be both different and better in the future. Grenny looked at the whole future that way.

GRENVILLE CLARK:

Notes

Erwin N. Griswold

My first recollection of Grenville Clark goes back to 1927. In December of that year, as a prospective graduate of Harvard Law School, I made the usual rounds of New York offices. One of the places where I called was Root, Clark, at 31 Nassau Street. I met Mr. Buckner on this occasion, but I have no recollection that I met Mr. Clark. However, *Law Review* students at Harvard frequently heard from those who had preceded them about the vitality and enthusiasm of the Root, Clark office, and about the persistent high standards of Mr. Clark.

When I returned to Harvard to teach in 1934, Mr. Clark was already an *eminence grise*. He was one of that august body, the Harvard Corporation, which Harvard professors know exist and which they understand, deep in their hearts, is a rather beneficent group. However, they are not only mighty, but remote, and there is very little contact with those who are carrying on the day-to-day activities of the university.

In those days, I did not ordinarily attend the Harvard commencement. However, in 1944, my great professor Austin W. Scott received an honorary degree, and I was there to join in the honors. This, I think, was the first definite meeting I had with Mr. Clark. In the meantime, though, I had heard much about him from my colleague and contemporary Professor Livingston Hall, who had spent some time in the Root, Clark office before coming to the Harvard faculty.

Thus, at the time I became dean of the Harvard Law School, in 1946, my contacts with Mr. Clark had been very slight. It was he, though, who extended the invitation to me to become dean of the school. Of course, I remember that interview vividly. He started by asking me if I would be interested in being considered for the post of dean. I replied that I would be interested. He then said that there was a serious possibility that the post might be made one for a term, and asked me if I would accept an appointment as dean for five years. I replied that I would not be interested in a term appointment, that being a professor at the Harvard Law School was the best position I knew of, and that I would not care to give it up except for the purpose of making a career of the deanship. He did not seem surprised. We discussed the matter a bit further, and he then asked me if I would accept appointment at the pleasure of the Corporation, which was the basis on which all administrative appointments were made. I replied that I would accept such an appointment. He reminded me that the Corporation's action would have to be confirmed by the Board of Overseers. And so the meeting ended.

Years later, I referred to this meeting in a conversation with Mr. Clark. He said, in substance: "Yes, there were some who favored a term appointment, and I was instructed to ask you about that. Of course you were right. I thought so at the time, and I have found no reason to change my mind."

Shortly after I took on the duties of the dean's office, I heard from Mr. Clark in connection with the work which he was doing with Louis Sohn. Mr. Sohn had been a student of mine in 1939–1941, and I had been much concerned about him because he had been separated from his native country by the war. I had high regard for him, and I was much pleased, both for Mr. Clark and Mr. Sohn, when I heard that they were working together on plans for postwar world organization. I cannot say, though, that I had anything to do with making the contact between them.

Mr. Sohn was a Research Fellow in international law at the law school when I became dean. During the first few months, Mr. Clark talked with me two or three times about Louis Sohn, expressing great appreciation for the work he had done, and indicating his great potential capacity. I do not now recall the details, but in February 1947, Mr. Sohn was appointed a lecturer on law, and thus became a member of the faculty of the Harvard Law School, where he has been ever since.

My next contact with Mr. Clark came in 1949 when we were trying to raise $1,500,000 for the law school through the original Harvard Law School Fund. This was a large sum at the time, and the going was not easy. As is inevitable, in the case of a law school which is worth its salt, there were alumni who were unhappy about speeches and activities of some professors. There was at that time a considerable "red scare" and there were those who thought that the Harvard Law School was "a hot bed of communists," generally having in mind some of our sturdiest, most independent, and clear-thinking professors.

It was at this time that one of our alumni, Frank Ober, of Baltimore wrote a letter of discontent about the law school. In due course, there was published a response from Mr. Clark, and this became famous as the Clark-Ober correspondence. Mr. Clark's statement was a stirring reaffirmation on behalf of academic freedom and intellectual independence. It was in accordance with a great Harvard tradition, and Mr. Clark was the man to say it forthrightly and effectively, as he did.

I remember, though, that I had some mixed feelings about what occurred. As a matter of fact, I was not consulted in any way, and did not know that Mr. Clark's letter had been written, or was going to be written, until after it was published. At that time, I was trying very hard to do my part to raise the funds needed to provide very modest dormitories and dining facilities for students at the Harvard Law School, something which should, indeed, have been done long before. The money was not rolling in, in fact, and, frequently, I wondered whether the publication of the Clark-Ober correspondence might not have a considerable chilling effect. I wondered whether the same points could not have been made in a more conciliatory manner. I had no question whatever about Mr. Clark's position, and the propriety of restating it. I wondered whether it would not have been just as effective if it had been stated in a somewhat less vigorous manner.

Perhaps I was just annoyed because I had been left out of the discussions which led to Mr. Clark's letter. At any rate, we raised the money and finished the dormitories and dining hall. Everything worked out all right, and the Clark-Ober correspondence was a useful background for later episodes in Harvard's history.

Beginning in the 1950s, I had more contact with Mr. Clark. This was usually over the telephone, generally from Dublin. When my secretary told me that Mr. Clark was calling, I knew that I was in for a long session. The conversations were always interesting, and generally involved some cause in which Mr. Clark was interested. In later years, I had more contacts with Mr. Clark arising out of the Dartmouth Conferences which brought together groups of Americans and Russians.

It was in 1961, after I had attended the Second Dartmouth Conference, which was held in Russia, that Mr. and Mrs. Clark invited my wife, Harriet, and me to come to Dublin for a weekend. Thereafter, we were invited on a number of occasions. The Clarks were always exceedingly kind to us there. It was a beautiful place, and we enjoyed our stays there very much. Because Harriet could not go upstairs, Mr. Clark gave us his bedroom. We were grateful for this, and I was concerned, since it meant that Mr. Clark had to walk upstairs himself. When Mrs. Clark died and after Mr. Clark had remarried, we were invited to Dublin and were again received with the same generous and friendly hospitality.

During these times in Dublin I often persuaded Mr. Clark to talk about various episodes in his career. He talked extensively about Felix Frankfurter and Henry L. Stimson; about his role in connection with selective service in 1917–1918, with particular reference to conscientious objectors; about law practice in New York; about Andrew Carnegie; about Harvard notables over a long period of years; about world organization, and the World Federalists; about the NAACP Legal Defense and Educational Fund, to which he gave great strength; and so on. These were great moments, and we greatly valued the friendship extended to us.

I last saw Mr. Clark in Cambridge in the October before he died. He had not been well for many years, and his illness was closing in on him. However, he was cheerful and animated. He talked in terms of the future, and of things to be done. He was tireless in the cause of good and determined not to give up despite the obstacles that lay in the way. In some ways, he was a bulldog. Sometimes, he seemed to hang on too hard. I wish we had more like him.

GRENVILLE CLARK:

Operator Extraordinary

Kingman Brewster, Jr.

The formidable, impressive "Mr. Clark" soon became "Grenny" to all his associates. Without any shrinkage of stature, there was puckish delight which added a glow of light to the glowering, stubborn tenacity. Through it all the brightest thread was a capacity for moral outrage and high idealism.

Grenny would like to be known, also, as an "operator." The political arts and games—not the so-called science of the same name—were his constant enjoyment and avocation. Never were goals, called unrealistic by skeptics, better served in practical pursuit. More people found themselves doing and saying and endorsing things they never would have dreamed of on their own, as a result of being goaded, cajoled, wheedled, kidded, and sometimes duped into it by Grenny.

I was such a willing victim. When I felt I could not join him as a "host" for the Second Dublin Conference in 1965, then perhaps I would be a "co-sponsor." Then since Alan Cranston couldn't make it, perhaps I would join Grenny as "co-chairman." Then when I arrived "we" had decided that it would be better if only I were chairman. So there I was; and I loved it!

It was the cheerful doggedness and the total selflessness in the cause—whatever the cause, though my association with Grenny

159

was limited to world federalism—which were the inspiration. It still is, in part because of the extraordinary vividness of the man in his physical person. With a chin to rival Leverett Saltonstall and eyebrows to compete with Learned Hand, the thoughtful, chuckling person is still, happily, a brooding omnipresence in image as well as in spirit.

GRENVILLE CLARK:

Stalwart Defender of Academic Freedom

James B. Conant

Grenville Clark was a powerful man—a stubborn opponent or a formidable ally. In the latter capacity he was a source of strength on more than one occasion to the president of Harvard University. Clark had already made his reputation as a New York lawyer and public-spirited citizen before he was elected a member of the Harvard Corporation. That was shortly before that body chose me to succeed A. Lawrence Lowell as president of Harvard. Mr. Lowell had firmly established Harvard's adherence to the principle of free inquiry. In his annual report for 1916–1917 he had spelled out the reasons why the governing boards of a university should not attempt to place restraints on what a professor said.

In my first talks, as a new college president, with Grenville Clark as a member of the Harvard Corporation I learned how deeply Clark felt concerning the doctrine of free inquiry. He urged me to continue the tradition which President Lowell had so clearly set forth and which as a matter of fact was implicit in all that Charles William Eliot had written during the forty years that he was Harvard's leader. Clark warned me that some alumni would disagree and perhaps raise the issue publicly. Indeed, I was already hearing echoes of criticism of certain Harvard professors who were close to Franklin D. Roosevelt and who were said to be endangering the nation by their radical views. The Corporation met every two weeks in term time. Almost from the start, one item on the agenda was very likely to be related to a consideration of some aspect of academic freedom. Always Clark would express his opinion forcefully and always on the side of defending free inquiry and the rights of professors to express their views.

In spite of a deep depression and a global war, demands kept arising from without the university that alleged radical professors be silenced or fired. The onset of the Cold War in 1947–1948 gave a new twist to the old arguments. In 1949 I received a letter from a Harvard Law School graduate, Frank B. Ober of Baltimore. It was another version of the old, old story. Harvard was taken to task because the university had made no effort to control what some professors were saying publicly. Their activities, according to Ober, were giving aid and comfort to communism. I turned to Grenville Clark for assistance. I knew no one could write a better defense of Harvard's position. Clark agreed to write Ober. He produced a long letter which may stand as a classic defense of the rights of professors to express their views.

GRENVILLE CLARK

William L. Marbury

———————◆———————

During the fight against President Roosevelt's court-packing plan in 1937 I learned at firsthand to respect Grenville Clark's skill as a political strategist and to appreciate the extraordinary tenacity with which he relentlessly waged an uphill struggle to final victory. Later, when I served under Judge Patterson in the War Department during World War II, I heard from Edward S. Greenbaum and Howard C. Petersen the extraordinary story of how, almost single-handedly, Mr. Clark pushed through a reluctant Congress the Selective Service Act of 1940, an even more remarkable example of his generalship. So that when, in 1947, he called me on the telephone and inquired whether, if invited to do so, I would be willing to serve on the Harvard Corporation, I suppose that I should have suspected that this was a tactical move in a campaign to achieve some much more important objective.

It was not until much later, however, that I learned that my candidacy was a part of a bitter struggle for control of Harvard University between President James B. Conant and influential Boston alumni headed by "Bill" Claflin, the treasurer of Harvard College. As a result of Mr. Conant's absences in Washington during World War II, the reins of power at Harvard had been allowed to fall into Mr. Claflin's hands, and when the war ended Mr. Conant found that Claflin was reluctant to give them back. The situation became increasingly tense and finally climaxed with the resignation of Henry James, a member of the Harvard Corporation who had been advised by his doctors that he had an incurable cancer. Claflin immediately proposed a candidate from the Boston financial community who could be counted on to support his views, and Conant responded by urging my appointment. The Corporation by a divided vote sent my name to the Board of Overseers, and the fight was on. For many months all kinds of pressure were brought to bear on the members of the Board of Overseers, including the threat of Claflin and another member of the Corporation to resign if I were elected. Mr. Clark enlisted Judge Patterson—himself no mean fighter—on the Conant side, and the controversy apparently stirred up very high feelings among some of the alumni who were scandalized at the idea of selecting a man who was not a graduate of Harvard College.

Of all this I remained blissfully ignorant, since no rumors of the controversy reached as far as Baltimore. In the end the Claflin forces surrendered, and to my astonishment I received a telegram from Judge Patterson saying that my name had been unanimously approved by the Overseers. I could not imagine why he was in any way interested and was still completely in the dark when I paid my first visit to Cambridge. At that time Mr. Clark arranged to have some of my old friends meet me at lunch at the Somerset Club and in addition invited Mr. Charles Francis Adams, Mr. Ralph Lowell, and a few other equally outstanding pillars of the Boston community. At the end of the lunch he handed me a brochure and said, "Don't let this go to your head." I found in it a complete summary of my past history and about a dozen letters from people with whom I had been in contact from my college days down to the year 1945. I have kept this brochure and will pass it on to my children with the injunction not to take it too seriously, since it was a campaign document.

GRENVILLE CLARK AND THE DEVELOPMENT OF THE INTERNATIONAL LEGAL STUDIES PROGRAM AT THE HARVARD LAW SCHOOL

David F. Cavers

Progress toward the law school's International Legal Studies Program began in the autumn of 1946 when Dean Griswold created a Committee on International Legal Studies in response to a proposal for expanded instruction in foreign and comparative law made by Professor Fuller, seconded by a proposal I made for an expanded research program in the international area. Lon Fuller was named to chair the committee, but, since he had his hands full with a broader study of the school's educational program, he soon asked to be relieved of the chairmanship, and I was appointed in his stead.

I devoted extensive work to curricular plans that would embrace more than simply the conventional courses in public international law and comparative law. We saw a need for instruction and research that not only would reflect the rapidly expanding law of world organization but also would examine the intertwining of

public and private laws, both foreign and domestic, that was resulting from the growth of world trade and investment, as well as
manifold problems of economic development in the new countries.
It seemed essential, moreover, if this expansion were to exert an
influence beyond the United States, that Harvard's program of
graduate law study should attract law-trained students from many
parts of the world.

Grenville Clark learned of these activities in September 1947
and expressed a lively interest to Dean Griswold, who referred him
to me as chairman of the committee. We had first formulated our
goal as the creation of "a school of world law," a concept especially
appealing to Mr. Clark. We remained in frequent contact, not
only by letter and memorandum but through a number of long
conversations and occasional phone calls. Later, when critics of the
"world law" concept noted that only a fraction of the courses
could accurately be described as such and we shifted from that
phrase to "a world school of law," Mr. Clark did not like the
change, but he did not let his disappointment diminish the help
that he was giving to us.

Once our goal had been defined and plans for its realization developed, we faced a formidable problem, namely, how to secure the
substantial funds needed to sustain the enlargement of faculty,
fellowships, library, and working space that a world school of law
would entail. One of my principal duties became the drafting of a
brochure that would at once explain our objectives and attract financial support.

The brochure that emerged from the drafting process reflected
many of Mr. Clark's suggestions. We decided to send it in draft to
a group of outstanding men in the field of law and international
affairs both at home and abroad. Mr. Clark was especially helpful
in guiding the distribution of the draft booklet and in bringing
our project to the attention of potentially helpful people. However, this was only one aspect of his continuing efforts to assist us
both in meeting our financial problems and in appreciating the
possibilities of our endeavor.

We decided not to send out a final version of the brochure but
instead appeal directly to large foundations. Various attempts to
interest them, especially the Ford Foundation, yielded no immediate results, though possibly they exerted some influence on the

thinking of foundation officials and their advisers. By the end of 1949, however, we had begun to feel quite discouraged. Our hopes of being able to attract the very substantial funds we thought needed to enable us to build "a world school of law" were at low ebb. At this point, on January 4, 1950, Mr. Clark wrote a memorandum to Dean Griswold with the advice, "Let down your buckets where you are," recalling the message to a ship becalmed and short of water, its captain unaware of the fact that it had already reached fresh water at the mouth of the Amazon.

That counsel was accompanied by a detailed set of suggestions for creating a "Harvard Institute of World Law" on a small-scale, pilot-project basis. Dean Griswold was attracted by the idea but thought we would need $500,000 for a five-year program. However, when I assembled the committee to assess our chances of getting started with or without funds, I found them convinced that we should do whatever we could with the resources at hand.

When we put our heads together, we realized that, with the recent addition of a number of younger men to the faculty (among them Louis Sohn, Kingman Brewster, Robert Bowie, Harold Berman, and Arthur von Mehren), we had substantially enlarged our capability to offer a program in international legal studies without outside financial assistance. With Dean Griswold's support, we were able by 1951–1952 to double our offerings in the fields of world order, world economy, and the comparison of legal systems. These offerings were listed together in the 1951–1952 catalogue as comprising a "Program in International Legal Studies." Moreover, we laid plans for an international research and training program in taxation in cooperation with the United Nations Fiscal Division. This came into being the same year under the direction of Stanley Surrey, supported by a Ford grant. We also initiated several other international research projects.

As these developments were going forward under the impetus of Mr. Clark's suggestion, we continued to seek financial support from foundations. Now, however, instead of having merely aspirations to point to, we had a going concern. We had let down our buckets. Our own potentialities had been released, as he had foreseen, and we were also providing leadership for a number of other law schools.

After obtaining several smaller grants for specific objects, we succeeded in January 1955 in obtaining from the Ford Foundation a grant of $2,050,000 to endow two chairs, provide funds for fellowships, and furnish the nucleus of a building fund which, when matched, made possible the International Legal Studies Wing of Langdell Hall. We were able to bring back Milton Katz to fill one of the new chairs and be director of the program.

At the same time and subsequently, the Ford Foundation made grants in lesser amounts to several other leading law schools. The basis was laid for broadening the horizons of the once parochial legal educational system in the United States. Not only Harvard but also all the major law schools, and many smaller ones, have come to give to studies in international law (broadened to include world organization) and to the problems of world economic development a significant place in their curricula.

One result has been a much greater flow of graduate law students to and from the United States than ever before. Moreover, as a consequence of enhanced student interest, we now have fifteen new student-edited reviews in international fields.

On January 17, 1955, I wrote Mr. Clark, in reporting our Ford grant, that his had been "crucially helpful counsel." Without that counsel and his earlier encouragement, probably we might have come in time to realize our own potentialities, but the process would have been slower. Moreover, delay could have been costly in *élan*. In 1950, we were moved by the realization that, even in law, the United States had to become a part of a world society. Though we are still short of the goals Grenville Clark envisaged, I am sure he would take satisfaction in the progress toward world legal education that he did so much to bring about.

PART VI

Family, Friends, and Neighbors

A DAUGHTER'S VIEWPOINT:

Lighter Moments—and Many Exposures

Mary Clark Dimond

My father liked to relax sometimes by taking off in the car into the New Hampshire countryside to seek out the small town cemeteries, as many who absorb and care about history are prone to do.

One hot, dusty day we set out in the direction of Nelson, and a bit unsure of our way, we spotted a boy with a fishing pole walking along the road. We stopped, and thinking to adapt his language appropriately, my father asked: "Could you tell me, please, how to find the local buryin' ground?" A moment of thought, and our young man replied with a strong New England twang, "Wal, now, it depends wot kind of berries ye was lookin' fer." This incident, of course, relayed when we got home, became one more of a collection of stories that gave the whole family many a good laugh.

On most such expeditions we talked little and had happy peaceful times, even though my father was a very bad driver, in no way ever mechanically inclined, and with little respect for such items as stop signs, especially if the roads were clear, and with no lack of courage when it came to attempting the roughest of roads or "overlooking" a no trespassing sign. In all of his career as a driver, however, he was arrested only one time, for driving around Harvard Square the wrong way.

His great curiosity about all things enticed him now and again into forbidden areas. One day he climbed an iron fence near the Green Park in London as his children watched rigid with embarrassment, the better to read an historical legend, mumbling as he went that the worst that could happen was that he'd be put off the premises. He was, though he and the guard were thoroughly enjoying each other's company before the incident was over.

I was eighteen and, with much New England conscience inherited in me, when I returned home from college for Christmas I was unable to refrain from confessing that I had taken two flying lessons on the sly. My mother was much offended, my father very solemn, and I was virtually confined to my room for several days. Finally, a visit from my father, and we endeavored to analyze the reasons for my excessive behavior, and the effort was made to impress on me the seriousness of my aggression. The lecture finally ran out, and there was a long pause, and then a look from him, and then the question, "What was it like?"

As a young boy in New York City, my father was taken weekly to the Metropolitan Opera, where the Clarks and their cousins had a box. Although much of this time was spent at tag and ingenious games of hide and seek in the great semicircular corridor and the little red plush parlors through which one went to one's seat, he nevertheless absorbed enough to develop a great love for Italian opera, and he had always a strong desire to sing at the top of his lungs as though to fill a great arena with glorious sound before an enthralled audience. In the rather low-ceilinged parlor in Dublin of an evening every now and then he would demonstrate his powers, and no one could deny that he knew his "Celeste Aïda," and that his volume was indeed immense even though his ability to carry a tune did not exist. His audience could not endure for long, and then quite soon he himself would collapse in howling disarray.

On other evenings before the open fire, he would tell his "grizzly bear" stories with wide gestures and enthusiasm. These were good stories of a very dry humor of the northwestern guides with whom he camped and hunted, and often until we knew their variety better, we would ask at the end, "And then what happened?" He would be a little put out at this, and declare, "Well, that's not the point." He regaled us with anecdotes of Pomfret school days, certain of these many times over, and with each telling they were more funny to us than the last. He also told of incidents of the conventional trip to Europe with classmates the summer after graduation from Harvard. We enjoyed most, I think, a tale of their last day in Paris. They were about to leave and remembered they had not yet visited the Louvre. On the way to the railway station, they instructed the taxi driver to let them out at one door, then to go quickly to the other side of the building while they ran as fast as they were able through the Louvre to rejoin their cab, to catch their train in time, and to be able to say that they had indeed "been to the Louvre."

He also read aloud many of his favorite stories of adventure, and, over and over, parts of *Uncle Remus*, much of Kipling, Sir Walter Scott, the novels of John Buchan, most of Shakespeare, and even the dialect of Milt Gross with gestures and vigor. He enjoyed Owen Wister's *The Virginian*, having known the author in the latter's late years, and repeated often a favorite quote from this book, "When you say *that*, smile." Every year he rendered Dickens' "Christmas Carol" on Christmas Eve, with his voice becoming more and more unsteady as he neared the end. He played cards with us, a game of hearts or some mild bridge; he taught us elementary poker, and he required that we know chess.

He was a true outdoorsman and sportsman, would have his children learn not only to camp nights in a row, rain or shine, on the "forty acre lot up on the ridge," but to sense and appreciate in silence the section of primeval forest back in the woods and to stop and hear the sounds of wild life around us. We would drink the pure cold water from a hidden spring, and tramp through the underbrush and over fallen rotting, moss-covered trees, following the mountain streams or the old stone walls which dated back to when the mountain had been cleared for grazing—many such hikes in the rain and often at a great pace for short legs. We climbed often by various routes to the summit of Mount Monadnock to look over the land, much "as Cortez . . ." He put excitement into such things for us for he so loved them himself, the sight of a deer, geese in flight, picking blueberries into a tin pail tied around his waist, on rainy days the great bonfires of brush which had been cut to preserve the pastures, and times of jumping from the high rafters in the barn and then roughhousing in the luxuriant hayloft. At other times, we walked the three miles around Dublin Lake in the rain, meeting certain of the summer residents, who made a habit of this on such days. I remember the bright orange lizards who would appear and scuttle off only on days like this, and my father's collection of debris he would have accumulated by the end of our walk, unable as he was to leave a discarded can or bottle in sight, even if he had to wade into the lake to get it. It was not unusual that he would awaken us at night to have us see northern lights or the shooting stars of August, and he worked to have us recognize the planets and constellations and understand the reasons for their position in the heavens at various times of the year.

My mother and he both loved farming on the small scale that it was. We had chickens and cows most of my life, and in earlier years two or three pigs, a flock of sheep, which became too complicated, and finally beef cattle, about a dozen of these, two of whom one morning were found missing. There was a big hunt before they were discovered on the golf course especially enjoying the putting greens, and the hoof prints which resulted were hardly popular with the local players. We had a vegetable garden, and really knew what the tops of carrots and beets looked like. We dug potatoes and picked beans, peas, corn, cut asparagus, and brought in the squash and pumpkins at the summer's end. There were plums, pears, crabapples, peaches to be gathered, there were strawberries in June and raspberries and wild blackberries later in the summer. My mother made watermelon rind pickles, orange marmalade, and currant and grape jelly from the sour Concord grapes which covered the trellis in her flower garden. We could pluck a chicken or a duck, we dug worms and cleaned our own fish. I could never milk a cow, but often got a squirt of warm milk in the face, and watched the separator afterward produce cream so heavy that we spooned it onto our cereal and berries. And we would rake, hoe, dig, mow, and learned to use an ax, hatchet, a sickle, and even attempt to scythe. There were strict admonitions on handling many of these, especially a pitchfork.

There were work horses on the place before tractor days, and later the two riding horses. I could drive the tractor, although I do not remember that I was very useful doing this. My mother and father both studied quality of pasture and crop rotation, and one year we won a prize for the best wheat at the county fair (it was the only wheat exhibited). The sugar maples were tapped in the spring, and in early years maple syrup was made in the little sugar house in the woods near the Indian stone which was so often pointed out to us, a large boulder which had been hollowed from the grinding of grain. The sugar house is no longer there and the ice house is gone, another favorite and forbidden place. Cut from the lake nearby, the supply of great squares of ice lasted buried in sawdust through until the next winter.

If my father had decided upon a certain plan, adverse conditions were not likely to deter him from trying. I can remember us on horses on Long Island attempting to ride through a ferocious stinging blizzard, the snow of a depth the cars could not manage, to get to the doctor for a measles shot for me. The weather was too wild and we did turn back, but not before his own frisky animal had bucked him off into a snow drift. I think this was the same storm which prevented the trains from going into New York, and the next day he started off down the center of the railroad track nineteen miles from the city and his office, with his high boots on and his briefcase on a sled. He won out this time.

My father cared to see us excel in whatever we did, and he worked and enjoyed with us a wide variety of sports, but expected, too, that we measure up at our school work. He had us learn early to ride, and I was a very small girl on a very large horse galloping at a four-foot fence or being run away with clinging to the saddle and yelling "Help!" with what breath I had, a little before I was ready to handle such episodes. We were taught to use a shotgun and rifle, golf, tennis, swim, to use a bow and arrow, to fish, canoe, and sail. In winter, we practiced fancy skating with him, we went skiing, and there were hair-raising toboggan rides, spectacular sledding, and magical days of traveling cross-country on snowshoes. Many a Sunday we spent flying large box kites of a kind I can no longer find. Two of these would lift us from the ground and carry us along.

He could be a stern taskmaster, especially with lessons, departing from the assignments we might have been belaboring, because he detected a lack of basic knowledge. On a cruise ship in the West Indies I was taught to differentiate between the legislative, executive, and judicial branches of our government, such that I could never forget, though the day's assignment had become quite lost in it all.

One day he came upon a young woman drowning as we rounded "The Point," canoeing on Dublin Lake. She had come too far from the shore, and was in very real distress. My brother and I were small and not yet swimmers, but we went to her and she grasped in panic the side of the canoe, tilting it dangerously. I recall my father's formidable capacity to command on this occasion, exacting absolute obedience from all concerned, and thus he accomplished the rescue. We brought the woman ashore to a cluster of anxious friends, who took over, and went on our way.

He was highly disciplined himself and worked very hard. Told to relax at times, he would go to a movie for an allotted hour, and after sixty minutes rise and leave, to our consternation, sometimes, at a moment of great suspense in the story.

He also sought a change of pace with a detective story, but for a time only, and it was a rare one that he remembered so well that he could not read it again one day, simply using it as a distraction, with equal enjoyment all over again.

He was very perceptive about people and would challenge us to summarize the character of "so-and-so." He had a compassion, too, for young people and especially when we were sick, he would come to the bedside and rather awkwardly pat us on the head, quite hard, for he was strong, but he felt badly if we were sad or hurt.

He enjoyed the rituals of Christmas, Easter, Thanksgiving, and, above all, perhaps, the Fourth of July with a joy and exuberance even greater perhaps than our own. I can see him clowning and dancing in exploding firecrackers, and making elaborate preparations for the evening display of fireworks, for which event he was the referee and possessor of the "punk." A human of natural good will, he loved to give presents on the slightest or no excuse. He would come up from New York for the weekend when we were children bearing an armful of packages, a practice which my mother finally curtailed as extravagant and bad for us. Even so, although my mother had been responsible for assembling a

Grenville Clark before the turn of the century. Taken in Burlington, Vermont.

Mother of Grenville Clark, Marion deForest Cannon Clark.

Grenville Clark as a small boy. Taken in New York City, circa 1890.

The young Grenville (x), aged eight, seated with his brother, his Griswold cousins and their tutors.

Grenville Clark (left) with Mary, Harry, and Julian Clark. Burlington, Vermont

Grenville Clark (x) and classmates at Pomfret School. Pomfret, Connecticut, 1895.

Grenville Clark (x), member of Porcellian Club, Harvard College.

Grenville Clark (x) and the Harvard Debating Club, 1900.

Grenville Clark (right) and Harvard classmates on Alpine peak, summer 1903.
"How fast can you get from sea level to the highest nearby point available?"

Grenville Clark big game hunting
in the Northwest, 1904.

Grenville Clark's grandfather, Le Gran
Bouton Cannon.

Grenville Clark.

Louis Crawford Clark, father of Grenvi
Clark, circa 1917.

Grenville Clark's son, Grenville, Jr.

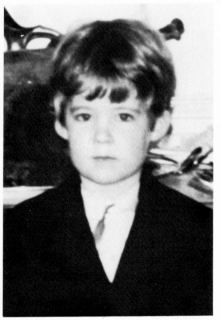

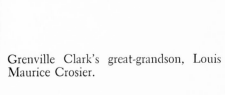

Grenville Clark's grandson, Grenville Clark Thoron.

Grenville Clark's great-grandson, Louis Maurice Crosier.

Fanny Dwight Clark, 1888.

Fanny Dwight Clark, circa 1903.

Fanny Dwight Clark.

Grenville Clark and Fanny Dwight Clark.
"Just married."

Grenville Clark during World War I.
Washington, D.C.

Grenville Clark and Eleanor Dwight
Clark. Long Island, New York, circa 1915.

Mary Clark Dimond; Eleanor Dwight
Clark, deceased, December 1921; Gren
ville Clark, Jr., 1921.

Grenville Clark with three Spencer grand-
children in Dublin, New Hampshire, circa
1960.

Root, Clark, Buckner, Howland and Ballantine office dinner at the University Club, January 24, 1921. Seated, clockwise from lower left: Reed B. Dawson, George A. Stevens, Emory R. Buckner, William P. Palmer, Maxwell Steinhardt, Mortimer Boyle, Alexander B. Royce, Vanderbilt Webb, Cloyd Laporte, Bernhard Knollenberg, Radcliffe Swinnerton, George E. Cleary, Loyal Leale, Hamilton Rogers, Clinton Combes, Alfred C. Intemann, Silas W. Howland, Senator Root, Elihu Root, Jr., Willard Bartlett, Arthur A. Ballantine, Grenville Clark, Clarence M. Tappen. Standing, left to right: Henry Jacques, Jerome Franks, Ashton Parker, Ralph Catteral, Leo Gottlieb, Ellis W. Leavenworth, Robert P. Patterson.

The Corporation of Harvard University, circa 1945. Front, left to right: Dr. Roger I. Lee, Grenville Clark, President James B. Conant. Rear, left to right: Paul Cabot, Charles A. Coolidge, William L. Marbury, Henry L. Shattuck.

"Ceremony in the rain." Harvard Tercentenary celebration, September 19, 1936. 1) Franklin D. Roosevelt, 2) Grenville Clark.

Grenville Clark and Edward M. Day. Svartisen Glacier, Norway, summer 1937.

Grenville Clark in Dublin, New Hampshire, circa 1937.

Grenville Clark. Kerhonkson, New York, 1926.

Grenville Clark on vacation. Ribaut
Club, Florida, circa 1933.

Grenville Clark swimming with his grands
Tom Thoron. Dublin, New Hampshire, Oc
ber 1964.

Grenville Clark fishing the Mill Pond. Dublin, New Hampshire, May 1962.

Grenville Clark with Louisa Clark Spencer. Long Island, New York, November 1931.

Grenville Clark and Fanny Dwight Clark with Louisa Clark Spencer on vacation at Reginald S. Fincke plantation outside Charleston, South Carolina, circa 1932.

Grenville Clark relaxing in Dublin, New Hampshire, circa 1932.

Grenville Clark on visit to Mary Clark Dimond at Rancho Santa Fe in California
with his grandson, Grenville Clark Thoron. 1965.

Grenville Clark. "Newspapers were
a staff of life." Ireland, 1963.

Grenville Clark. November 1963. Photograph by Mary Kersey Harvey.

Grenville Clark at home on Long Island. April 1963.

Grenville Clark receives an honorary degree from Dartmouth College in June of 1953. Those pictured on that occasion from left to right are as follows: Back row: Dudley W. Orr, Beardsley Ruml, Sherman Adams, Grenville Clark, Governor Hugh Gregg of New Hampshire, Charles J. Zimmerman, Lloyd D. Brace, and Thomas B. Curtis. Front row: John R. McLane, Ernest M. Hopkins, John J. McCloy, President Dwight D. Eisenhower, President John S. Dickey, Lester B. Pearson, Joseph M. Proskauer, Harvey P. Hood, and Sigurd S. Larmon.

In the garden in Dublin, New Hampshire, from left to right, Dr. and Mrs. Paul Dudley White, Grenville Clark, Professor Alexander Myasnikov, and Senator Joseph S. Clark.

The Clark house in Dublin, New Hampshire, in 1953 on the occasion of a family wedding, has been in the family close to one hundred and fifty years. *Boris Studios*

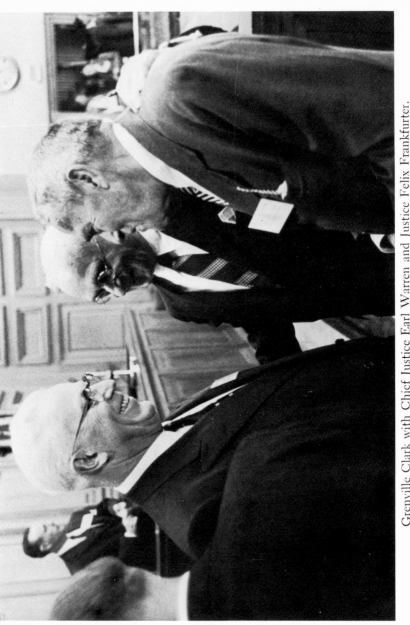

Grenville Clark with Chief Justice Earl Warren and Justice Felix Frankfurter.

enville Clark. Hotel National, Mos-
w, USSR, winter 1964.

Grenville Clark. Hotel National, Moscow, USSR, winter 1964.

Grenville Clark at Dartmouth College, Hanover, New Hampshire. November 6 1964.

Grenville Clark with Dr. John S. Dickey just off the train to go duck shooting in Swanton, Vermont. November 1964.

generous assortment of Christmas presents well ahead of time, Abercrombie and Fitch on Christmas Eve each year was assaulted by him in remarkable style.

Always he could laugh and did so as often at himself as with others. He never teased, but one got away with nothing when around him, not even a passing thought. I remember speaking with some nonchalance the words in Greek of that saying he respected, "Nothing too much." Immediately, from him: "Is that all the Greek you know?" It was, just about.

He enjoyed human beings, and cared not at all for artificiality. He could be extravagant, yet he could as easily live simply, for he was not dependent upon material things. His dignity was the same whether dressed for the office or in very tattered country clothes. He brought a French Canadian illiterate farmer who helped with the haying for many years to the court in Keene so that this man could become a citizen, and the judge had to ask which of the two it was who had come to be naturalized.

He loved a good joke, and while he did not regularly partake of alcoholic beverages, and then only moderately, it would astonish me when he enjoyed a "drunk" story out of all proportion. He would be quaking with laughter over a rather trivial incident, and I traced this as perhaps deriving from exposures of his college days at the Porcellian Club.

One Sunday he took us for a walk in New York on Park Avenue when we were at the "tricycle riding" age. We were enjoying the sensation of riding over some iron grates above the basement windows of one of the old palatial houses. After a time, a very formal butler appeared and admonished us all and requested my father keep us from this sport. My father was so indignant over what he considered an arrogance at being told to restrain his children on the public sidewalk, he retaliated immediately and with pleasure by jumping on the grates of the house of "Old Man Blumenthal," with whom he happened to be slightly acquainted.

One could say that he did not swear. When he was severely annoyed or distressed, his words were "Oh dear, oh dear, oh *dear* me!", with a characteristic emphasis such that one knew something was really wrong. There were a number of expressions he used often, not original with him, and usually with reference to people: "There is too much ego in his cosmos," "He bit off more than he could chew," "He is overeducated for his intellect," or "He is a fair weather friend." He would speak of "cash money" with a twinkle, and he would, if he thought we were a bit short on funds, offer us a bit of "soap." A phrase familiar to northeasterners: So-and-so didn't die, he "kicked the bucket." When he was stumped, "I'm buffaloed." One secretary of state of long acquaintance, though he sometimes deferred to him, he could refer to as "an old woman."

There were "club dances" in Dublin on Saturday nights, and he would come and watch a daughter and choose the moment to "cut in," and then invariably remind one of his inability to dance, which was unnecessary, since he could only circle in one direction. And so we did, with some exuberance, clockwise only.

One evening my mother and father had already eaten a hearty evening meal at seven o'clock when they realized they had forgotten a dinner engagement, one which required stiff shirt and black tie and was scheduled for eight o'clock. They managed to arrive not more than twenty minutes late, and my mother reveled the next day in describing my father, who, as though to make up for this near serious *faux pas*, not only ate an enormous second dinner, but with vocal enthusiasm took large second helpings.

Half joking, but with an underlying seriousness, he did not have patience for such formalities as automobile licenses and passports. His feelings about the latter were illustrated on a trip to Antigua the year before he died. Before landing, he was asked to fill in the usual blank, which had a space for the number of his passport. Not having the latter with him, he relished inventing a number of the correct length and writing it in to the appropriate space.

He had a wide variety of friends, and any friend in need got what he needed. I know that a congenial spirit prevailed among the members of his law firm. Let me again picture him as he would stand and render in full voice the songs and lyrics which had been composed annually for the "office dinner," performing until we were bent over and he himself wiped from his eyes the tears of laughter. He would have commented on the cost of the legal hours of work put in by the firm's lawyers to compose the lighthearted to outrageous program, but he would chuckle, "It was worth it."

Grenville Clark's galaxy of friends and acquaintances throughout his life was a varied and impressive array. A daughter met through him at home such persons as Richard E. Byrd, who spent two summers in Dublin as he negotiated and worked to accumulate funds for his last trip to Antarctica. Harold J. Laski spent an evening with us in New York, where he appalled my father by relating how the Russians systematically exterminated a percentage of their population who did not agree with the tenets of the Communist regime. Reinhold Niebuhr and my father upset my mother's careful timing of dinner one evening by deciding to have a martini not more than ten minutes before the meal was announced. Martinis were rarely served in our house, and a remarkable hunt ensued before a dusty bottle of gin and a remnant of sweet(!) vermouth were discovered. On a spring vacation in Washington, we were taken for a formal call on Franklin D. Roosevelt in the Oval Office at the White House. And I remember, too, going to call on former Justice Louis D. Brandeis, then in retirement and greatly revered by my father. I once attempted small talk with Herbert Hoover, of which the latter did not have very much to offer. We sat on the steps of a cottage in Jasper, Canada, one summer vacation and talked with Charles Evans Hughes, whom my father always referred to, not without affection, as "Old Brushface." I remember Lord and Lady Halifax, and my being particularly impressed by the silk print she wore which had small British lions all over it. Robert Maynard Hutchins came to stay with his wife at the time he was the young handsome new president of the University of Chicago.

So great a variety of people came and went: Governor John G. Winant of New Hampshire, later to become ambassador to England, A. Lawrence Lowell of Harvard, and Robert Moses of New York State Park Commission fame. I lunched with Mrs. Theodore Roosevelt at Sagamore Hill on Long Island, and several times saw Clement Attlee, who was a contemporary of my father's. For an evening at the Berkeley Hotel in London, Mr. Attlee sat with us trading humorous incidents of their lives with my father for almost three hours, laughing again and again with delight. Later that week we lunched with the former prime minister at the small apartment he occupied at the Inns of Court until his death. He had given up a beloved place in the country, where he had also once welcomed us on a bleak August afternoon just after his wife's death. In 1967, I asked Mr. Attlee to write a reminiscence about my father, not aware of how feeble he had become. Nevertheless, in an unsteady but determined hand, he replied:

"I only met Grenville Clark in his old age though I knew of his great career and of the great services he did for his country and for the world. I had myself become convinced that we could only attain world peace through the establishment of world law. It was therefore with great interest that I read the great work by Clark and Sohn. Here we had the blueprint of what we desired to see established.

"Clark was a man of great personal charm and his conversation was good to listen to. I had the pleasure of staying with him in Dublin, New Hampshire. Undoubtedly, he was the most distinguished man in our movement and his loss cannot be exaggerated."

Of countless anecdotes I heard at the dinner table or later around a fire, was the story of my father taking Al Smith to his college club, where the latter stood on a table and sang to the assembled company "The Sidewalks of New York." I heard of his encounters with Winston Churchill in 1936, and of the occasion he had the opportunity to maneuver Charles A. Lindbergh and Eddie Rickenbacker into a position where they spoke to each other once more after a deep rift in their relationship had kept them apart for many years. All of the Theodore Roosevelt clan were friends, and warm words have been written me in recent years by both Ethel Roosevelt Derby and Alice Roosevelt Longworth. The latter recently wrote: "I am sorry I have no particular recollections of Grenny, except that we all had many good times together sixty or seventy years ago!"

I attended as a girl a performance of *Madame Butterfly* with my mother and father and one of the firm's bright and attractive young lawyers and his wife, the former later to become the justice of the Supreme Court John M. Harlan. I remember the latter's concern when the opera so overwhelmed me that I burst into tears at the end and was led home consumed by this tragedy.

Visits to Dublin of Robert Frost, who was driven over each summer from Vermont for a stay of several days, were wonderful and exhausting. He talked delightfully, almost exclusively about himself, and so incessantly that it was necessary for my mother and father to take him on in shifts. Their attempts to shorten the conversational day by giving him breakfast in bed were never successful beyond the hour of eight-thirty, when he invariably appeared, alert and ready for company. Felix Frankfurter was often with us, with his calm and beautiful wife, the daughter of a Unitarian minister. She was perfect for the irrepressible Felix, not above rebuking him at times, and she would drive him over from Vermont while Felix, who did not ever touch the wheel, talked, read, or wrote sitting beside her. His boundless energy and conversational capacities poured forth late into the night. These were sparkling memorable sessions.

I remember my father's sorrow and disappointment as well at the premature death of the Right Honorable Hugh Gaitskill, whose likely destiny was to be prime minister of England. He had been forthright and outspoken in his support of Grenville Clark's plan for world peace through world law and might have been the head of state my father sought to promote his plan throughout the world. As he closed a speech delivered in Paris in 1962, his words were the following: "One last thought. The progress of this cause requires the active support of governments. It has been suggested by a distinguished American, Mr. Grenville Clark, that the British Government is well qualified to take the initiative—because of its political experience, because of its world-wide connections through the Commonwealth, because it is not a super power, because, though an important and loyal member of NATO, it is not fanatical in its attitude to Communism. Whether these qualifications are valid or appropriate, it is for others to say. In any case, the less individual nations arrogate virtues to themselves the better. But for my part I should be proud to see the British Government, in association with other like-minded governments, take a full part in this enterprise. It is very much the kind of role I believe my country should play in the world today. I am sure that many others—in Western Europe and the Commonwealth and elsewhere—would gladly join with us."

Perhaps the greatest moment of all for this daughter was the opportunity to rescue Albert Einstein from falling down a scullery stairway at the Princeton Inn in Princeton, New Jersey, where he had come for a meeting of those who had convened at the first Dublin Conference some months earlier. This gentle, diffident man whose only confusions would be in the area of small matters, not only cheerfully accompanied me to the meeting room, but in the course of the meeting I observed him as a vote would be requested, "All in favor, please stand." Mr. Einstein would stand. "All against, please stand." Mr. Einstein stood again.

My mother and father visited with President Nasser who afterward wrote a charming letter to my mother, and Jawaharlal Nehru entertained them in India, sending a very large white official limousine to pick them up as their ship docked, greatly to their embarrassment. My father went on a salmon fishing expedition with the painter Frank Benson, a trip which reinforced a dislike for that sport which eased only in later years when we would pull a few trout from the millpond near our house before dinner, successfully, that is, if our hooks landed in the water instead of a tree.

I have touched on but a fraction of my memories of times with my father and events and people to which he exposed me. It was indeed a "liberal education" to have had this father as a guide, mentor, and friend. I would like to close by recalling one more event of my early life. Picture yourself a very serious student at Radcliffe College majoring in philosophy as I was and imagine the inspiration drawn from a number of visits for tea with the Alfred North Whiteheads in their book-lined apartment in Cambridge which overlooked the Charles River. I even came to know them well enough to call by myself on occasion, in some trepidation, to sit in awe and reverence, listening to this cherubic and articulate man with his great incisive mind. I especially remember his observation to the effect that satisfaction and comfort with a present situation should not deter one from taking on a new opportunity, that one should not stand still in life, but, on the contrary, have the courage to leave behind that which was happy and secure, move on, and take up the new challenge.

MY FATHER'S FRIEND

Elizabeth Jay Hollins

———◆———

Mr. Clark was a friend of my father's, perhaps the friend whom he loved and valued the most. It was a friendship dating from college and law school days but one which increased enormously in intimacy and closeness through the years, the reverse pattern of most college friendships. Because he was my father's friend, a figure from my childhood, he always remained "Mr. Clark" to me even when people younger than I, and perhaps not even as involved in his work as I became, called him "Grenny." And in his affectionate manner toward me, which made me feel very proud, was always the background of his deep affection for my father. I think I represented old strands in his life, and it gave him pleasure to see me independently involved in the work that became the consuming passion of the last third of his life and which few of his old friends supported. My adult friendship with Mrs. Clark too, though quite freshly arrived at, had in it more intimacy because of this old background.

The Clarks lived on Long Island within commuting range of New York, as did my family. The Clarks chose what was then considered a small place at East Williston where Mr. Clark could walk to the station. Even as a very unsophisticated child I was aware that this was not a "fashionable" thing to do in sporting, high-powered Long Island society and I can remember my father chuckling with affectionate amusement and approval about this typical ability of Mr. Clark to go his own way. The Clark children were all a bit younger than I, so I never knew that house through going there "to play" and it was only years later, when Harry was working closely with Mr. Clark, that we went there together and I stepped into that sudden extraordinary pool of quiet in the midst of the noisy, garish, crowded development that by then surrounded it. Mrs. Clark had created her own world quite as much as any Zen gardener. Both the Clark houses that I came to know, the one in Dublin and the one at East Williston, had a direct simplicity, an unpretentious, stripped, cultural elegance combined with strong individuality that was Mrs. Clark's doing but which I always felt suited Mr. Clark well.

My father and Mr. Clark were both lawyers, both of "old New York" families, both public-spirited. As a child I was fairly unaware of what their mutual concerns were, but one of my early memories (I *hope* I was very young for this!) is of sitting next to Mr. Clark at lunch in my parents' dining room and noticing certain purple birthmarks high up on his big forehead. Since I associated him with my father's involvement with the Plattsburg movement preceding the First World War, I decided that these were heel marks made by the trampling of some German officer's boot when he lay almost dead in the mud! A much later, as well as a far more realistic and more continuous memory is of the whole Clark family coming to tea on Christmas afternoons. This was the time of day when we had our tree (with *real* candles, at my mother's insistence, while my father with agonized forebearance simply saw to it that there were buckets of water under the piano and behind the wing chair). As we became surfeited with our own orgy of present-opening, the door would open from time to time as a few close friends of our parents would drop in; but always the Clark family. Their arrival on Christmas afternoons—Mrs. Clark, in a hat, with a sort of beige silky dress, Mary D., Grenny, Louisa, Mr. Clark usually last with his big head (big forehead, big jaw, those friendly eyes) even then thrust forward—is part of the warmth that surrounds my memories of life in my parents' house. It meant much to my mother that the Clarks, with characteristic feeling, continued the custom a good many years after my father's sudden death.

Mr. Clark was always a favorite person to have come to the house at any time. He had a way of really speaking to you, even if you were only twelve years old, and of listening to what you might say as though it quite conceivably might be of interest. He treated you with respect as a person and you felt it was genuine respect, not just patronizing kindliness. This spontaneously friendly, interested, egalitarian treatment of other persons that I felt so strongly as a child always seemed to me one of the chief characteristics of Mr. Clark, and when I read *World Peace through World Law* I felt this same quality in the careful, detailed reasoning behind the proposals. I said this once quite forcibly, to surprisingly good effect!

It was in February 1960. Harry and I were on our second trip for Mr. Clark in relation to the translation, publication, and discussion of *World Peace through World Law* in other parts of the world. We were in Madras, India, which is the seat of a university, and which was also the home of C. Rajagopalachari, a very distinguished and then still fairly powerful "elder statesman," patriot, and scholar. Through a series of complicated efforts Harry finally arranged an appointment with him. It was a hot evening in southern India. The Madras representative of the Oxford University Press, an old Gandhian himself, had brought us out to this suburb. We were sitting in a small round palm hut of utmost simplicity which seemed to be the office of this thin, forceful, aristocratic old man in a homespun dhoti of flawless whiteness (there was a modern typewriter in the midst of this Gandhian home-madeness and the young aide, or perhaps disciple, who made us tea had evidently been taking dictation). Harry and I were trying to persuade our host to read *World Peace through World Law* and to encourage discussion of its ideas. But he would have none of it. He was busy, and he prejudged adversely the human understanding (or lack of it) in the work of any American.

Presently he asked Harry about himself, how he happened to be doing this, and Harry explained his active involvement with the United World Federalists since the end of the war. Then he said to me, "And are you an international lawyer?" Very startled and not at all sure how he regarded the place of women, I hastily explained that I was not a lawyer of any kind but that I had known Mr. Clark since my childhood and not only did I agree with his ideas but I knew at first hand the man's fair-mindedness and respect for others—and I told about childhood encounters. Rajagopalachari almost snapped, "What you say is important. You may leave the book with me." We left soon after, having made him promise to read at least the introduction. The next morning, while we were eating breakfast at our hotel, a runner arrived with a note from Sri Rajagopalachari, "I am at page 16. This man is everything you say." Again at noon, another note by runner, "I am at page 65. A just and great book. I am reading with close attention." And two weeks later he sent us the enormously enthusiastic review he had written for the paper *Swaraj*. He had seen the value and regard given even-handedly to the concerns of all persons behind the dry legal rhetoric of the proposals. My childhood Mr. Clark was fully vindicated.

In the early 1930s I married and left home, though I often returned to my parents' house to visit. My father and Mr. Clark saw a great deal of each other during this period so I often met him there. There are some things that stand out in my mind:

In the summer of 1934, a lighthearted article I had written about living on a schooner was published in the *Atlantic Monthly*. When I saw Mr. Clark, after congratulating me, he said, "Now Betsy, tell me: how much did they pay you?" I said, "One hundred fifty dollars." (I think that was the figure. Writers were paid a whole lot less in those days.) Mr. Clark chuckled. "Why, that is exactly what they paid me. How do you suppose they figure it?" Mr. Clark had also had an article recently published in the *Atlantic*. (I am mortified to remember that he had taken the trouble to read my piece but I, with the arrogance of youth, never bothered to look up his.) He was pleased to have had an article in the *Atlantic*, delighted to find we had been paid exactly the same. It was a new field to him, so of course, since we live in a money economy, he was interested in the money. In the 1960s, when I would go with Harry for those long (and treasured by both of us) working sessions in Dublin, I never could get over how much time he spent going over the money in hand and the budget in meticulous detail; he wanted to have each hundred dollars and where it came from clearly in his mind. Understanding the place of money, he also understood very well the limitations of being short of it. There must have been countless people for whom he quietly eased some money out of his own pocket. For instance, Harry and I were aware that Mr. Clark was distressed that such a distinguished man as Clement Attlee came to this country on lecture tours in his old age because he needed the money, and that Mr. Clark made many little arrangements to help out on this score. We did *not* know until some years after Mr. Clark's death, when we were visiting Ruth Wight in the basement of the Dartmouth Library, where she was laboring on the immense task of ordering Mr. Clark's papers, and I dipped at random into one of the files, that Mr. Clark had directly paid for some expensive dental work for him. He had written Lord Attlee's dentist in London, explaining that he wanted his distinguished old friend to have the best. He had followed up by letter on how the work had gone. Not merely the generosity, but the delicate feeling and the attention to the practical detail were typical of him.

Or, for instance, my diary records that April 30, 1935, was my parents' twenty-fifth wedding anniversary and that at dinner that evening everyone made speeches and read poems for the occasion, that Dr. Derby sang, that Uncle Eddie sang, and that "Mr. Clark also made a gallant attempt." I did not know until thirty-five years later, when Louisa told me, that one of Mr. Clark's favorite dreams was that he was a famous professional singer. (He had no voice at all!) It was so surprising and yet so indicative of the unexpectedness and *fun* of this rich, complex, diverse, very human man.

Hitler was rising in power in the thirties and the world picture was darkening. My father, who had had several heart attacks, was wearing himself out with concern and the person he talked about as the *only* person with constructive ideas was Mr. Clark. One spring morning I took a ride with my father (in moderation, one of the few forms of exercise allowed him). As the horses jogged along side by side under the dogwood of the Broadhollow Woods, he said in a way I was always to remember, "Grenny Clark is the only truly great man I know. His thinking is so far ahead of his time that he probably will not be recognized during his lifetime but mark my words because he will be. He is developing some ideas now that have to do with peace. I will not live to see them recognized and I doubt if even you will. But Stephanie (my oldest daughter, born September 1936, my father's first grandchild) *may*." I thought of this conversation in Copenhagen in the summer of 1953 when we were attending the conference of the World Association for World Federal Government and Max Habicht, the Swiss lawyer and Federalist, said to the entire assembly, tapping a copy of the small book *A Plan for Peace*, "No one here has put forward anything comparable to the sophistication and depth of thinking of this Plan."

Mr. Clark's peace-thinking had a long history. Another time I was home; the news in the papers was very dark; Mr. Clark was at dinner. They were discussing Clarence Streit's proposal of the immediate union of the Atlantic democracies. My father seemed all for it, while Mr. Clark was explaining why such a concept of common citizenship with a small part of the world did not go far enough, and somehow I glimmered an all-inclusiveness of view I have never forgotten. At that moment both my father and Mr. Clark had been convinced for some time that Hitler must be stopped, that to this end the United States must enter the war, that, in order to be effective, what later became the Selective Service Act must be passed. Even while totally taken up by the necessity of defeating Hitler, Mr. Clark could hold in mind at the same time a larger concept.

It is impossible to speak of my father and Mr. Clark during those years without speaking of Mr. Clark and the telephone. Those telephone calls would go on for hours (just think of how many people through the years must have come to know them!). They are one of the distinctive memories of my parents' house during that period. The telephone would ring, usually at mealtime. It would be Mr. Clark for my father. Mother would at once send some child to tell the cook to hold dinner for forty-five minutes. It was very familiar, twenty years later, when Harry was working closely with Mr. Clark. If it were Mr. Clark on the telephone I would simply walk into the kitchen and turn off whatever was cooking. I knew those telephone conversations.

During the winter of 1940–1941 Mr. Clark used to telephone my father, who, through orders of his doctors because of his heart, was cut off from the fully active involvement he would have chosen, almost literally every evening. Years later, sitting beside the fire in the living room in Dublin Mr. Clark told Harry and me that on the evening in March that my father died (suddenly, sitting in his chair after dinner), he (Mr. Clark) had come home much later than usual from a meeting. He had thought it was really too late to telephone, but he had felt impelled to do so. Dr. Jessup (Everett C. Jessup, Mr. Clark's friend and doctor and also my father's) an-

swered the phone and said simply, "He's gone, Grenny," whereupon Mr. Clark had gotten in the car and come over. Two days
later a long tribute to Delancey K. Jay appeared in the *New York
Times* in the form of a letter by Mr. Clark. The hours he must
have devoted to writing it (and with characteristic thoroughness,
seeing to it that the *Times* published it without delay) were taken
from urgent, behind-the-scenes, foreign-policy activity of considerable importance he was then engaged in. It was a small instance of
something I noticed strongly in the later years of knowing him. He
never got mixed up about what was important, and public involvement, however important, would be put aside for the ties of private affection.

MEMORIES OF GRENVILLE CLARK

AS PATIENT AND FRIEND

Paul Dudley White, M.D.

———————————◆———————————

I doubly appreciate this opportunity to present on the one hand my medical contacts with a remarkable human being who taught me and other physicians so much about the vicissitudes of health, in particular, the relationship of the psyche and the soma, and on the other hand, the interweaving of our personal medicolegal interests and of our efforts in the promotion of world peace. It is this contact with the mental and spiritual qualities, aspirations, and accomplishments of his patients that so intrigues and enriches the life of the physician, often much more than do the physical findings. In Grenville Clark's case there was often more than in any other patient of mine that I can remember an extraordinary interdependence of body, mind, and soul. Hence I shall present herewith an all-too-short account of my thirty years both as a physician of his and as a friend.

I met Grenville Clark first on September 12, 1936, in my office at the Massachusetts General Hospital whither he had been referred to me by Dr. L. F. Richards of Nashua, New Hampshire, for an appraisal of the condition of his heart, for which he had been recently rejected for life insurance because of the finding of a loud apical systolic murmur, and also for consideration of his general health. This was a few months more than thirty years before he died at the age of eighty-four.

Since this story of mine will doubtless be read by some physicians and since it may be of interest and value to many laymen, I shall present in concise but reasonably comprehensive manner the ups and downs of his physical health throughout his life, greatly benefited by the useful advice which he received from his team of physicians, and the care by his devoted family, in particular by his first wife, Fanny, and his second wife, Mary. Among his many medical advisers to whom I would pay tribute and with whom I have corresponded over these thirty years were Dr. L. F. Richards of Nashua, New Hampshire, Dr. W. W. Herrick of New York City, especially Dr. Andrew Foord of Kerhonkson, New York, Dr. Everett Jessup of Long Island, New York, and Dr. Greene Fitzhugh of Boston; also, Dr. Fuller Albright, Dr. Joseph Aub, Dr. George Smith, Dr. Arthur Allen, Dr. Bernard Jacobson, all of Boston; Dr. Donald Clark and Dr. Theodore H. Lee of Peterborough, New Hampshire; and Dr. Richard Snowman of Keene, New Hampshire. I would add that contrary to the experience with the results of some such superabundant medical advisers there was a delightful and effective cooperation in the care of Grenville Clark, whose intense spirit demanded as much freedom as it did control.

Suffice it to say that not only did that loud heart murmur come and go within a very few years while Grenville was still a middle-aged man, but so did "essential" hypertension (of unknown cause) even up to 185 systolic and 110 diastolic, also, a decade later after the heart murmur had largely cleared. Ventricular premature beats varied very much in their frequency from year to year and even from week to week and day to day and hour to hour; on June 20, 1950, and March 21, 1966, they even occurred every other beat. His electrocardiogram also varied very much as to ST segments and T waves. They were quite normal when I first saw him but gradually in the years that followed, little or not at all related to other findings or symptoms, they would be occasionally abnormal, the STs depressed and the T waves of Leads 1 and aVL and the left ventricular chest leads flattening out or even becoming inverted on occasion, especially in Leads V_4, V_5, and V_6 and most prominently in the early 1950s when he was probably under the most severe accumulated nervous strain. The heart size also varied considerably, being greater when measured by the transverse diameter by ortho-diagram in full inspiration by 1.0 to 1.5 cm. during the early 1950s than earlier or later. We were never able to diagnose coronary heart disease since he had no angina pectoris or diagnosable episode of coronary thrombosis. It seems reasonable to blame an excessive secretion of catecholamines (adrenalin and nonadrenalin) under stress for also all these changes in the so-called parameters (physical measurements). This also fits in well with the strains of his life, which were many. And we should, I believe, apply to many others the lessons we have learned from Grenville Clark in his psychosomatic medical history.

A word about definite diagnoses that were made in the long life of Grenville Clark. In childhood he did have scarlet fever and diphtheria, which might have injured his heart temporarily without leaving any important scars; he had typhoid fever at twenty-one, tonsillectomy at forty-one, nervous prostration at forty-three requiring a rest cure of eighteen months' duration, varicose veins of both legs at about the same age, and pneumonia at forty-nine, all this before I myself first saw him as a patient. He was always low in his basal metabolic rate but did not have myxedema. He constantly took thyroid medication, which was of doubtful benefit. In 1956 his gall bladder full of stones was removed with a clearing of biliary colic and he died finally of lymphocytic lymphoma of seven years' duration. Autopsy showed acute perforation of the duodenal wall by the lymphoma. His heart was slightly enlarged with a moderate amount of arteriosclerosis of the aorta and coronary arteries, only slight arteriosclerosis of the cerebral arteries, focal or patchy fibrosis of the heart muscle, and slight "rheumatic" mitral valve deformity with insufficiency—which explains the heart murmur.

In retrospect I believe that his considerable longevity was made possible by the frequent periods of rest at critical times imposed by doctors and his wife and grudgingly accepted by the patient himself, and this longevity made possible accomplishments of all sorts, in particular, political measures to aid the government in both World Wars and, finally, internationally, the promotion of world peace.

I would like in closing to quote from letters of Grenville Clark himself to reveal somewhat the nervous stresses which so threatened his physical health.

From Grenville Clark, February 18, 1947:

"How about this world government subject of mine? It is the subject I am most interested in and the one to which I think I can contribute the most. On the other hand, the doctor is emphatic that there must be a connection between my heart condition and putting in highly intensive thought on the problem, which, admittedly, is a terrific one. In any case, I would drop the day to day planning, telephoning, etc., on this subject and confine myself to writing without deadlines. Moreover, I intend to 'lay off' the subject entirely throughout the rest of '47 except perhaps for collecting some material with a view to later writing. I have already declined a number of requests for speeches and articles this year and have told the people I have been associated with on this that they should count me out of all active work for some time to come and perhaps indefinitely. For the rest of '47, the only work I have in mind doing is some quiet, slow writing up of a Memoir of my public activities 1939–46 and the continuance of my Harvard connection. (There will be no deadline on the Memoir, which I may not even publish, but want to write up as a record of some things of importance on which I alone have the real facts.) However, I would like, if possible, to look forward to doing some systematic writing on the world government subject next year—a book reviewing my ideas—the completion of which would require at least a year at a slow pace. Can I reasonably look forward to doing this sort of thing?"

Letter to Mr. Elmore Jackson, American Friends Service Committee, from Grenville Clark, May 10, 1951:

"After long reflection, I have the conviction that if I can go to Moscow this summer (under proper conditions and as a purely unofficial private citizen) and have an interview with Mr. Stalin, I could do something of consequence towards alleviating the present tension and to help towards disarmament and a stable peace. If you can aid in obtaining an invitation for me, I should appreciate it.

"This is not a new idea with me. Over five years ago, it was suggested to me by one of our leading citizens who was in Moscow with Secretary Byrnes in December, 1945; and it has been proposed to me by several others of good judgment.

"On the one hand I would hope to suggest to Mr. Stalin some methods whereby disarmament could be achieved, without sacrifice of essential interests either by the Soviet Union or the United States, and whereby relations between East and West could be greatly improved. On the other hand, I would hope to bring back from Mr. Stalin some statements, specifically approved by him, which, when reported in this country, would forward these purposes.

"I believe that this summer is the time to go, in view of the trend of events and the desire of hundreds of millions to find a new way towards disarmament and peace.

"I would wish to stress to Mr. Stalin the all-importance of progressive and enforceable disarmament as the inexorable price of peace; to express the view that this object is attainable and should be made the one great goal of both the Soviet Union and the United States and to suggest specific ways and means whereby this purpose can be advanced. I would then hope to receive such encouragement and ideas from him as, when reported to those in authority in this country, would promote this purpose, help to relieve the prevailing tension and bring about a true cooperation for disarmament and for genuine and stable peace in the interest of both peoples and of the whole world."

GRENNY IN THE 1930s AND 1940s

Lewis W. Douglas

I first met Grenny Clark in the spring of 1932. Without any particular knowledge of his views about servicemen's compensation, I introduced what was called an economy resolution in the House of Representatives. I was the only Congressman from Arizona where the number of veterans amounted to approximately 21 per cent of the total voting population. In addition to the World War I veterans, there were a good many Spanish war veterans as well.

The resolution I had introduced was inspired by the rather startling news or so it was in those days—that the budget deficit of the U.S. government would amount to something just under one billion dollars.

Pursuant to this resolution a committee of the members of the House was appointed. I was on that committee, as was John McDuffie of Alabama, who was its chairman. Of course, the principal item—there were three or four principal items—was veterans' compensation, then something of the order of $750 million to $800 million in expenditures annually. Most of this was paid to veterans with nonservice-connected disabilities.

Because I had introduced this resolution and because I was attempting to work on this question of veterans' compensation, Grenny came to see me in Washington. He told me of his very deep feelings and strong convictions regarding veterans' compensation and of the fundamental responsibility of an American citizen to bear arms in time of trouble and in the defense of his country. I was wholly sympathetic with his views and from that moment on we worked together.

I tried on my part to make a very careful analysis of the entire area of ex-servicemen's compensation going as far back as the War of 1812. Interestingly I found that there were twelve widows of veterans of the War of 1812 still drawing compensation. At any rate, the efforts of the Economy Committee of the House, in conjunction with the Senate, produced substantially nothing in the spring of 1932.

I saw Grenny immediately after the adjournment of the Congress. Meanwhile he had organized the National Economy League. The entire emphasis of this organization focused on soldiers' compensation and especially upon the ex-servicemen with nonservice-connected disabilities, that is to say, those whose disability was not connected directly with their military service. The activities of the Economy League were well known. There had developed the view that certain diseases, especially tuberculosis, were connected with the exposure to which veterans were subjected during their military service and that did not appear in perceptible and diagnostic form for five or six years after discharge. This was known as the presumptive period after the period of service. Under this extraordinary extension of the presumptive period, far beyond anything which science and medical testimony could support, a vast group of pensioners had grown up. This is not to suggest that they were lacking in patriotism. A large part of them in Arizona were friends of mine and fine men.

It became very difficult to face the issue of removing from the pension roles a host of my friends whose disability could not in fact be connected with their war service. So, while Grenny was working through the Economy League to build up public sentiment in favor of reducing this vast millstone, as it were, around the neck of the federal budget, I was trying, without detailed knowledge of what he was doing, to analyze the situation very carefully in Washington.

Then President-elect Roosevelt invited me to be director of the budget and to sit as a member of the cabinet. At the time of the inauguration all the banks in the country were ordered closed. The situation was threatening. With the external support of Grenny and the Washington help of General John F. Hines, who was the director of the Veterans' Administration, Dean Acheson, Swager Sherley, and several of my friends in the House, including John McDuffie of Alabama and Cliff Woodrum of Virginia, the Economy Act was drafted and went to Congress with a presidential message on the tenth day of March 1933. Within a relatively short time this piece of emergency legislation was enacted with the emergency clause, and the reductions were put into effect.

I was shocked as I have seldom been shocked to discover, after about thirty days, that by some unintended interpretation of the law, many of the directly service-connected wounded men suffered a reduction in their compensation. Immediately I reported this to the president and recommended the establishment of reviewing committees all over the country to review the case of each service-connected disabled veteran and to restore his benefit to its previous level. This had the effect of reducing the amount of saving previously estimated, but it also had the effect of belatedly attempting to rectify an injustice for which I, and I alone, was responsible.

All this rather captured Grenny's imagination. He was at the time on the Corporation of Harvard. I rather suspect that he suggested to President Conant that there be an LL.D. honorary degree conferred upon me at the June commencement. There I saw Grenny and indeed continued to do so over a long period thereafter.

When in 1934 I severed my relationship with the New Deal—more especially because of irresponsible spending of the public funds and the behavior at the London Economic Conference, I saw a great deal of Grenny in New York. Even while I was chancellor at McGill University I used to see him often when I crossed the border.

As the clouds of war began to gather in the late 1930s, we saw even more of each other. I returned to the United States. Grenny was most helpful with the Committee to Defend America by Aiding the Allies. He called together, I shall never forget, a group of the Plattsburg Civilian Military Training Camp Veterans of 1915–1916 at the Harvard Club and announced his purpose to have drafted a selective service act. This he did with the aid of one or two others. He, however, was the dominating force. The legislation was taken to Washington. I remember seeing him during that summer in his room at the Carlton Hotel, where he and Howard Petersen were canvassing the various members of the House and of the Senate. The White House had refused to endorse the legislation; the general staff and its chief, General Marshall, had declined to endorse it.

Nevertheless, with that dogged determination for which he was so very famous, Grenny kept trying to find somebody in the House of Representatives and some member of the Senate who would introduce legislation which had the endorsement of neither the White House nor General Marshall. At last he discovered James Wadsworth in the House and Senator Burke, a lame-duck senator from Nebraska, to introduce the legislation. He spent most of his time soliciting among the members of both houses, arguing with them, trying to persuade them that the hour would come when we would need selective service, that the war would break over the shores of our country and that it was vitally essential to our national existence that the selective service legislation be enacted.

A number of us testified before both houses. At last, in the very middle of a presidential campaign, 1940, the miracle happened. The Congress passed the selective service legislation. To Grenny should go all the credit for this remarkable achievement. It proved to be all he prophesied. It became one of the solid foundations of the development of our military strength. It saved many months, possibly a year, at a time when minutes were the difference between victory and defeat.

Also in the spring of 1940, Grenny played an important role in persuading the president to form a coalition cabinet. His persuasiveness resulted in the appointment of Frank Knox as the secretary of the navy and that indomitable character, Henry L. Stimson, as secretary of war.

Often during this period Grenny would come to see me in my office at 34 Nassau Street. On several occasions he asked whether I would not act as secretary of war. I always reminded him of the differences that had existed between President Roosevelt and me during the early days of the New Deal and that his suggestion was quite beyond the realm of acceptance by the president and, although I think that he suggested my name, when it received a very powerful rebuff on the banks of the Potomac, he promptly switched to Mr. Stimson, who was a "rock of ages," a man of un-impeachable integrity and great moral strength.

After 1940 our paths crossed less frequently. More and more, Grenny became occupied with his work on disarmament and world peace. We remained friends. He was a towering figure, one of the patriots within the orbit of my acquaintance and a person of extraordinary mental powers and moral courage. He was one of the greatest *private* public servants of this century.

REMINISCENCES OF GRENVILLE CLARK

Lyman V. Rutledge

In the summer of 1952 after I had retired from the ministry and finished a tour of duty as executive director of the Star Island Corporation, I told my friend and mentor, the Rev. Dr. Charles E. Park, that I desired to return to the pulpit if there was any church in the United States small enough to accept my services. Within a few weeks he suggested that I might be interested in Dublin, New Hampshire. I was much pleased by the prospect. He put my name through the proper channels and I received a formal invitation to "occupy the pulpit" for two Sundays in August. After morning services the second Sunday, Mr. Henry Allison handed me an envelope, cautioning me not to reveal its origin. It turned out to be a penciled letter from Grenville Clark dated September 28, 1952. He was not on the committee to select a minister but had asked Dr. Park to suggest a name, and when he saw that I was interested he felt that I should not be induced to accept a call without knowing the condition of the church (which had been without a settled minister for two years, and had only eighteen voting members). In his letter he asked me to phone him personally, which I did, and he told me then that if, knowing the situation, I was willing to accept, he personally would guarantee my salary for five years, and so stipulate in his will. That was my introduction to Grenville Clark.

During the years that followed he took an active and decisive part in building up the church. I had told him and others that my ambition was to restore the church to a condition which would command the full-time services of a younger man. One day by his fireside he asked me how large an endowment the church should have, and I answered fifty thousand dollars. He replied: "That's just the figure I had in mind." So we started the campaign—which the congregation thought impossible—and soon had the full amount pledged. Then he surprised me by suggesting that we should double the amount. That too was soon pledged, and the campaign, extending over seven or eight years, came to its climax with the provisions in his will, that thirty thousand dollars be added to the endowment if a similar amount were raised within two years after his death. I understand these conditions were met, but I do not know the full amount of the endowment finally achieved. Whatever it is today, Mr. Clark is the real benefactor, and without his quiet efforts my feeble services would have accomplished virtually nothing.

Personally Mr. Clark fulfilled his original promise many times over. In 1953 when I underwent major surgery he covered my bill at the hospital, and pledged me not to tell. Once—or twice—I received letters and generous checks from the cashier of a New York bank with the impersonal note that a friend of mine who wished to remain anonymous, wished me to have the enclosed. On other occasions he would send a gift, a few hundred dollars, to the treasurer of the church to be handed to me either as gift or salary over and above my usual stipend from the church. In the spring of 1957 I decided that I should resign from the church, but when the news reached Mr. Clark he took immediate action, without consulting me! He engaged accommodations at a lodge in Stowe, Vermont, instructed the church committee not to accept my resignation but grant a leave of absence for three months, and then told me to absent myself from Dublin for that period and consider the resignation afterward. All this within a few hours, at no expense to either the church or myself. I continued as minister of the church for three more years, during which time Mr. Clark seemed to command me as private chaplain. It was my privilege to preside at the wedding of Margaret Spencer, to conduct the funeral services for Mrs. Clark, and perform the ceremony for his marriage to his second wife.

In one of his early letters to me in 1953, he had suggested

dropping formality between ourselves. Some years later I was greatly amused when, sitting by his fireside I spoke of Charley Park, and he chided me for being so informal in referring to so distinguished a man as the Rev. Dr. Charles E. Park. I was happy to tell him that the distinguished minister of the First Church in Boston had ordained me into the ministry in Billerica in 1910, and we had continued on the first-name basis during all the years since. He then told me once more that Dr. Park had presided at his wedding in 1907, and had recommended me for the Dublin pulpit.

During my last years in Dublin Mr. Clark became more and more solicitous for my welfare, and made every possible excuse to reimburse me for some fancied expense or insist that I accept a fee for some service, whether I deserved it or not. He exacted a pledge that if I ever needed anything I would let him know. Finally on December 9, 1966, during the last days of his long and painful illness, he sent a little note which spoke so eloquently of his great heart and kindly interest. I did not know how to answer. I felt as if he really wanted to give me something, but I could not accept it with a clear conscience. So I wrote a brief note trying to tell him how deeply I appreciated his continued interest and valued his acquaintance above anything he could do for me; that my financial obligations had all been met. This I delivered in person, and that was our last brief interview at Outlet Farm.

The funeral service in the little church in Dublin only a month later overwhelmed me. No one can ever know how deeply I regretted my own inability to voice the tribute of love and respect which a multitude of silent hearts longed to hear spoken. A part of that which I spoke is as follows:

"It was true of Mr. Clark that no matter how broadly his interests might roam throughout the civilized world, he had the same intimate kindly interest in all his neighbors, in those who carried out his instructions in the humblest manner, in those who cared for him.

"And who would have suspected that this friend and neighbor of ours whom we felt that we knew so intimately—and who was so deeply concerned for all our interests, and for all our little problems—was at the same time a man whose sheer strength, wisdom, judgment, experience attracted the best people from the nations of the earth—those who are responsible for the conduct of great nations and governments, those who were promoting some great cause seemed instinctively to find the path that led to Mr. Clark's mountain rendezvous.

"We do not know, the world may never know, how much of the human problem has been so carefully examined and mature judgment given to those who came, seeking that which cannot be secured by money, or power, or prestige, but which springs from a noble heart, a clear mind, and above all, a generous spirit. He had faith in humanity. He believed that the human race would develop and nations would find their way.

"This is a description of his whole attitude toward national and international problems. It was that spirit which led him long ago to present to his friends in Washington the plan for Plattsburg which was followed undoubtedly to the salvation of America at a time of crisis—whose principles are still recognized as valid for the training of men to defend our country.

"It was that spirit which led him to his quiet but effective work in the forming of the United Nations Charter.

"And it was his vision, which went far beyond that of most of the delegates there, which could see that this charter could not be passed by the nations gathered there, in a form strong enough to be ultimately effective.

"So it was his hand that had written into that original charter one little paragraph which called for a revision. And through the twenty years since, he has been working on the possible revision of the United Nations Charter.

"How many people in the world know what they owe to the hand that wrote that paragraph, because that little passage looks forward into the indefinite future to a time when the nations can establish what was to Mr. Clark the one essential for peace in all the world: world peace through world law."

A DUBLIN FRIEND

Edric A. Weld

There have been many whose contacts with Grenville Clark have come about through affairs of state or world law. Mine started from the fact that I completed my mentally assigned term as rector-headmaster of Holderness School in 1951, and my wife, Gertrude, and I took up all-year residence in Dublin for a period of "rest and recuperation" in our family home. It was our good fortune that we lived less than two miles down the road from the Clarks, and passed the house every day on our way to the store and post office.

As neighbors we were invited to tea, and were privileged to look out the window at a vista of Monadnock that was far more striking than any from our house. But the superb view became to me the least important feature, as Grenny began to discuss whatever affair was closest to his overriding concern on that particular day. He would say, "I want to pick your brains," as I am sure he said to hundreds or thousands of others. Surely to a younger man, there is no more flattering approach to a discussion, and I used to jump in with all four feet. Gertrude had an equally happy time with Fanny, and we looked forward eagerly to the next invitation.

It so happened that we had returned from a visit with family in California and were asked to call a few days later. On that particular afternoon he had just received a desperate appeal from the committee fighting the teachers' loyalty oaths in California— which left them subject to prosecution for being "subversive."

They had to have a brief prepared in thirty-six hours from Saturday P.M. to Monday A.M. As a New Hampshire clergyman asked to conduct marriages in the state of Massachusetts, I had been required to go to the state house in Boston each time and sign a loyalty oath to uphold the constitutions of the United States and of Massachusetts—in a form that did not upset me at all. So the differences between the Massachusetts oath (of nearly two hundred years' standing) and the California oath were fresh in my mind and provided a basic approach which Grenny developed that night and the next morning and telephoned to California with the result that the California court declared the loyalty oath unconstitutional. I suppose I never felt as useful a citizen before or since.

There has been much talk about "mind-expanding" drugs. Grenny had the ability to listen as much as he talked. So, when he did talk, his friends were listening eagerly. Of all my friends, contact with Grenny was the most "mind-expanding" experience I have ever had.

In closing, I hold it important not to omit reference to Fanny's part. Without her cordial welcome and the enjoyment of her company, we would not have come so often. I am sure she was an indispensable element in Grenny's wealth of contacts and his worldwide influence.

A SMALL BOY'S GRANDFATHER

Grenville Clark Thoron

———————◆———————

Some men sow the ground, some the minds of men.
Pascal, Pensées

In recalling a few memories about my grandfather, Pascal's words come back to me very appropriately. Grandpa implanted many rich "seeds" in my mind at a formative period. In time, those ideas have grown very large.

At age thirteen, I was less acquainted with what Grandpa did than with his strictly human side. That summer in Dublin we spent more time together than we ever did. He was a vitally affectionate and interested human being. His professional life was about as removed from me as the rings of Saturn. I could have probably best described it then as so many long-distance phone calls, the contents of which I could only guess.

Gradually I came to know him as so pre-eminently the lover (not too strong a word, for he was a passionate person) of democracy and civil rights. However, he went one step further than most people. He proceeded by some highly personal and independent principle of fairness. The Constitution and the law books were only his base; his own private judgment was far keener and more refined than any written law. He was always one to reserve his opinion on any matter. To give a rather homely illustration, he invariably aggrandized a person's accomplishments, not from a sense of loyalty or friendship but from an inward scale of deservedness. Coming up from Dublin Lake, Grandpa would call out to no one in particular that I had single-handedly paddled the canoe across the lake. There might be a quarter part truth in the claim. Although you were not fooled, such compliments never failed to warm your heart.

Grandpa was supremely interested in the individual. He held little store with position or title. He once praised his friend Dr. Paul Dudley White in a manner which could easily be applied to himself, saying that Dr. White was not above treating an impoverished farmhand (at no fee) as readily as he would Queen Elizabeth. He was drawn to humble men, and notwithstanding all his higher callings, he remained exquisitely the simple and modest man. I remember him leaving for a phone call. Thirty minutes later he returned. A young man had called, saying, "Mr. Clark, my grandfather told me long ago that if I got into difficulties I was to call you." It turned out that the man was literally drowning in a sea of troubles, as if he had been saving them up for years, all the way from larceny to women. Grandpa set about advising him in each case and ended by referring him to a capable lawyer at his old New York law firm.

Humility always impressed me as Grandpa's most distinguishing quality. Genuine humility is difficult for the Western mind to understand. It is often mistaken by less charitable persons for diffidence, self-doubt, or cowardliness. A man's enemies would probably be quick to call it weakness. Nor is it something cultivated like good manners. Grandpa's humility was not falsely adopted but native to him. It resulted from a thorough knowledge of his enormous powers of mind and an equal measure of inherent moral strength. He had a vein of moral probity as deep and firm as the granite bedrock of New England. When it became obvious to him that the country was into too wide a commitment in Southeast Asia, I remember Grandpa vigorously remonstrating against President Kennedy's actions; Kennedy was the man over whose election he had been so enthusiastic and for whom he held out such great expectations. Grandpa foresaw all that came about, that knowing the relentless nature of history, the conflict there would be a sticky affair, difficult to disengage from, a moral scar on the national conscience. Grandpa's own nature would not permit him to scamp an issue. He felt each issue strongly and took a stand "on principle."

Grandpa was constantly plumbing people's depths (he would say "picking their brains"). He often would make up games or pose hypothetical questions to test me during our many walks together. Sometimes I was surprised at my own answers. He always made you think you knew more than you did, and sometimes you did!

A game involving figures, for which Grandpa had a special penchant, he played with the local natives during a trip we took to northern New Hampshire. Whenever we stopped at a country store or old inn, he would ask the proprietor: "Now what is the elevation here?" Invariably, the man, either not sure himself or believing Grandpa would not know differently, would throw out some arbitrary figure. Grandpa would come back to the car chuckling and tell us that the old fellow was off by a 100 or 150 or 500 feet.

I could fill pages with the stories he told, his remarks and opinions, and the advice he gave me. I remember an unusual number of his statements because what he said always seemed important or he would put a subject into striking and original terms. Maybe it was because he made you want to learn from him through his own very informal and Socratic approach. Grandpa was my best teacher. He remains a great influence. He taught me what no school has taught me, namely, to think on my own and to think well of my own thought.

GRENVILLE CLARK
AND SELECTIVE SERVICE

Lewis B. Hershey

Pearl Harbor found the United States unprepared for war, as has been the situation in all our wars. There was one exception to the general unpreparedness. The United States had a million men in the armed forces and a system established by law which was prepared to procure whatever additional manpower might be required. The Selective Training and Service Act of September 1940 became the means by which the Selective Service System was established and the men inducted. It was legislation secured under circumstances far from favorable. Indeed, army planners had never believed that such a law could be enacted prior to a declaration of war.

The Selective Training and Service Act was passed by Congress in the early autumn of 1940. It followed a summer-long hard-fought legislative battle. The original sponsors of the legislation were a self-styled group known as the National Emergency Committee of the Military Training Camps Association of the United States.

The dynamo of this committee was Grenville Clark. Without his tireless energy, unusual ability, influence in many areas, and, perhaps most of all, dogged perseverance, the law would not have been enacted. I was only a major at the time but General Marshall had selected me to work with Clark's group. He was tireless. And what a man with the telephone! Several times I was interrupted at breakfast by long-distance phone calls from New Hampshire.

An example from many—the secretary of war had to be replaced in order to have an incumbent favorable to the prospective law. Grenville Clark secured the assistance of Mr. Justice Frankfurter in recommending this action to the president, and President Roosevelt selected their good friend Henry L. Stimson.

Another example of the obstacles met and overcome was the negotiations required to get the bill introduced into the House and Senate. The nature of the proposed legislation was not conducive to attract legislators to be the sponsors of compulsion. Senator Burke of Nebraska, an anti–New Deal Democrat, introduced the bill in the Senate, but after he had been defeated in the primary for another term.

In the House, a minority member, Representative James Wadsworth, had been a proponent of the unsuccessful Universal Military Training Act in 1920. It was a further advantage to him that he came from a safe Republican district.

The initial draft of legislation presented by the group led by Grenville Clark provided for a wide registration with obligation for military service for the younger and other service for the older. This, like a multitude of other conflicting points, was adjusted before the bill was introduced, or on the floor, or at times in the conference committee of the House and Senate.

The result of this civilian initiative was the enactment of the first peacetime draft in American history—a result which no military or political expert would have thought possible at the time.

There was no other individual who contributed to that result as did Grenville Clark.

THE CLARK FAMILY
FINANCIAL CONFERENCES
Edward P. Stuhr

———————◆◆———————

Shortly after I joined the Fiduciary Trust Company in the early 1940s, I was assigned management responsibility for the Grenville Clark accounts, a task I accepted with trepidation. Not only were the funds involved unusually large, but G.C. was somewhat of a legend—an outstanding citizen, a lawyer of great repute, and a founder of the Trust Company. Our first meeting was an unforgettable experience. I had spent innumerable hours boning up on every conceivable financial question that might arise, only to be treated to a broad brush discussion of economics, politics, social trends, financial philosophy, and queries about my own background. Just as I slipped into a relaxed frame of mind, G.C. began to pepper me with sharply penetrating comments on the securities portfolio. It soon became clear that his association was to be a liberal education, which, over the years, I enjoyed to the fullest.

Each summer, usually in late July or early August, depending on G.C.'s vacation schedule, a meeting was arranged at the Clark home in Dublin, New Hampshire. His "vacation," in effect, constituted abandoning temporarily certain day-to-day activities so that he could concentrate more effectively on matters of greater import. I would drive down from Maine, or, if this proved inconvenient, a rendezvous on the Maine Turnpike would be planned with military precision. Other regular participants in the conference were Grenville Clark, Jr., a lawyer by training and an independent investment counsellor by profession, and his two sons-in-law, representing the interests of G.C.'s two daughters. A morning session began at about nine o'clock, with a break for lunch, followed by an afternoon session lasting until five or six o'clock in the evening. On occasion, the discussion stretched through part of a second day.

The Clark home in Dublin is most conducive to quiet contemplation. It overlooks Dublin Lake on one side and Mount Monadnock on the other. The gardens, ruled over by Mrs. Clark, seemed to thrive on loving care and the wonderful Dublin climate. We would gather in the big living room around the fireplace, where more often than not a low fire burned, even in midsummer. G.C. required a fair amount of floor space because he invariably had numerous piles of documents spread on the floor around his chair. He used a loose-leaf notebook to jot down ideas, comments, and decisions. He often wrote informal letters by hand on pages torn from the book. After a few preliminaries concerning the health and activities of family members, including mine, the financial conference would get under way. The first order of business was a wide-ranging discussion of the economic background and outlook and other factors which might affect stock prices. G.C.'s sources of information and his keen sense of analysis and interpretation resulted in an exceptionally good track record. It was an open forum and each of us was able to speak his mind and to disagree, but finally, a decision was always reached. With an almost imperceptible twinkle in his eye, G.C. would ask me to put down in writing the level of the Dow Jones Industrial Average on the date of our next meeting a year hence. This was a pleasant little game and I played it enthusiastically, always offering outrageous alibis for failure to hit the mark.

Preparation for these conferences meant considerable work. The format showing the family holdings was unique for those days. It consisted of long sheets of analysis paper listing total holdings of each security, holdings of individual family groups, cost, market value, income, and columns for estimated capital gains tax as well as net market value of each security after deducting taxes. G.C. rationalized that measuring one's wealth by total market value was a delusion because the tax lien on the profit always existed. Changes in market value were stacked against the rise or fall in the Dow Jones Industrial Average for the period, a forerunner of the performance emphasis which developed in later years.

Stocks were listed by industry groups and each industry was reviewed from the standpoint of whether the percentage of the total fund invested in it was too high or too low in relation to its prospects. Each individual company was then examined and accorded a buy, sell, or hold rating. It was a most effective and orderly procedure, and at the end of the meeting a written summary would serve as a starting point for the next meeting. The performance record over the years was outstandingly good, largely a testimonial to G.C.'s guidance and acumen. He had a capacity to recognize change and capitalize on it, and some of this quality in time rubbed off on the rest of us. He had the courage to act on his convictions, especially when things looked bad. One maxim I have never forgotten: "Buy when the blood is running in the gutter." And this he did with great success during the depression of the 1930s.

The family financial conferences are no more, and each summer I think of them and feel a sort of void. I realize now what a privilege it was to know and to work with Grenville Clark.

NO NOBEL PEACE PRIZE

WAS AWARDED IN 1967

Mary Kersey Harvey

Ever since I had met the man in 1960 at the first Dartmouth Conference at Hanover, New Hampshire, my conviction that the Nobel Peace Prize should go to Grenville Clark had grown to almost obsessional proportions. I finally decided to try in my own way to do something about it.

In London, on a literary scouting mission for McCall Publishing Company I learned from Patrick Armstrong, clerk of the Parliamentary Group for World Government, that several MPs and two British Nobel Peace Prize winners had put forth Clark and Sohn and the book *World Peace through World Law* for the award several years earlier. Had a dual award been made during the history of the Prize? I asked Patrick. He thought not. Perhaps his federalist-minded MPs would now support a single nomination, I ventured. Patrick thought they would indeed. Thus my self-assumed role as catalyst in the effort for Mr. Clark began with the notion that the dual approach had not and could not succeed due to lack of a precedent and the knowledge that British support for the solo nomination would be as strong as it had been for the dual one.

Upon my return to New York, I telephoned Randolph Compton, who had, at the urging of Mr. Clark, helped found the Fund for Peace. Randy was a long-time UWF officer, bound to both the cause and the man. I tried out the idea of a single nomination and the thinking behind it. Randy concurred enthusiastically, but cautioned that the cost of mounting such an effort on an international scale—the only scale, we both agreed, one could conceive of—would be high. He didn't see how money could be obtained and how, without it, the effort could succeed. There was a further problem. A section of the American Federalists, Randy pointed out, led by William Sheehan, a high official in the International Air Transport Association and chairman of the executive council of WAWF, had, for some time, been committed to the dual nomination. As a first step it would be necessary to encourage this group to modify its position.

Grenville Clark was, by that time, quite ill, having contracted blood poisoning on a visit to the Caribbean with his second wife, Mary. The newly acquired toxicity had triggered a latent old disease. The two were now working in tandem to defeat Clark's will to live.

In view of his condition I thought it imperative that we work for the 1967 award, nominations for which had to be in Oslo by January 31 of that year.

Since only a few months remained, Bill Sheehan and his group had to be reconciled within days. When I finally got Sheehan on the telephone I spoke frankly about the talks in London, of Compton's enthusiasm, and pressed the case for the solo nomination. Bill held to the view that Sohn's name, alongside that of Clark, was important in that Sohn was Polish-born. An "East-West ticket," he thought, would be more attractive to the Nobel Committee than a strictly American one.

Moreover, he said, any effort directed to the committee in Oslo ought to be stalled until Clark was placed in the spotlight as the principal speaker at the coming WAWF World Congress scheduled for Oslo in the summer of 1967. This visibility on the committee's home grounds, Bill contended, would serve to strengthen a renewed effort. I pointed out sorrowfully that it seemed all too possible that Mr. Clark would not be able to make it to Oslo in the summer of 1967. Our discussion ended amiably but inconclusively.

For several years Norman Cousins and I had talked about working for the Prize for Mr. Clark. We'd done nothing. It was now time to ask Norman to unleash his extraordinary resources and resourcefulness in the cause. It took me about two minutes to outline the case and the timing. Characteristically Norman replied with a question: "What do you want me to do?" After I had suggested he take the leadership in a worldwide effort to round up endorsements and nominations for Grenny, he smiled and said, "Of course. Just tell me what to do. Let's get started."

Compton's warning about money still rang in my head. Back at the office I made a few calls to people who might have helped solve the problem. But my heart wasn't in it. The thing to do was to plunge ahead, worry about money at another time. Later in the day a call from Ruth Wight, Clark's personal secretary, had the needed galvanizing effect. Mr. Clark, Ruth said, was going downhill. From that moment on I proceeded on my own time and resources, counting, of course, on the absolute certainty that Norman would too.

But first it would be necessary to clear it out with the main character, struggling to stay mentally alive in a Boston hospital. Several days passed during which I phrased and rephrased all the arguments in favor of the solo nomination, for Clark had been strongly committed to the dual approach. Finally I phoned Ruth Wight and asked her to take a reading, during his stronger moments, on Mr. Clark's views on the proposed new tack. They finally called back.

Grenny came on the phone. Like all his calls, it was a long one. He covered the progression of events since his decision to leave Washington, D.C., in the midst of World War II to work on a plan for United Nations Charter revision, the collaboration with Louis Sohn, then a young émigré law professor, and the previous attempts made on his and Sohn's behalf for the Peace Prize. The first had been put forth in 1959 by Henry J. Friendly and a group of his colleagues. Clark outlined this group's reasons for the dual nomination and strongly impressed on me his concurrence with their views.

I came on weakly with the thought that the dual approach, having been tried twice and having failed, might now well be abandoned. I wondered what would be lost by attempting a single nomination. It was almost inhumane to press an ill man on matters of such exquisite nuance. But he had telephoned me and I had had to respond. One thing became clear. Mr. Clark was grasping at straws, in despair of recovering. Several steps could be taken almost at once to give him hope. I went ahead and took them.

The first was to prepare the drafts of letters to leading jurists, legislators, and public officials in the United States and abroad which Norman Cousins would send out. These were rushed in batches by messenger to the *Saturday Review*. There they were typed, signed, and in the mails within days to points around the country and overseas. They produced the first wave of what eventually became an impressive sea of nominations and endorsements of Grenville Clark for the 1967 Nobel Peace Prize.

"They're sending me home to die," Grenny had said to Ruth upon his discharge from the Boston hospital. Her sobs came over the telephone as she recounted the experience. A next step was taken. I called Norman and told him about this new turn. We both said nothing. Then Norman: "What do you think we ought to do now?" I suggested that Norman write an appreciation of Grenville Clark and publish it in the *Saturday Review* on the occasion of Clark's eighty-fourth birthday. Norman had been thinking of doing something along these lines. The birthday idea crystallized it. Within a few days "Aristocrat of Peace" was rushed to the typographers, galleys pulled, a set airmailed in advance of publication to Mr. Clark in Dublin. Ruth Wight reported that he read them with tears streaming down his cheeks.

Another step: I arranged by means of some intricate inter-office gambits to have an in-depth interview on world order with Mr. Clark by the historian Richard Heffner published in *McCall's*. It had lain sidetracked for months.

All of this had the effect of at least temporarily turning the tide. Mr. Clark rallied. He wrote us, in a short note, "I am beginning to see the light at the end of the tunnel."

Upon returning from a business trip to Europe in early November Bill Sheehan learned of the new Nobel Prize effort. I hastened to fill him in on what Norman and I had been doing. We had rushed ahead in his absence due, in large part, I said, to the gravity of Mr. Clark's illness and to the closeness of the deadline for Nobel Peace Prize nominations (January 31, 1967).

Bill was understandably somewhat shaken by this turn of events and wrote forthwith to Clark to ascertain his views on the switch in strategy.

Four days later, in a burst of renewed energy, Clark replied to Sheehan, sending copies to Norman and me. The letter was a long and careful recapitulation of what Clark had outlined to me telephonically about a month earlier.

Three days after the arrival of Clark's November fourteenth letter, another came, striking in its attention to detail and its resolute adherence to the cause of Federalism.

Under the impact of the two documents, Bill, Norman, and I held a meeting and agreed to have the temerity to disagree with Grenville Clark. Our decision was to continue the effort for the solo nomination and we told him so. Sheehan was appointed to express our views to Clark.

His trusted legal aid, Robert Reno, was brought on to the team. Marion McVitty, UWF's UN observer, and Clark Eichelberger, founder of the United Nations Association, took responsibility for talking to certain United Nations leaders. Lance Mallalieu joined with Patrick Armstrong in working for support from Canadian and British MPs. I, in addition to other tasks, helped back up the efforts of the president of Pro Deo University in Rome, who held interviews with certain cardinals. Harry Hollins, president of the World Law Fund, began canvassing educators and parliamentarians in many countries, including India, from which he had recently returned.

As Sheehan pointed out in a hastily scrawled letter to Mallalieu, "Time is of the essence." All of us had full-time jobs. We kept meetings to a minimum, burned up the cable and long distance wires, ran typists and messengers ragged.

By the beginning of the new year, 1967, a torrent of nominating letters and endorsements from public figures had rained on Oslo. But within twelve days Mr. Clark was no longer ours. He died January 13, 1967. No Nobel Peace Prize was awarded in 1967.

PART VII

---◆◆---

World Peace

GRENVILLE CLARK

AND THE WORLD LAW FUND

Harry B. Hollins

During the many occasions when Betsy and I met with Mr. Clark in Dublin, New Hampshire, in the ten years from 1957 to 1967, I always feared that we would not get through the rather lengthy agenda. The subjects ran from G.C.'s world plans in 1957 for the translation and distribution of *World Peace through World Law* to the initiation of the World Law Fund's World Order Models Project * in 1966. The discussion would focus, at the start, on whatever most concerned G.C. at the moment, whether it related to the agenda or not. It might be of a draft of a lengthy letter to President John F. Kennedy about the ever-worsening situation in Vietnam and G.C.'s concern that the vastly superior wealth and technology of the United States would be used "to crush" North Vietnam, or perhaps detailed plans for Governor Stevenson to present copies of *World Peace through World Law* to Khrushchev and to a few other USSR leaders. (At a meeting shortly after his return in 1958, Stevenson told us with some amusement that in typical G.C. fashion copies of *World Peace through World*

* The first phase of this project was completed in 1972 as eight regional teams of scholars and public figures turned in their manuscripts and essays. The assignment of the teams was to construct models of alternate world systems to achieve four interrelated values: warlessness, world economic welfare, world social justice, and ecological stability.

Law had been sent to Moscow by every available means. The result was that Stevenson had a dozen or more copies to present to various officials.) During these relaxed discussions on what seemed to me peripheral subjects, it would inevitably turn out that many of the agenda problems had been thoroughly aired so that the final half hour was left to summarize the conclusions which we found had, by some mysterious process, been reached. We always concluded with the agenda covered and an immediate plan of action laid out.

By 1960 we had already met a number of times with G.C., all memorable and all followed by assignments, but in the fall of 1960 Betsy and I were asked by G.C. to spend three days in Dublin to discuss "a matter of some importance." Our welcome by Mr. and Mrs. Clark at the front door of Outlet Farm was as warm as always. Betsy had a special relationship with both Mr. and Mrs. Clark dating back to her childhood. I was a relative newcomer to this triangle, although I had known G.C. slightly when I was an undergraduate at Harvard in the early 1930s. On this occasion in 1960, the outward appearances were the same. Mount Monadnock was still looking down on the old red brick farmhouse and Mrs. Clark's garden; the fire was carefully laid in the living room, and Mrs. Clark and Betsy had their walk through the garden. But there was a difference—a difference which became apparent as we settled around the fire for the first of three sessions. Instead of following the usual procedure, G.C. went right to the point of our three-day visit. He told us that he had contracted a form of cancer and that while he might live for a number of years, he had insisted that his doctors give him a reasonable estimate. As he put it, he had a 50-50 chance of living better than a year. This estimate was to change G.C.'s plans and was also to change radically my own life.

My first reaction to the brief, factual description of his new problem was to recall the many occasions when G.C. used the relationship of a doctor and his patient to illustrate the diagnosis, prognosis, and prescriptive process for dealing with serious problems whether they be medical, economic, social, or political. He used it repeatedly, not only to differentiate between symptoms and root causes, but also to reaffirm his faith in the courage and sound judgment of most people, *provided* they understand the true nature of their difficulty. In a very real sense, this faith in the sound judgment of people gave impetus to his boldness both of thought and action on war and peace issues, on civil rights, and on many other matters. To make a right judgment in the fall of 1960 on his future plans, he required the best professional judgment on the diagnosis and prognosis of his new affliction. It was far from hopeful.

The discussions over the next three days centered on how G.C.'s illness affected his views on what should be done. G.C.'s plan to this point had been to complete by July 1961 a special project he had started with Earl D. Osborn in 1958 through the Institute for International Order to aid the translation and distribution of *World Peace through World Law,* and then to start a more extensive educational program commencing July 1, 1961. It was as part of this first project that Betsy and I, in nonprofessional capacities, had traveled to England and Denmark in 1958 to facilitate distribution of *World Peace through World Law* throughout the British Commonwealth and Europe. Then, in early 1960, we had taken an extended trip to Egypt, India, Burma, Southeast Asia, and Japan for the same purpose.

The more extensive project, due to commence in July 1961, was outlined in a letter written by G.C. in June 1960 to Earl Osborn. It projected a six-year educational program with an annual budget of $60,000 to be directed by G.C. from Dublin and buttressed by the efforts of numerous volunteers. G.C.'s contraction of cancer made for a different set of conditions which changed his plans in one important respect—he could no longer count on directing the educational effort himself.

Everyone I know who worked with G.C. for any extended period had to acknowledge his profound influence. This resulted in part because his actions coincided to a most unusual degree with his professed views (and G.C.'s views were radical in the sense that he was interested in root causes rather than symptoms) and in part because he was a great teacher who used anecdotes and analogies to drive home his points. I do not recall how many stories came up at this meeting—Baruch seeking his advice in the 1930s on how to identify himself in the hearings before the Senate committee and G.C.'s advice to tell the committee the truth, namely, that he was purely and simply a speculator in the

stock market; G.C.'s visits in two consecutive summers, while he
was at Harvard, to a small town in Montana which made the
transition from a community governed by six-shooters to a law-
abiding society under a sheriff; G.C. and a judge getting stuck in
a ditch while driving into Boston, and finally giving up until a
farmer who understood the principle of leverage arrived on the
scene and with *specific, practical suggestions* to revitalize their own
flagging efforts, got the stuck vehicle rolling; and many others
including, perhaps for sheer amusement, his story of getting
locked out of his house in New York in his nightshirt on a summer
evening with no one in the house.

But the meetings over these three days focused on how to set
up an ongoing educational project that would help people all
over the world understand that world anarchy was incompatible
with peace and economic welfare. Until this was clearly understood he knew that the best brains would be wasted in attempting
to cope with the symptoms. G.C. had done historical research on
the twenty years prior to the Constitutional Convention in 1787
and had discovered throughout this period a continuing discussion
about theories of government that were absorbed to a marked
degree not only by the leading public figures of the time but, most
important, also by the people. To duplicate this kind of discussion
and understanding—but on a world scale—was to be the assignment which G.C. scheduled to begin some eight months from our
meeting, and he was asking me to help. I accepted the challenge.

Several years later, seeking support for the program that had
evolved out of these meetings in the fall of 1960, known over
many years as the World Law Fund, I had a meeting with the
executive vice president of one of the larger foundations. This
man concluded that such a project should not be undertaken
unless one had $5 million assured funds. G.C.'s nature worked dif-
ferently. From somewhere deep within him he was compelled to
act as a private citizen when the occasion called for action—no
matter what the odds. One of his law associates told me that over
the years he had seen G.C. take on various public issues which no
one else would touch and that somehow he had pulled them off.
He went on to say, however, that on the issue of peace G.C., in
his opinion, had set his big jaw on to a problem which even he
could not chew.

Thirteen years have passed since these meetings. The project which G.C. outlined and which we discussed for three days in the fall of 1960 commenced operations the following July. This project has expanded to an over-three-million-dollar one to date. Annual grants of $75,000 came from a foundation established in 1965 by G.C. and his wife, Fanny Dwight Clark, the terms of which were such that the principal and interest were to be expended over ten years with 60 per cent of the funds going to the World Law Fund and 40 per cent to the Legal Defense and Educational Fund of the NAACP. Thus did G.C. provide for two main public issues to which he devoted his life after 1945.

For myself, I miss the meetings with him more than I can say.

TRIBUTE TO GRENVILLE CLARK

C. Maxwell Stanley

Grenville Clark lives in my memory as an indelible inspiration: a thinker who envisioned world peace under world law; a stalwart man who dedicated his great energy to this end. His calm but passionate commitment to the goal he shared with World Federalists encourages us to forge ahead, even when the obstacles seem mountainous and progress minuscule. Although Grenville's lasting outreach was chronicled in the monumental *World Peace through World Law*, written with Dr. Louis Sohn, I particularly treasure my personal contacts with him.

In the mid-1950s he made one of his rare appearances before the United World Federalists Executive Council in New York. There, with followers at his feet, this great prophet spoke with unusual frankness of the difficulties of reversing historic patterns, specifically those of national sovereignty and reliance on military force as ultimate tools of diplomacy. How true his prediction that the world must stand on the brink of disaster before nations would surrender (or delegate) an iota of their freedom of action. We can only hope that the experiences of Cuba, Vietnam, and the Middle East will cause leaders to stare into that brink and reassess.

My fondest recollections of Grenville Clark center around his week-long participation in June 1965 in the Conference on the United Nations of 1975 and the World Congress of World Federalists which followed it in San Francisco. The congress, jointly sponsored by United World Federalists and World Association of World Federalists, convened on the twentieth anniversary of the United Nations. As president of UWF and chairman of the WAWF council, I was deeply involved in conference planning. We needed several articulate Federalists in San Francisco to stimulate the congress program and to offset an anticipated lackluster performance at the symbolic session of the U.N. General Assembly scheduled there that same week. To provide a podium for a strengthened United Nations, the Stanley Foundation sponsored a gathering of world leaders in what became the first of a series of Conferences on the United Nations of the next decade. In addition to Grenville Clark, the group included two past presidents of the General Assembly, General Carlos P. Romulo (Philippines) and Sir Zafrullah Khan (Pakistan); plus Adebo (Nigeria); Buron (France); Fairweather (Canada); Houman (Iran); Lannung (Denmark); Peal (Liberia); Quintanilla (Mexico); Rossides (Cyprus); van der Stoel (Netherlands); and Yukawa (Japan); with my son David as *rapporteur*. The conferees, many accompanied by their wives, met for five days at Vallombrosa, a quiet wooded retreat some twenty-five miles from San Francisco. We discussed the United Nations day and night, seeking ways to make it more effective as a tool to achieve world peace through world law.

As conference chairman, I marveled not only at the power of Grenville's commitment but also at the openness of his mind. Much credit goes to him for the resulting conference statement calling upon nations of the world to get on with the task of strengthening the United Nations. One paragraph of that document came directly from Clark: "Like an individual who delays needed surgery until his condition becomes desperate, the world has delayed the major operation which is essential to save the United Nations. If the surgery waits too long, the patient may die."

Equally impressive was his willingness to embrace an idea that he had heretofore rejected, namely the incorporation of economic and social functions in his plan for lasting world order. By 1965 Grenville was well known, and sometimes criticized, for advocating a pure legalistic approach to world federal government with powers strictly limited to those essential to international peace and security. At Vallombrosa the conferees thoroughly examined the importance of economic and social development in a strengthened United Nations. Face to face with dedicated Federalists from developing nations, Grenville tested their contention that a world development program was needed as much as universal disarmament, a strengthened peace force, a revised Security Council, an improved General Assembly, an altered voting system, and a strong International Court of Justice. After spirited debates, he joined them in the concluding conference statement in advocating world development as all essential to peace. That his conversion was not a passing fancy became evident at the Second Dublic Conference that October. There he again urged that economic and social development be a part of a broader approach to world peace through world law

A few days after the Stanley Foundation Conference, while speaking to the WAWF Congress in San Francisco, Grenville summoned assembled Federalists to examine anew how they expected to gain peace and law in the world. He startled the more conservative Federalists by suggesting, among other things, that perhaps the time had come for Federalists to march in the streets.

Such open-minded energy in a man of eighty-two reveals another side of his greatness. Many are indebted to Grenville Clark for his tenacious but judicious crusade for world peace through world law. The greatest tribute we can pay to Grenville Clark is to emulate his example to the best of our abilities.

GRENVILLE CLARK,
THE GREAT INTERNATIONALIST

Simeon O. Adebo

Like many others interested in the cause of an ordered world, I knew Grenville Clark by reputation long before I came to know him in person. The monumental work that he produced with Louis B. Sohn, *World Peace through World Law,* will remain a permanent memorial to his dedication to that cause.

It was in San Francisco in June 1965 that I first made his personal acquaintance. The World Federalists were holding their congress there and had invited me, among others, to attend and make statements on different aspects of our disordered world and what might be done about them. Grenville Clark was, naturally, present, for wherever two or three people were gathered to hold serious discussions on this subject, he was almost always sure to be with them. Listening to my contribution, he apparently felt that I was a young man that would be worth taking under his wing and encouraged in this field. So, following the session at which I made my presentation, he took me aside and introduced himself —as if he needed introduction to anyone in that assemblage of admirers of his leadership. He told me he had been impressed by my statement and what he called my obvious sincerity. He would like a chance to pursue the subject further with me, especially the question of how to reform the United Nations to increase its capacity to help bring about a world ruled by law and justice. Could I spent a weekend with him at his home in Dublin, New Hampshire? I said I would be delighted to do so. He said that it would give him added pleasure if I brought along my wife and our children as well.

The weekend was one of the most rewarding of my life. Not only did it enable my family and me to share the peace and tranquillity and the material comforts of Mr. Clark's lovely home, but also included an early morning swim in the lake which was a daily routine exercise with him. I had several hours of private discussion with him, during which he told me how he came to make the cause of a reformed United Nations his most urgent priority and how he thought it might be pursued. He was resolved to continue helping it onward, physically and financially, to the end of his days and he liked to think that people like me, and others in the United States and elsewhere, would continue the struggle, whatever the odds, after he was gone. He was visibly moved with joy when I told him that he had more followers everywhere than he thought and that I was sure we would do our best.

There was one point on which I had to confess that I differed from him. Grenville Clark was convinced, right to the end I think, that the best way to update the United Nations Charter was to convene a world conference (such as was envisaged in the charter itself) to go over all the existing provisions. This view, of course, has many supporters and was one that I shared and joined in pressing upon the U.N. General Assembly during my first two years as permanent representative of my country to the world organization. But experience in the Assembly had persuaded me that such a conference would be long and tedious, that it was unlikely to achieve our aims, and that it might result in some of the good provisions in the current charter being weakened as a price for concessions in other directions. It would, I thought (and still think), be better to concentrate on the chapters that need the most urgent attention, or the lacunae that need to be urgently remedied, and press for action on that, as the Afro-Asian members of the General Assembly, with support of our Latin American colleagues, did successfully in 1964–1965 to secure the enlargement of the Security Council, the Trusteeship Council, and the Economic and Social Council.

Regrettably, I was never able to make another visit to Grenville Clark's New Hampshire home. But that one visit was enough to leave indelible in my memory the impression of a tireless believer and worker for world peace whose sterling contributions to the cause remain a continuing source of inspiration to fellow believers in the cause.

GRENVILLE CLARK

Sir Alexander J. Haddow

My personal acquaintance with Grenville Clark was a happy outcome of a letter which I had written to the London *Times* on
March 30, 1954, dealing with the hydrogen weapon, scientific
responsibility, and a proposal for the establishment of a scientific
concilium within the United Nations. Mr. Clark came to see me
in London not long afterwards, and the contact thus formed grew
rapidly into a close friendship which endured to the day of his
death. Our later meetings were frequent, whether in Boston,
Dublin, New Hampshire, or in London. He was more than sympathetic towards my own interests in the then Parliamentary Association for World Government, in the Parliamentary Group for
World Government, and in the Conferences on Science and
World Affairs (COSWA), while in turn I myself learned much
from him on charter revision and charter reform. It was through
these discussions that I gained the further pleasure of acquaintance with Louis B. Sohn and hence of valuing their massive joint
contribution.

Our paths were thrown even closer together in the years following 1962. In the summer of that year our mutual friend, Paul
Dudley White, and I while attending the International Cancer
Congress then being held in Moscow, received invitations on behalf of the Chinese Academy of Medical Sciences to travel together to China in the spring of the following year. On return to

London my own invitation was confirmed, but unhappily Dr. White was informed by the Chinese authorities that his own visit would not after all be possible because of the then unsatisfactory state of Sino-American relations. In the circumstances, Dr. White and I decided to travel together or not at all; but the position was ironically unhappy, since no greater friend of the Chinese people can be imagined than Paul Dudley White. Characteristically Grenville Clark at this point showed the deepest interest and concern, and over the next two or three years moved every endeavour to bridge the gulf. Throughout the whole of this time the U.S. governmental authorities could not have been more helpful. Although the venture failed in its primary purpose, I still like to think that these efforts were not perhaps entirely lost upon the Chinese and may perhaps have made a modest if silent contribution towards the general improvement of trust which appears to be developing today. At any rate, this experience provided the writer with great insight, if such were needed, into Grenville Clark's humanity, idealism, and tenacity.

Added to these qualities were his kindliness, generosity, warmth, and charm, and a shining valiance expressed not only in the courage with which he defended freedom, liberty, and individuality, but also in the resolution and indeed cheerfulness with which he confronted the years of his troublesome and tiresome illness. His life was cast against a backcloth of a marvellous epoch in American history. No man could have done more for his country, and no man could have done more for the greatest cause of the twentieth century, which is the abolition of war. For these and for many other things we shall hold him in ever-grateful and ever-affectionate remembrance.

GRENVILLE CLARK AS I MET HIM

Einar Rørstad

———————◆———————

Who is Grenville Clark? This was the question I asked myself on board the *Bergensfjord* in June 1959 while crossing the Atlantic Ocean on my way to meet Grenville Clark, having accepted an invitation from him to come over to discuss questions in connection with his book *World Peace through World Law* and various translations into other languages.

Of course I knew from different Americans I had met that he was a highly respected man in the United States. I also felt that I knew him as an outstanding and dynamic personality through our correspondence. But beyond that I did not know very much.

However, during the next weeks I learned quite a lot from numerous personal talks in Dublin, New Hampshire—in his wonderful home, the house where a "monumental work" was born, overlooking Dublin Lake and Mount Monadnock. Then I realized how well this man deserved the description: America's Statesman Incognito.

After all our talks, in his study, in the garden, or driving around Mount Monadnock, I became convinced that I would always work for this man, even when he was gone. How can warm friendship, mutual respect, and a "father-to-son feeling" suddenly develop and stay on forever between a famous man of eighty and an unknown youngster from Norway? I don't know the answer: I only know it happened!

There occurred five years later an example of how impulsive

and dynamic he was and how expediently he acted when he had made up his mind.

Friday, November 13, 1964, in the late afternoon or early evening my telephone rang at Haslum outside Oslo. It was an urgent call from Dublin, New Hampshire, U.S.A. Grenville Clark's voice came through, intense, excited, encouraging. How are you, Einar? Fine, I said. Now listen, he went on. I am going over to Europe in a week's time, to spend one week in London and one week in Moscow, and here is my question: Where would you like to spend a week with me? I winked to my wife, Lillemor, and said, as if it all was a big joke, of course, I prefer Moscow! That's what I hoped you would say, Grenville Clark said laughingly. But what about your wife, will she come along too? I'd like to meet her, as I have never seen her. I repeated the question and said: it seems as if Lillemor is fainting. His happy, gay, hearty, and catching laughter filled the receiver. Wonderful, he said, I'll be seeing you in the Hotel National, Moscow, December first. That's a date. But, there is one condition, he added—I'll not permit you to spend one penny of your own money.

My wife and I were regularly knocked out. When I finally could speak again I said to Lillemor: Now you understand better all the things I have told you about Grenville Clark.

This was Friday, the thirteenth. And still there are people who claim that Friday the thirteenth brings bad luck.

Moscow, December 1964, with Grenville Clark, a week never to be forgotten. Our personal talks, our whole group having vodka and caviar together overlooking the Manege Square and the floodlit Kremlin, and with Grenville Clark as the natural group leader. His talks with outstanding Russian scientists, the meeting in the Institute of State and Law when he discussed *World Peace through World Law* with a big group of Russian lawyers, and when you really had the feeling that he was only fifty-five or sixty years again, sparkling, brilliant, to the point, witty if necessary— the eminent, piercing advocate of world law. Everyone present, regardless of nationality, had reason to be impressed.

Lillemor and I have three children, two daughters of twelve and seven who never met Grenville Clark, but always talked about him as if he was their best friend in the world, and who pointed at his photo on the wall and said to their playfriends: That is Grenville Clark!

We also have a little boy, just over a year old. He cannot speak yet, but he will. He has a letter from Grenville Clark which he will be able to read one day. Then he will point out a certain photograph on the wall and say to his friends: That is Grenville Clark!

Grenville Clark! And the way we feel about him in Norway!

In my opinion it is a great shame that he never got the Nobel Peace Prize because the awarding committee will never find a more worthy candidate.

"America's Statesman Incognito," that is true. But Grenville Clark has also written his name into the history of the world with his monumental work for world peace, in the chapter called "A World Federation."

He has said himself that as a young man he was greatly influenced by Charles W. Eliot, the president of Harvard for forty years, from 1869–1909, a man he has characterized in the following words: "Great vigor of mind and great reliability of character, very high principles, very insistent on speaking the truth under all the circumstances no matter how hard it was, great shrewdness in selecting men, teachers, a man of immense range of ability."

As a personal friend and collaborator of Grenville Clark, I feel entitled to use the very same words about Clark himself. He was a true statesman of the world—probably the greatest one in modern times.

GRENVILLE CLARK

Stanley K. Platt

My many memories of Grenville Clark involved an idea whose time has come, namely, that the world *can* be governed.

I recall an evening in Minneapolis in 1952, when John Cowles, Sr., principal owner and editor of the Minneapolis *Star* and *Tribune*, told Norman Cousins: "I regard Grenville Clark as one of, if not the greatest living American—but most people do not even recognize his name."

There was in 1959 a visit that my wife, Martha, and I had in the simple guest cottage back of his home outside of Dublin, New Hampshire: We were among the first allowed to see him after a serious illness. Mrs. Clark greeted us and let us know that the visit must be brief. She called and Grenville Clark descended a narrow staircase, his great craggy head bent forward, a massive and impressive figure—like Moses on the mountaintop pointing the way to the promised land.

He greeted us warmly in his encompassing, friendly manner. As we sat in his book-lined room, he told us of his conclusion that leadership for U.N. Charter transformation would be most effective if it comes from the smaller nations—because the United States would oppose it if the USSR proposed it and the USSR would oppose it if the leadership is centered in the United States. As we left and looked out over the beautiful scene before us, I was reminded of how very appropriate it was that Grenville Clark's telephone number was Dublin 1.

I also remember a dinner before the Second Dublin Conference began in October 1965. Pope John had issued his *Pacem in Terris* Encyclical and Pope Paul was about to arrive in New York to address the United Nations. My wife, Martha, seated next to Grenville Clark, remarked that she suspected that he had influenced Pope John's thinking as expressed in *Pacem in Terris*. Mr. Clark responded with a twinkle: "He was a Pope and I am a Unitarian, but we were as thick as thieves."

Among the few who attended both of the Dublin Conferences (1945 and 1965) was Kingman Brewster, Jr., president of Yale University. He presided with great skill and patience over the four days of deliberations which led to the Second Dublin Declaration, proclaiming the essentials of an effective world organization to prevent war. However, it was Mr. Clark who served as host, who developed the concept, detailed the plans, issued the invitations, set the tone, and defined the goals. When the weather turned bitter cold, he ordered new blankets from a New Hampshire blanket factory and brought in emergency spare heaters for the conference hall, which was the barn-studio of the deceased artist Alexander James.

We had arrived early and I was visiting the studio with G.C. He was planning assignments and evidently was wondering about the acoustics. He asked me to go to the lectern and to say a few words. Embarrassed but challenged, I did so. He said nothing but I assume that he concluded that the acoustics were satisfactory. Guided by G.C.'s wisdom and diplomacy, the conference resolved many a controversy and moved toward the later adoption of the Second Dublic Declaration—still another step toward a humane and peaceful world, a personal tribute to the vision and leadership of Grenville Clark.

RECOLLECTIONS OF GRENVILLE CLARK

The Rev. Gerard G. Grant, S.J.

━━━━━━◆━━━━━━

I first met Grenville Clark in the Commodore Hotel in New York at a Pacem in Terris Conference. It was the end of a session as I was filing out. And here was this gentleman about whom I had read so much and whose name was already a household term to me. He stopped me, looking up from his chair, and took my hand. Yes, he knew all about me; no, he wasn't busy and would I sit with him for a few minutes? I did and while I cannot now recall the trivia we dealt with on that occasion I was left with a lasting impression of a warm and witty person whose wisdom gathered through the years permitted him to find a bit of humor in even the most serious occasion.

He was kind enough to invite me with a number of others to the Second Dublin Conference in 1965. Here he was the generous host but a bit too preoccupied with what was for him an opportunity to recapture the initiative of twenty years before. He had the text of the Declaration all prepared and we delegates found that our sole task was to discuss and then decide but certainly not to change. It must have been a minor shock to him to find that his friends saw the world somewhat differently from the way in which they had viewed it in 1945.

The press conference called for Thursday morning to witness the signing of the Declaration had to be cancelled when it became clear that far too many participants had reservations that would prevent them from affixing their signature to the document in its original form. And yet Clark, disappointed as he must have been, was able to comprehend their viewpoints and to accommodate himself to the changes they suggested. He was large enough to embrace another man's opinion. I became part of the small drafting committee that worked through the autumn to polish the Declaration into its final form.

My last meeting with him came a few months later at the final session of the Dublin Conference held at the New York Bar Association. He was much feebler then but wit danced in his eye and he still had a gracious moment for someone he had known only briefly in his varied career.

I have carried away from those meetings a sense of deep gratification that I had known such a man even slightly. He was a large person in the ambit of his views and the breadth of his knowledge. If he wasn't necessarily a man for all seasons, he certainly was one for his country and for the world. Certainly his studies on the subject of organizing the peace must be regarded as foundation stones of the much greater work that will come in the future. But above all, because in the last analysis a man is great for what he is more than for what he does, Clark must be counted among those men of stature that underpin a country and who, while they have never held public office, have contributed more than most elected leaders to the welfare of their fellow man.

It is my faith that we will be judged in eternity more for the amount of love we have given to our fellow humans than for anything else, and in his gentle way Clark welcomed into his circle of friends not only great achievers but also rather small persons like myself. For this I shall always be grateful to him and for this I toast his memory.

GRENVILLE CLARK

Muhammad Zafrullah Khan

———————————— ◆ ————————————

I had known Mr. Grenville Clark through his valuable contributions to the promotion of world peace and had become familiar with his ideas on the subject which were spelled out by him jointly with Professor Sohn in their well-known book *World Peace through World Law*. That book approached the problems of world peace in a concrete fashion, indicating how the Charter of the United Nations could be amended, article by article, to enable the United Nations to maintain peace and promote justice more effectively in the world.

I had the great honor and pleasure of meeting Mr. Clark at the First Stanley Foundation Conference at Vallombrosa, near San Francisco, in 1965, where the discussions centered around, as they do during these conferences, the future course of the United Nations. Mr. Clark impressed all of us by his dedication to the idea of a world community based on equality of all peoples and nations and by his devotion to the concept of world peace based on law. It was easy for us to agree with him that without acceptance of the rule of law we cannot have effective peace.

The work commenced at Vallombrosa has continued over the years. The fifth conference in the series met at Fredensborg, Denmark, in the summer of 1970. The report of that meeting clearly reflected the spirit with which Mr. Clark had imbued us five years earlier. He would have liked in particular the emphasis in our statement on "the need to halt the arms race in both nuclear and conventional weapons," on involving the United Nations "to the maximum feasible extent in arms control and disarmament," and on developing the role of the United Nations "in supervising agreements in this field."

I know also that Mr. Clark was much interested in the work of the International Court of Justice. He would have been disappointed in the continued reluctance of states to submit disputes to the court. He understood well that without a wider acceptance of international adjudication as the normal way of settling legal aspects of disputes between states, the rule of law cannot be established in the world community. It may be hoped, however, that a change in international climate will occur which will make his dreams come true.

THE PRINCETON CONFERENCE OF 1946

I. A. Richards

Mr. Clark invited me to attend his Princeton Conference in January 1946 to consider what the bomb might imply. I was unforgettably impressed when I arrived by the ease and *sweetness* with which he was greeting and making at home the miscellaneous persons joining the assembly. He had hidden arts—unimaginable to me—of bringing people swiftly into contact even with very otherwise-minded folk. And it all seemed, as I watched it, as simple as breathing.

The conference went its way. Mr. Clark as chairman was somehow making every contribution seem really to contribute—when a little folded *note* reached him. After half a minute, he rose and told the conference that Albert Einstein would like to join in our deliberations. After that, we sat hushed. Entered unobtrusively a surprisingly small personage, arrestingly dressed in gray flannel trousers (of varying hue) topped by a black knitted spencer and supported upon natty black suede shoes. Above all that, was a tangled mop of Skye-terrier-style locks (hiding the eyes), strangely reproducing the brown-blue-yellow-gray shades of the voluminous "flannel bags."

This apparition had us a little daunted. Not at all so Mr. Clark. Swiftly and skillfully, Einstein was seated to listen to our deliberations and be the cynosure, the dog's tail, the center of attraction for all our eyes. I wish I could recall who, so stimulated, said what. But whatever was said, the party-colored Skye-terrier locks shook and swung and nodded in approbation. Suddenly, that compelling figure rose. It had been inconspicuously writing a note for Mr. Clark. When he had left, Mr. Clark unfolded the note and read it to us. It said: "I will be happy to vote for any conclusion at which your conference arrives."

Mr. Clark's inflections and his gentle humorous smile as he conveyed the message to us are for me more than a memento. They are a monument to his sympathetic, patient, statesmanlike comprehension of the problems of Meetings and Men.

AN INCIDENT IN ENGLAND

Patrick Armstrong

———————◆—◆———————

It was 1965. I remember Grenville phoning me from the Berkeley Hotel, where he always stayed when in London. He had just returned from a visit to Moscow. He had been encouraged by the decision of the new Labour government in Britain to create for the first time in the history of the country a minister for disarmament. The appointment had been long delayed and was awaited with much interest. The announcement that Lord Chalfont, until then known as Alan Gwynne Jones, defense correspondent of the *Times* and not a Labour party member, was to be this minister came a few days before Grenville's arrival in London.

Grenville asked me to arrange an interview, which duly took place in the foreign office. On arrival there we were supplied with a guide to show us to the minister's room. He set out down the corridor with us following. After walking for some time it became clear that the guide neither knew where we were going nor who we were looking for. He asked us to repeat the name of the minister and found considerable difficulty in enunciating the word "disarmament," which he seemed to be hearing for the first time. Was this, we wondered, symbolic of the foreign office policy on the subject? As we continued on, our guide inquired of other porters who passed us, the second one of whom believed that our destination could be found in the former India Office annex. This proved correct and we were finally ushered into the minister's presence, being probably among the first visitors he had received.

Grenville took no time at all in presenting a most powerful case for an initiative by the new minister along the lines advocated in his various proposals in *World Peace through World Law*. The minister made some rather skeptical noises, indicating that he was most unlikely to follow any of this advice. To which Grenville then said: "My dear young man, you are defeated before you have even started." The minister was rather startled, smiled nervously, and shortly afterward the interview ended. However, the time had not been wasted entirely. We heard later that Lord Chalfont had phoned the prime minister and said: "There is a most extraordinarily outspoken American who has been in my office. I think he ought to see *you*." And so he did, no doubt telling the prime minister something as prophetic as he had already told Lord Chalfont.

THE GOVERNED TEMPER

Stringfellow Barr

———◆———

When World War II ended, Grenville Clark convoked the so-called Dublin Conference of October 1945. Two loose groups were represented, later to become the United World Federalists and Federal Union, Inc. The latter group had been organized by Clarence K. Streit, author of *Union Now*, whom I had known at Oxford around 1920 when both of us were American Rhodes Scholars. Federal Union, Inc., was urging that the Western democracies federate, as the thirteen American colonies had done, and then hope that other countries would organize free government and apply for admission to the new Union. As time passed, more and more members of Federal Union, Inc., felt that Streit was too doctrinaire and too fond of "free enterprise," thus making it impossible for socialist countries to join. For Streit, no Federal Union could endure if some members practiced free government and others remained under dictatorships. Federalists who considered Streit's party line doctrinaire, self-righteous, and, in the case of some Federalists, reactionary, tended to drop out of Federal Union and join United World Federalists.

When the Dublin Conference assembled, I was shocked by the speed with which anti-Streit forces took over; and, rightly or wrongly, I thought our host, who was chairing, was helping to get action without hearing Federal Union's side of the argument. I therefore protested and, I am afraid, made some pretty biting remarks. Mr. Clark flushed and prepared for battle. Then he caught himself and made such a handsome apology that I felt thoroughly unjustified in my attack—and thoroughly won over to him as a person.

A few years afterward, when I was president of the Foundation for World Government, we were able to make a modest grant of $5,000 to help Grenny—as he had become to me—and Louis B. Sohn with *World Peace through World Law*, a book I greatly admired. After 1957, when I was living in Princeton, Grenny, with or without Mrs. Clark, sometimes showed up and asked my wife and me to luncheon to keep me posted on his efforts. But I think I would never have come to recognize the quality of this man had it not been for two things: the quick heat of his flare-up at the Dublin Conference and the large generosity of his apology. As it was, I vainly added my plea to the pleas of stronger voices to secure for him the Nobel Peace Prize. The man had greatness in him and the kind of public spirit that the founding fathers of this Republic showed. God rest his soul.

GRENVILLE CLARK

Carlos P. Romulo

———————◆———————

I met Grenville Clark for the first time in the United Nations. He approached me in the delegates' lounge and introduced himself, without benefit of an intermediary.

"My name is Clark, Grenville Clark," he said. "I wonder if I could exchange views with you, General Romulo."

I had heard about him, of course. He had been at work on a plan for disarmament and was then broadening his studies to include proposals for revising the United Nations Charter. I was myself in the process of pushing through certain proposals for revising the charter, and it was because of this that he had sought me out.

When we sat down, Clark said, "I know you're having difficulties with your plans for a general conference as provided for in the charter, and I'd like to help in a humble way."

As he saw it, there could be no world peace without world authority. He explained earnestly that the United Nations was the basis for a world authority, but that it would be necessary to overhaul the charter in order to turn the organization into a supranational body with powers to enforce the will of the world community.

I was engaged, during this period, in expounding the idea of a world government, and I was beginning to feel increasingly that perhaps the idea was far in advance of the time. But as Clark talked to me about his project that first time, I realized that he was not a mere visionary. On the contrary, he was a profoundly practical man, and he was in command of all the technical details needed in revising the United Nations Charter. He knew its weaknesses and he knew exactly how it could be strengthened.

I came away from the conversation with Clark convinced of his sincerity and deeply impressed with his devotion to the United Nations and to the cause of peace.

We saw each other a number of times after that first meeting and inevitably the talk would turn to the United Nations. He was an engaging man with considerable powers of persuasion, and I could sense the dynamic element in his personality.

Over the next several months, I received copies of his pamphlets and articles, which I still treasure, along with numerous pointers which I found to be valuable to my work. I remember showing one of his letters to the late Dag Hammarskjöld, the secretary-general of the United Nations, and the latter, not an easy man to impress, said, "I have great respect for Grenville Clark. I think he knows the United Nations better than most of us do."

During a conference in San Francisco under the auspices of the Stanley Foundation, Clark arrived, happy to be helpful as usual. One day I suggested that we work together on a draft in connection with a working paper needed in the morning session.

"Do you think we could ask your secretary to type the draft?" I asked.

His answer both surprised and amused me. "Oh, no," he said, "that's not my secretary; that's my wife."

I congratulated him, and then chaffed him about his failure to inform me that he had remarried. He smiled. "You know how lonely you could be when you're alone. It's difficult; I need a helpmate." After a thoughtful pause, he added, "Marriage is a blessing if you choose well. I think I have chosen well."

At work, Clark was an impressive performer. No detail was too small to escape his attention. As I discovered during that conference, he never committed anything to paper without having thoroughly weighed its pros and cons. A semanticist, he went through sentences, analyzing syntax and the proper use of words with a care that would have taxed the patience of a lesser man.

But it was on the subject of the United Nations that he showed his true mettle. He had a vast wealth of knowledge on the subject, and he could trace every provision of the Charter of the League of Nations, as well as the Treaty of Versailles, from all of which he would quote provisions word for word, entirely from memory. On several occasions, he explained the equivalent provisions of the United Nations Charter and the League's charter, tracing their similarities with an easy mastery that I envied.

Clark's knowledge of these subjects seemed to me inexhaustible, but he was no pedant. During these discussions, he leavened the hard work of drafting with amusing anecdotes, which I heard for the first time, about the drafting of the Treaty of Versailles.

It was a privilege to have known and to have worked with such a powerhouse of ideas. To listen to him was to be enthralled by the spontaneous flow of his knowledge of the United Nations and his wisdom in the changes he wanted made and his sound proposals to correct them. Grenville Clark is irreplaceable. His mind was a reservoir of great ideas on how to establish and maintain world peace and his memory will be ever green to all those who know, as I do, his dedication to the ideals of peace and human understanding and his contributions to achieve both. There will not be another Grenville Clark.

MEMOIR OF A MAN

Alan Cranston

October 15, 1973
Washington, D. C.

How strange to write at this particular time of that giant, Grenville Clark—now, when the country is shaken by war and Watergate, by the departure of Spiro Agnew and the coming of Gerald Ford; when the lawlessness so feared in the streets has been found reaching so high in our government; and when violence and anarchy in the world threatens all of us as fighting rages in the Middle East.

I see Clark, when I look back upon his life and work, and forward to his effect on unfolding history, as one of the founding fathers of a world where one day there will be law.

Our paths, Grenville Clark's and mine, crossed because of our common interest in peace. While I was in the army in 1945, I wrote a book—*The Killing of the Peace*—telling the story of a great struggle in the United States Senate, showing how a handful of men kept us out of the League of Nations after World War I. My purpose was to make it less likely that the same strategies would succeed again if isolationists sought to keep us out of the United Nations after World War II.

I wrote a few pages of *The Killing of the Peace* late at night inside the very walls of the Pentagon, and I alluded in the book to Henry L. Stimson, who was presiding over the army in 1945 as secretary of war, because in the course of the battle over the League

252

of Nations he had joined Elihu Root in an action that seemed to be part of the grand strategy of the League's enemies. So I was in the Pentagon, still in uniform, but increasingly concerned with the coming struggle for lasting peace, not long after Clark resigned as Stimson's aide to turn his full attention to peace and the prevention of World War III.

Soon after the peace that followed Hiroshima and Nagasaki, Clark instigated the Dublin Conference to examine the state of man in the atomic age, and to consider the steps requisite to survival and enduring peace in this new and unprecedented circumstance.

Clark's resolute response to the bomb, at the age of sixty-four, was in deep contrast to that of H. G. Wells, then seventy-nine, whom I had admired from afar for years. In an anguished essay which I happened to read at about the time of the Dublin session, Wells said, "This world is at the end of its tether. The end of everything we call life is close at hand and cannot be evaded. . . . The writer is convinced that there is no way out or round or through the impasse. It is the end."

Most of those who responded to Clark's call and came to Dublin were seasoned men of affairs—such as former justice Owen Roberts, Thomas K. Finletter, soon to be secretary of the air force, Robert D. Smythe, one of the creators of the bomb, Senator Styles Bridges, former governor Robert P. Bass, Edgar Ansel Mowrer. But Clark, in a way that was typical of him, invited also some younger people of energy and, perhaps, promise. Among those who came were Kingman Brewster, now president of Yale, Cord Meyer, Jr., now high in the CIA, and Norman Cousins, who then, as now, looked like Cupid and who seemed very young then but had already shown his talents on the *Saturday Review*. Norman persists in the belief that a slim young man still in naval uniform dropped up from Boston for a few hours one afternoon— John F. Kennedy. I imagine I was invited because my book had somehow come to Clark's attention.

It was my use of a quotation from George Washington, in the climax of a heated Dublin debate between those who wanted to seek an extension of the rule of law in the Atlantic world and those—led by Clark—who wanted to strive for world law, that caught Clark's attention and led to our close collaboration.

The words I used had been spoken by Washington at a turning point in the Constitutional Convention, when those who thought the creation of a more perfect union was an impractical dream seemed about to prevail at Philadelphia. Washington had risen then to say, "It is too probable that no plan we propose will be adopted. Perhaps another dreadful conflict is to be sustained. But if, to please the people, we offer that which we ourselves disapprove, how can we afterward defend our work? Let us raise a standard to which the wise and the honest can repair. The event is in the hand of God."

Those words later came to symbolize to me so much that Grenville Clark represented. Sometimes, when I've had my own moments of doubt about our ability to surmount the intricate and vast problems of our time, I've renewed my strength by reflecting upon the standard set by Clark, and his supreme ability to achieve.

Clark arranged for me to chair a committee to carry on the work started at Dublin, and afterward he remarked to me, "When you quoted Washington at that point, for that purpose, you caught my fancy."

I didn't fully trust Clark at the outset! I'm abashed to admit, as I analyze now my first feelings about Clark, that my qualms were partly due to an ignorant western suspicion of Wall Street. My concerns were strengthened by the very name of his law firm —Root, Clark, Buckner and Ballantine. Elihu Root and Theodore Roosevelt, with whom Clark was closely associated in World War I, had been leaders of the successful struggle to keep our country out of the League of Nations—and were hardly heroes in the book I'd just written. I was not reassured, either, by Clark's close association in World War II with Stimson, whom I generally admired but whose role in the League struggle I questioned. I also held Stimson largely responsible for what I still feel history will deem President Truman's most dubious decision—opening the atomic age by dropping the bomb on Hiroshima without first giving Japan a brief opportunity to surrender.

I'm by nature far from suspicious—but I just wasn't sure what Clark was up to.

It didn't take long for me to decide, though, that he was absolutely straightforward, utterly without guile or cunning. I know a man who is perfectly capable of using the skills of persuasion to work his will; he prefers to trick others into doing what he wants

—for the sheer joy of engaging in trickery. I know another, also possessed of great persuasive abilities, who prefers to force others to do his bidding—for the sheer exhilaration of exercising power. Not so Clark. He was, I'm sure, constitutionally unable to practice deceit of any sort. And he shrank from the direct use of power, having no hunger for it. One of those who was at Dublin, Louis Fischer, in his magnificent biography of Gandhi, wrote in words equally applicable to Clark, "Power gave him no pleasure; he had no distorted psychology to feed. The result was a relaxed man."

My original questions about Clark were soon answered as we worked together. Doubts were replaced by appreciation and admiration, and then by affection, too.

We became closer than I, at thirty-one, had even been to any man that much older except my father, who I always called "Father." I didn't know what to call Clark. We started out as "Mr. Clark" and "Alan," but as time went on I began to feel awkward about this—"Mr. Clark" seemed too distant and formal as our intimacy grew. I noted that he referred to his first wife, Fanny, as "Mrs. Clark" and that he addressed his secretary as "Miss Maloney." I suspected that I was the only one of us who was uneasy, and supposed that my concerns arose because my free and easy western heritage differed from his more formidable and formal eastern background. Yet I didn't like this "Mr. Clark" business, and it seemed to me to have reached the point of ridiculousness when, one warm New Hampshire afternoon, we went swimming together in the nude in a secluded pond off in the woods. So, as we were dressing, I asked him what I should call him.

"An older man is usually complimented when a younger one feels at ease enough with him to call him by his first name," he replied.

He was Grenny from then on.

Soon after my appointment as "chairman" of the Dublin Conference Committee, it became clear that my principal responsibilities were to help execute Clark's strategies and to carry—physically —his ideas and his probing questions to people in high and far places. Soon I was scurrying around the United Nations Assembly at Lake Success—where I explored Clark's views with the American delegation and with Romulo of the Philippines, Spaak of Belgium, and other U.N. founding fathers. Then I was visiting the

United Nations in its London session, where I conversed with, among others, a glowering, rising young Soviet diplomat named Andrei Gromyko. Next I was flying to New Delhi to convey Clark's view to Nehru; to Devadas Gandhi, son of the Mahatma; to Ambedkar, the incredible untouchable who wrote India's constitution.

Ambassador Chester Bowles helped arrange these Indian interviews for me, incidentally, and apparently the toughest to set up was with Ambedkar. A newspaperwoman told me she had requested an interview with this remarkable man, who had written a huge number of books on constitutional and related weighty matters. The appointment was granted, but Ambedkar asked the first question:

"Have you read my books?"

"No."

"Then I have nothing more to say to you."

End of interview.

The persevering reporter struggled painfully through Ambedkar's books and, eventually, again sought to see him. Appointment granted. First question, again, from Ambedkar:

"Have you read my books?"

"Yes. Every one of them."

"Then I have nothing more to say to you."

End of interview.

I think Clark was more fascinated with this tale of a fellow constitutionalist than by almost anything else I ever reported to him.

I visited, too, the Japanese Diet in Tokyo, and presided over a Clark-inspired conference in Princeton, where new and further Clarkian thoughts were refined and ratified by an assemblage as small, diverse, and potent as Dublin's. One participant was Albert Einstein, and after a while I noticed that he was raising his hand to vote aye, and then again to vote no, on every issue.

"Why?" I asked him during a break.

"The people on both sides are so nice," he explained, smiling apologetically. "I can't vote against any of them!"

As I rushed hither and yon, while Clark sat and thought, I became aware that there were others performing other functions in Clark's scheme of things. There was Louis B. Sohn, solid, sober, and scholarly, collaborating with him on his masterwork, *World Peace through World Law*. There was Robert H. Reno, a young and able attorney in New Hampshire, performing legal chores related to world law. There was Thomas H. Mahony, a charming and thoughtful Catholic lay leader and Boston attorney, doing likewise. I came to wonder how many more were helping Clark pursue other goals in his compartmentalized life, striving to fathom the mysteries of the Soviet Union, working on the Harvard Corporation, and other affairs.

Most stimulating and rewarding were my visits with Clark up in his Dublin hideaway, or off in his more formal Long Island home, or in the quiet libraries of one or another of his clubs in New York City. There we would analyze hour upon hour every possible aspect of, and every conceivable development regarding, some situation in contemporary politics or diplomacy relevant to peace. Or we would conjecture with equal thoroughness upon the entire universe of twists and turns that might be available to yet unborn actors on the human stage in some time far in the future, as Clark methodically sought to consider every foreseeable category of events that might threaten peace or liberty in a world of law. I developed the feeling that almost nothing was unforeseeable to Clark. Nor, incidentally, was anything "foolproof" to him. I remember an incident when somebody wanted to use that word in a declaration attempting to define procedures and restraints that were required to prevent an atomic war. "*Nothing* is foolproof," Clark snorted.

It was a thrill to watch his mind—one that was at once that of a great corporate attorney and that of a stern and exacting military man—consider a vast array of almost inconceivable options and factors, assigning to each what he judged to be its appropriate weight in the realm of possibility.

I've never, ever, known anyone else who combined as deep a concern for and grasp of infinite detail with a seeming ability to cast his mind out beyond the horizons to the edge of infinity.

It was in the course of these sessions that I picked up his habit —still with me—of having a yellow legal pad handy to help keep orderly, and to preserve, the processes and consequences of reflection.

Always nearby, too, was the precious and ageless "Miss Maloney" with her incredible files on everything that had ever interested (or might one day interest) Clark. Up at Dublin, she would emerge instantly from a structure out back, apparently with whatever it was that Clark required. If it was on Long Island, she somehow had almost everything he needed right there at her fingertips, too.

Clark had a remarkable capacity for turning things off—suddenly dropping everything for a swim or a stroll right in the midst of a vital task facing an impending deadline. Sometimes it was for the purpose of sorting things out under New Hampshire's quiet, red-gold autumn leaves; sometimes plainly to give his mind an absolute rest. And it was done to rest his weak heart on the orders of Dr. Paul Dudley White as administered by the stern Fanny, who would often barge in on some schedule of her own to banish me and to lead an obedient Clark away to his bed for a nap.

The strength and scope of that mind, combined with his resolute determination and his powerful face . . . those heavy brows, yet kind eyes, stern jaw—all this marked by that angry red splotch on his face that added still more character, as a beauty spot enhances a striking woman's face—always instilled a sense of confidence in those around him that whatever Clark undertook Clark would accomplish.

As I learned of his long record of accomplishing arduous goals, small and large, and as I observed his achievements at first hand, I found it difficult to doubt that with Clark devoting all his powers to the creation of world law, world law indeed would come.

His own faith was as strong and certain as that of Woodrow Wilson, who had said in the last eloquent words of the last great speech of his life, "There is one thing that the American people always arise to and extend their hand to, and that is the truth of justice and of liberty and of peace. We have accepted that truth and we are going to be led by it, and it is going to lead us, and through us the world, out into pastures of quietness and peace such as the world never dreamed of before."

Though it was too vast a vision to come in Clark's time, he did, I believe, lay the foundations and outline at least some of the shape of world law that will indeed come in its own good time.

Clark was not, of course, infallible. I watched him make what now—in retrospect—were plainly mistakes in judgment.

He flatly predicted, and really believed, that world law would be achieved before now. He was wrong, obviously.

And it was a deliberate decision of his to use the term "world government" to describe his prescription for the world's ills. This was an honest mistake, if ever there was one, for he wanted to describe precisely what he had in mind, and he concluded no other term would do so. But those two words meant to many others, who never bothered to read his detailed explanations, something quite different from what they meant to him. They aroused visions of a vast superstate interfering in national and community affairs and in the private lives of everyone—something Clark most assuredly wanted to prevent, not provoke. He forever sought to make it clear that what he was advocating in the world institutions he envisaged was—in the words of the Dublin Declaration—"closely defined and limited powers" restricted to those matters plainly and directly related to war prevention. Just as so much of the Constitution of the United States is designed to limit the powers of our government in order to protect the people against abuses of authority that could lead to tyranny, so the main thrust of the world constitution he wrote with Louis B. Sohn was to limit narrowly the powers he believed were needed on a worldwide scale to keep the peace.

Clark was endowed with a rare ability to identify his own mistakes. He could abandon his position on a fundamental matter, even though he'd only adopted it in the first place after one of his long and penetrating exercises in logic. Thus he deserted his original and carefully thought-out view that the delegates to a world assembly should be selected on a basis of weighted representation—taking into account population, literacy or education, and economic development. He eventually turned about, deciding that only a system of representation based upon population—with upper and lower limits to accommodate the vast differences between, say, China and Iceland—would be fair, democratic, and acceptable.

Eventually, at the end of 1952, after one false start when I moved back west and back east again, I escaped to California, determined to devote my attention to business and hopefully to politics, where I felt most of the great decisions of our time—like any other—would finally be made. I enjoyed living in California, and my wife, Geneva, and I wanted our family to grow up there.

I use the word "escaped" advisedly, however. When I returned to my native California I had very mixed feelings about putting a continent between myself and Clark. I suspected that unless I did so, I would almost never be able to resist his requests for assistance on this project or that. Not that I ever had reason to complain, nor do I mean to suggest that I felt in any way that I was being used, or manipulated. I was Clark's willing—indeed, eager—junior partner in work I looked upon as enormously significant, on assignments so compelling that it was hard not to give them priority over all else. And I viewed collaboration with Clark as a classic education, something I felt I never quite got in any school. But I did want to focus on my own hopes, dreams, plans.

So, with one final overseas mission for him to Asia that followed my return to California, our time of intimate collaboration came to an end.

Until his death, though, there was a close relationship carried on by mail and memoranda, and more often, by transcontinental phone calls that were sometimes interminable, as we weighed every dimension of some new—or newly foreseen—situation.

Sadly, there was less and less of this as Clark grew older, and as I entered elective office in the state government in California and had less and less time for anything except affairs immediately at hand.

Over the years, though, I've often found myself pausing when grappling with a complicated situation, and asking: "What would Grenny do? How would he approach this?"

I've wondered now and then how presidents and cabinet officers felt when, upon occasions when they had not solicited Clark's advice, they realized that Clark was somehow nevertheless affecting, perhaps determining, their decisions . . . if they realized it, that is.

As some citizens use campaign contributions to influence the actions of government—whether for private or public purposes, for good reasons or bad—Clark used his awesome persuasiveness and logic combined with a sure knowledge of how to reach and move the levers of power. He placed at the disposal of men occupying high office the fruits of his quiet and creative contemplation—something for which most of them had little time and few of them much capacity.

Would that there was a Clark inside Richard Nixon's White House. Or, more appropriately, a Clark as president in our troubled times.

But that latter, of course, was not Clark's way. He chose a different path.

October 24, 1973

My thoughts of Grenny, and my recording of them, have been interrupted by the incredible events of these particular days . . . President Nixon driving three of the men of highest integrity from his administration—Elliot Richardson, William Ruckelshaus, Archibald Cox; the storm of protest and cries for impeachment climaxed by the president's turnabout, and his handing over of some of the Watergate tapes, after all, to Judge Sirica; all this while the war rages on in the Middle East, Henry Kissinger is dispatched to Moscow, and Kissinger and Brezhnev place the matter of a ceasefire before the United Nations.

As I listened on a radio to Archibald Cox explaining his abrupt dismissal as special prosecutor three days ago, he reminded me so much of Grenville Clark. I don't think I've ever met Cox, but as I listened I felt at once—as I'm certain millions of other Americans must have felt, instinctively—that there was a man of absolute integrity and high intelligence, who'd been performing a most unpleasant duty simply because his country had called upon him to do it, though he'd much rather be not in Washington but up on the Maine coast, as Clark always preferred to be in his beloved New Hampshire hills. I read today that Cox had sat alone with a yellow pad outlining on it the thoughts and the sequence of events that he related to the American people, exactly as Clark would have prepared for such a report.

Just now, in the rush of one of those swift TV interviews, a newsman asked me to comment on the latest development overseas: President Sadat's request that the United States and the USSR dispatch troops to the Middle East to police the ceasefire. I thought at once of Clark, and recalled how he had thought out, so long ago, what would be wise and what unwise in just such circumstances. I replied, as he would have, to the effect that it would be better to send in troops from the lesser powers, not U.S. and USSR troops, whose presence—and potential involvement in the conflict—would create greater dangers than they might manage to prevent.

(A bit later, happily, that was the official response of President Nixon and Secretary Kissinger, and thereafter, we weathered the new dangers that arose when Brezhnev seemingly threatened to send in his troops even if we weren't going to send in ours.)

Late on this day, editing and revising a more formal statement prepared for me by my staff, I came to this sentence: "Since Israel's existence depends on American arms, any agreement we negotiate with the Soviet Union mutually to scale down the arms we are shipping in must include foolproof safeguards against deception or circumvention." Automatically, as Clark's stern condemnation of the term "foolproof" flitted through my mind, I crossed out that word and inserted "careful."

October 29, 1973

I was about to comment, when I was interrupted by current events a while back, on the course Clark chose of influencing the uses of power rather than seeking to secure it in his own hands.

Clark prized his independence and his privacy, even though in his own way he was a very public man. He was devoted to his wife and children, and knew the heavy strains imposed on the families of those in public life. He was remarkably thoughtful concerning the families of those who worked with him. He insisted that Geneva accompany me to Europe when he sent me there to the United Nations, and he often invited her and our first young son, Robin, to come with me up to Dublin.

He was committed, I gather, to his unique course long before his health imposed limits on his pace and activities.

I doubt that he feared his own corruption by power. Though, perhaps, wise soul that he was, he did have some such fears—

knowing how few, possessing power, have resisted its temptations.

There's a clue, perhaps, to Clark's attitude toward power in some words spoken once by Gandhi: "Banish the idea of capture of power, and you will be able to guide power and keep it on the right path."

I suspect that it may have been most of all that he placed vast value on the opportunity to reflect, to think things through, and feared to lose it. He knew, given the magnitude of the problems of our time, that there need be some thinking through—not performed outside the sweep of events and hard realities, but done by someone able to come and go from the vortex without becoming distracted or overwhelmed by it—someone with the capacity and the determination to get his thoughts to those in charge (to the degree that anyone is in charge) and to see to it that they gave due consideration to his analysis and the proposals he based thereon.

So it was that he fulfilled the role he did in preparing our nation for World War I and again for World War II—seeing to it in the latter instance that there were men in charge of our armed forces (Stimson and Knox) to whom Franklin Roosevelt would listen, and, who, in turn, would listen some to him, Clark. Clark tried, incidentally, to persuade Stimson, who abhorred interruptions and whose natural bent was to deal with only one major problem at a time, that he could handle his job in four hours a day, and that he should spend the rest of his time in contemplation.

And so it was that in his efforts to avert the World War III for which he knew we could not really prepare, and that no one could really win, he set about thinking through the alternatives, and affecting the thinking of those who would be involved, one way or another, in the decision-making.

It is remarkable how little the nation knew of the part Clark played in shaping its destiny in the time he lived and worked.

Today, in the decade after his death, his influence is still vital strong, alive—yet still little known and barely recognized.

I'm confident its effect will wax, not wane, as time passes. And I expect awareness and acknowledgment of Clark's role to rise. But he wouldn't have cared about that.

It was in 1945, the year I met Clark, that I also made another great encounter—with Lao-tzu, in the form of a poem. The Chinese philosopher described in it a concept of leadership that I've tried to be guided by ever since—though I confess that while seeking to hold elective office at this time of mass communications, name recognition, and like hallmarks of our current experiment in democracy, I've found it impossible to follow the concept fully.

I suppose Clark never read these words, but he adhered to their philosophy and fulfilled their standards.

To me, Clark is the leader Lao-tzu described some 2000 years ago:

> A leader is best
> When people barely know
> That he exists.
>
> Less good when
> They obey and acclaim him.
>
> Worse when
> They fear and despise him.
>
> Fail to honor people,
> And they fail to honor you.
>
> But of a good leader,
> When his work is done,
> His aim fulfilled,
> They will all say:
> "We did this ourselves."

PART VIII

---◆---

Important Letters of Grenville Clark

Theodore Roosevelt, Esq.
  Oyster Bay
    New York

Dear Mr. Roosevelt:

I have had a little scheme in my head for the last month or two that I should like very much to have your opinion about if I may trouble you with a short statement of it.

I have in mind to get organized a small military reserve corps composed of young business men, lawyers, etc., who would go through a very light sort of training to fit themselves to be of some use in case of any real national emergency.

I think a good many people have been thinking along this general line lately, but nobody knows what to do about it. The men of the kind I am thinking about will not join the militia, because the militia is liable to be called out for service in cases when there is no real national emergency. For instance, I have heard a good many men say that they won't go into the militia because the militia might be called to serve in an expeditionary force into Mexico, when they think that is a young man's job and that their obligations at home to their families and in their businesses are such that they should not be called upon to serve in Mexico— that there are plenty of young unmarried men throughout the country who ought to do that work. At the same time they want to do something.

To try to be a little more definite, I have in mind a corps of 150 or 200 men. I would make the age limits 25 to 35 on the theory that no one under 25 ought to be included because such men ought to be encouraged to go into the militia and no one over 35 because they would be a little too old if anything did come up. The men in the corps would be men of sufficient means to carry the expenses themselves. I have very little idea of what those exepnses would be, but I should think $100 or $150 each a year would carry it. I would have it arranged and understood not only that there would be no *legal* obligation on the part of any such organization to serve, but also that there would be no *moral* obligation to serve except in case of a real emergency. This is on the idea that we could not get the men to join if there were even a moral obligation to go out on a big strike or to Mexico or in similar affairs.

As to the training, I would try to accomplish so little that very likely you would think it not worth doing at all. In fact you may think the whole plan futile, and possibly it is, because I am almost absolutely ignorant of military matters. I would have available for two evenings a week 50 or 75 horses and would have a drill at Durland's or some riding place in town in two batches, once a week for each batch. Then I would have a certain number of days through the year for rifle practice, also a reasonable amount of book study and instruction on tactics, etc., by an officer. I should suppose we could get the assistance of the war department in this. As to insrtuction in drills and rifle practice, I should suppose that we could get at least the help of the state authorities. I would also have a short expedition into the country for possibly a week each year, no longer, for I doubt if it would be possible to get the men I have in mind even to go to the regular army maneuvers every year, even if they would let such a loose sort of organization go.

The plan would have in mind two general objects—first, actually to give the men who would join the organization some sort of familiarity with military matters, so that they would be of some, though of course not of much, use in any emergency; second, to furnish an example by showing that some of us at least recognize the lack of preparedness of the country for any emergency and our willingness to take some positive step, however unimportant in itself, to remedy the situation.

I have spoken to a few people about this and have had conflicting opinions. Some, like Lloyd Derby,* think the idea is a good one and say it is just what they have been looking for and would go into such a thing with enthusiasm. Others say they like the idea, but that it is too fanciful, that people will not take any interest in it until there is some real emergency in sight, and that though theoretically all right it is impracticable. Others say that the idea is all right but that this is not the time to put it forward, that everybody's attention is too much taken up with the

* J. Lloyd Derby, associate in Root, Clark law firm and brother of Roosevelt's son-in-law, Dr. Richard Derby

war and that we ought to wait and see what is going to happen after the war. If there is no disarmament, it will be all very well and a good deal more than I have in mind will be practicable. Finally, there are some who adopt what is apparently the administration view that it is a bad thing to stir up anything of the sort at all, that it will militate against permanent peace, etc. This last opinion is very scarce, I think.

My own difficulty is that I do not know whether what I have in mind is worth doing at all. I suppose that most military men would say that if we want to do anything of the kind, we have got to do it more thoroughly or not at all and would laugh at the idea. However, I am thoroughly convinced that it is not practicable to get anybody but the very young men, mostly unmarried, to undertake anything that involves much sacrifice of time or energy just at this juncture, so the real question seems to me to be whether it is worth while to try to interest the class of men I am thinking of at all. As to the specific proposition I have made, I have tried to make it specific simply to have something to talk about. Perhaps there is some other scheme for reaching the same lot of men that is very much better.

If this has the slightest interest for you I should very much like to talk to you about it and see what you think. I could come to see you in New York almost any time that you could spare me a few minutes.

Very truly yours,

GC JB

Hon. Wendell L. Willkie
109 East 42nd Street
New York, N.Y.

Dear Mr. Willkie:

I have been thinking about the talk that Sherwood *, Bell,**
and I had with you last week, and especially two subjects: (1) the
convoy question; and (2) your concern about keeping our civil
liberties, as related to getting into the war. I am moved to comment on these two questions.

Convoys. I feel virtually certain that the only reasonable assurance of "stopping" Hitler is to provide convoys, by which I
mean the use of American ships on a considerable scale, protected
by American naval vessels, both manned with American crews. I
believe that this will be necessary even to insure against a forced
surrender of Britain through the cutting off of their supply line,
not to speak of enabling Britain to sustain a sufficient war effort to "prevail" (using your phrase) over Hitler. Of course, I
cannot prove this, but all the evidence that I have heard and
read, pieced together, points to the conclusion that it is only a
question of time before this becomes apparent.

If this diagnosis is correct, the question is whether there is any
use in talking about it without recognizing frankly that convoying
would involve a state of war. (I say deliberately a "state of war"
because, as you will agree, the question of a declaration of war is
another matter and largely immaterial.)

In my view, there is no use trying to avoid the fact that convoying would involve a "state of war." I saw Senator Gibson †
quoted the other day as saying that his Committee might advocate convoys, but that even if a number of American ships were
sunk, this needn't mean "war." This statement seemed to me
highly unrealistic and misleading. I cannot believe that, if correctly
quoted, he had thought the matter through. In the face Hitler's
repeated warnings that American merchant ships and naval vessels

---

* Robert E.
** Laird
† Ernest W. (of Vermont)

would be attacked by every means possible, one must assume that our merchant ships would not be sent without our naval protection. In practice, an attack would be made against them and in practice our ships would reply. It is inconceivable that they would quietly submit to being sunk without an effort to prevent it by shooting back at submarines, surface raiders, or bombing planes. If this isn't an actual "state of war," whether or not declared, just what would it be?

You mentioned the possibility that Hitler, having the strongest motives not to get us actively into the war, might refrain from attacking our merchant vessels. But surely on consideration, I am sure you would agree that this is not a practical possibility. It isn't simply that to refrain from attacking our ships would oblige him to eat his words and lower his prestige. Beyond that, it is that it would be a military necessity for him to try to stop our ships from landing cargoes in Britain and elsewhere. If he did not do so, the picture would be that hundreds and hundreds of American vessels would steam into British ports, quietly unload, and shuttle back and forth across the ocean, with millions of tons of munitions, raw materials, and food, wholly immune from interference. Hitler would have to continue to bomb British vessels and find a way to leave ours strictly alone. Frankly, the picture is absolutely inconceivable to me. I quite agree that Hitler has very strong motives not to have us actively in the war, since it would probably mean the end of him. But, on the other hand, the situation that would exist if our vessels were traveling forth in large numbers immune from attack, would create a situation so intolerable for him that he could not stand it.

I think, therefore, that on a realistic basis, one has really got to dismiss the ideas (1) that we could send our merchant ships to Britain and have them attacked and sunk without going into a "state of war"; and (2) any idea that we could send vessels and have them immune from attack.

Therefore, I cannot avoid the conclusions, reluctant as they are: (a) that we must convoy if there is to be any reasonable assurance of resisting Hitler effectively; and (b) that we must face the fact that to do this will involve a "state of war" whether declared or undeclared.

You have, with great effect, emphasized the vital necessity of greater and speedier production. You have accomplished and are accomplishing much to that end. However, as Major Eliot * has so clearly pointed out, there is also the "Battle of Transportation," and all the production in the world will remain futile if the supplies and munitions cannot, in practice, be delivered in a sufficiently large and constant flow. If this can be done without convoys, well and good. But, however reluctantly, I am convinced that these convoys have got to be put in effect and that soon, regardless of the consequences, if we mean what we say when we declare a national policy of preventing a Hitler victory.

I mention all this because it seems to me that upon your personal position on the convoy question will, more than any other one thing, depend the policy of the country in that regard. I believe that the administration is going soon to see—perhaps they do already—that convoys are indispensable. If this issue is faced up to promptly and without unrealistic ideas that somehow or other it can be done without involving a "state of war," I think the country will back the policy. But, on the other hand, I think the country would resent sidling into the policy under impressions that somehow or other the consequences can be avoided. Time also will be of the essence, because if we refrain too long from taking the indispensable steps, the whole effort may prove futile and at best the task will be so much the greater in the long run.

I am most earnestly hoping that you will not hesitate to support convoy measures without delay.

Civil liberties. I share your zeal about wanting to preserve our essential civil liberties under all conditions. I have been concerned with that subject for over twenty years. Back in the times of hysteria and persecution that you speak of following the World War, I was interested in it. I was one of the supporters of Chief Justice Hughes ** in his magnificent efforts to prevent the socialists from being thrown out of the New York legislature in 1920 merely because they were socialists, and I took part in the defense that President Lowell,† of Harvard, made of Professor Chafee ‡ about the same time when an effort was made to force Chafee out of

* George Fielding
** Charles Evans
† A. Lawrence
‡ Zechariah

the Harvard Law School because of his protests at some of the methods and persecutions of that period.

In June 1938, by reason of my long interest in the subject, I made a speech (the address at the annual meeting of the Nassau County Bar Association) entitled "Conservatism and Civil Liberty." I had become convinced that the safeguarding of civil rights had become prejudiced by reason of the fact that it had mainly grown to be the concern of "leftish" elements. I gave them credit, but I also said that their activities were giving the impression that the conservative elements of the country—"conservative" in the real sense—were on the other side. I called on conservative elements of the Bar to take an interest in the subject. This speech was largely printed in the *New York Times* and attracted attention and led to the appointment in July 1938, of the Committee on the Bill of Rights of the American Bar Association. I was its first chairman for two years and worked hard at it. We recommended and brought about the appointment of over fifty similar committees by state and local bar associations throughout the country, which now exist. We intervened in the Supreme Court against Mayor Hague * in Jersey City on the issue of the right of assembly of unpopular groups; and we intervened in the Supreme Court against the validity of the flag salute laws as applied to religious objectors. We dealt with a great variety of other problems throughout the country. I believe that these efforts have borne fruit and that there are many more organized efforts than ever before to watch vigilantly against reactionary tendencies in times of stress like these.

On the other hand, I have learned from more or less experience that civil rights are relative, i.e., relative to the extent of the necessities of national integrity and independence. I think that certain things must be done in time of crisis to restrict rights and privileges that can and ought to be more strictly safeguarded in quiet times.

Moreover, I am not so apprehensive as you are, I think, about the permanent impairment of civil rights because of measures obviously necessary in a time of crisis and limited to the crisis. I think that if such measures are strictly limited to the necessities of the crisis, both as to substance and time, they can be thrown off

* Frank

with the ending of the crisis. I think that here we should be guided by experience rather than by pure theory, because social and political questions of this sort cannot be reduced to an exact science, and experience is the best guide. As to that, I recall that although even Lincoln resorted to arbitrary procedures in the worst times of the Civil War, it was not long after that war before we returned to usual procedures. I know what abuses there were during and after the World War and feel just as you do about them, but, after all, we did slough off that state of affairs within a few years; and, moreover, the lesson has been remembered. As to England, Australia, and Canada, I recall that during the World War, they instituted even stricter controls limiting the "liberties of the subject," and that all those countries got rid of these emergency restrictions not long after the war, notwithstanding that they had been engaged in a vast struggle over a long period. I am confident that England, after this war, if she survives, will go back to the traditional "liberties of the subject." I think that we can do the same even if we get involved in a great war effort, especially so because of the lessons which we learned from the last war, and especially because of the many agencies which have been set up to be vigilant against unnecessary or too prolonged restrictions upon our civil liberties.

My fear for a possible permanent impairment of our civil rights comes from a different direction. It comes from the apprehension that in case of a sweeping victory by Hitler, we shall almost inevitably have to become a virtually armed camp *over a long period of years.* As I read history, this is the sort of condition, as distinguished from the imposition of controls of a temporary character during a moderately short crisis, that would lead to permanent impairment. Supposing that through a Hitler victory, we had to keep millions of men under arms in our army and navy and besides that had to keep our industry mobilized on a war basis for a long time, this condition, it is clear, would involve a high degree of control over the activities of the individual, including perhaps the freedom of expression. If such a condition prevailed only for a short time and everyone understood that the measures taken were to meet a particular temporary crisis only, the controls would be thrown off at the end of the crisis by common consent. If, on the other hand, the controls had to continue for two or three decades, the people might conceivably get used to them and become callous to the impairment of their old rights. That is the thing that I fear. It follows, therefore, that, in my view, the real problem of safeguarding our civil rights is to make sure that Hitler does not win; and to that end, I am willing to submit to the temporary controls that would be necessary in a great war effort rather than risk the supremacy of Hitler, with all that it would imply, by taking measures that are "too little and too late."

I have an idea that if we talked this matter out, we would not find much, if any, divergence between us. It is a question of emphasis as between apprehension over short-term controls to meet a particular crisis, as distinguished from the effect of the longer-term controls that a Hitler victory would require of us.

I hope that you will find it possible to read this rather long letter. I write on an impulse and because of having thought so long and hard about the two points I have mentioned.

I want to say again that I think you did a great and wonderful thing in your trip to England and in your testimony in Washington.

Sincerely yours,

GC GM

Dublin, N.H.
June 2, 1945

The President,
  The White House,
    Washington, D.C.

Dear Mr. President:

I write to urge the immediate negotiation of a treaty with the Soviet Union, the United Kingdom, and France, whereby we will agree with them in definite terms to prevent or suppress a renewal of German aggression for at least twenty years. I mean a treaty such as was suggested by Senator Vandenberg in his speech of January 10.

The logic and necessity of such a treaty in the interest of world stability and in our own interest were clear enough when Senator Vandenberg made his proposal five months ago. But events since then have demonstrated and confirmed the urgent necessity for such a treaty.

Many people complain of and fear the Soviet Union's persistent policy of creating a buffer zone against Germany of "friendly" or subordinate states—Finland, Poland, Czechoslovakia, Rumania, Bulgaria, Hungary, Yugoslavia, and perhaps even Austria. But what seems to be little understood is that these protective measures by Russia are the logical and necessary consequence of her experience and apprehensions, in the absence of any *commitment* by the United States to aid in preventing or suppressing still a third German aggression.

Hard as it may be, we must try to put ourselves in the Russians' place. In both World Wars I and II, they were invaded by Germany through Poland. In both cases, the combined power of Russia, Britain, and France was insufficient to ensure defeat of Germany and her allies. In both instances, the aid of the United States was necessary to turn the scale of war. But in both cases, the U. S., from the Russian standpoint, came in at the last gasp—in 1917 after Russia had been at war for 32 months and was virtually knocked out; in 1941, after the war against Britain and France had gone on for 26 months, after France had been knocked out and when the Germans were within thirty miles of Moscow.

Another factor of prime importance is the colossal losses suffered by Russia in both wars—millions of dead in 1914–'18 and in this war probably five million dead soldiers and at least as many civilians.

Now that Russia has regained self-confidence and military strength, is it surprising that without any firm promise of aid from the United States, either directly or under the proposed San Francisco Charter, she should seek other methods of self-protection? I do not think so. On the contrary, it is inevitable and natural. This might have been mitigated if months ago we had made a treaty with Russia, corresponding to the Anglo-Russian and Franco-Russian treaties, or if we had proposed a general international organization of a sort that would have *ensured* our help in case of a resurgence by Germany. But we did neither. We made no such treaty. And as to the international organization, although Mr. Hull said after his return from Moscow in late 1943 that it would obviate the necessity for spheres of influence and alliances, the actual proposal was for nothing more essentially than an agreement to consult. Some people do not seem to realize this. But, as you know, the San Francisco Charter will carry no *agreement* on our part (or on the part of any of the Big Five) to apply sanctions, no matter how clear or formidable the aggression. We (and the others) will be free to abstain from sanctions, each at its own will, for any assigned reason or no assigned reason. Such refusal to apply sanctions can occur without violation of any obligation under the charter which will expressly permit any one of the Big Five to veto sanctions and thereby prevent the organization from functioning.

It is a pity, I believe, that a more effective international organization could not have been framed. It is a pity that, in default thereof, a firm treaty with Russia, Britain, and France was not made months ago. But these are not reasons for not acting now. On the contrary, they enforce the necessity of delaying no longer with the negotiation of a treaty for Europe such as Senator Vandenberg proposed.

It is not too late for such a treaty which, by giving definite security to Russia and incidentally to Britain and France, can still mitigate and arrest the tendencies now in progress and which, if unchecked, will, at the best, cause tension and suspicion and, at the worst, will build up to still a third world catastrophe in which we cannot hope to escape involvement.

Sometime, if we are really to have world order, we (and others) will have to modify our ideas about "sovereignty" and make up our minds to relinquish the unilateral veto as to joining in cooperative action to maintain peace. We will have to consent to be bound by the majority vote in this respect of a World Assembly in which we have a fair and full representation. But, although I hope that day is not far off, it is evident that we must wait for it awhile because we (and other peoples) are not yet sufficiently chastened or sufficiently mature to release ourselves from the old shibboleths of "sovereignty."

In the meantime, we have a problem on our hands in preventing a further hardening of "spheres of influence" and new balances of power and the lining up of an Eastern bloc against a Western European–U.S. bloc, all of which would perpetuate old methods and conditions which, by past experience, lead inexorably to vast armed conflict. We can stop this process by going direct to an American-Russian military alliance (taking in also Britain and France), thus cutting right across the tendency of Russia and Eastern Europe to line up against the West. This would relieve tension to an immense extent. It would provide the indispensable foundation for our close understanding with Russia for the longer future which is so necessary to world order. It would provide a bridge whereby we could hope to make better progress toward the really effective world organization which must be the ultimate solution.

These views are, I know, not merely my own, but represent the convictions of many others who have given thought to the subject.

By sponsoring such a treaty, I firmly believe that you would make a contribution to world peace of incalculable value—a contribution that you alone are in a position to make.

On this subject, I suppose that Secretary Stimson is being consulted. With his immense experience, there is certainly no one in the whole country better equipped to give wise counsel on this great question.

With great respect, I am,

Sincerely yours,
(Sgd.) Grenville Clark

Mr. Frank B. Ober
Baltimore, Maryland

Dear Mr. Ober:

Mr. Conant sent me your letter to him of April 26 and his reply of May 11. He suggested that I might care to write you regarding the "history and significance of the traditional Harvard policy" on freedom of expression for the faculties and students. I am willing to do this because I think your letter raises questions that go to the very life of Harvard and all other colleges and are, therefore, of vital consequences to the country at large. While I write at Mr. Conant's suggestion, I do so only as an individual—although I do believe that my convictions are held by the vast majority of Harvard men.

Let me say at once that your proposals—apparently to dismiss or censure two professors, and certainly to impose drastic controls on the activities as citizens of all professors—cannot and will not be adopted at Harvard, so long as Harvard remains true to her principles.

Those proposals are absolutely contrary to Harvard's tradition and all she stands for. By reviewing the history of freedom at Harvard under Mr. Eliot, Mr. Lowell, and Mr. Conant, I will try to make clear why this is so.

I. Analysis of your complaint and opinions.

At the outset, I summarize your letter—I hope adequately and fairly.

You first state your intention not to subscribe to the Harvard Law School Fund because of the part taken by Professor John Ciardi (Assistant Professor of English Composition), and by Professor Harlow Shapley, in two recent public meetings. It seems that you want them both disciplined. And then you go on with some general observations and recommendations for basic changes in Harvard policy in respect of the "extracurricular activities" of all professors.

Concerning the two professors, your complaint as to Professor

279

Ciardi relates to his speaking at a Progressive party meeting in Maryland called in opposition to certain bills "directed at communism" proposed by a commission of which you were chairman. You say: "But the so-called 'Progressive' campaign against the laws enacted in Maryland was not debate, but vilification and falsehood—the usual Communist weapons," and "they attempted to foment hatred and prejudice in the typical Communist way." As to what Professor Ciardi said at the meeting, you say: "His own speech was not reported to any extent and I do not know what he said." So you do not complain of anything he said; nor do you question his motives. But you indicate that he ought not to have addressed that meeting at all because "Communists were actually using the Progressive party, and the meeting Ciardi was reported to have attended was addressed by Marcantonio and other fellow travelers in the usual way—so he must have been aware of its nature." You add that "the meeting gained some respectability by the statement that a Harvard professor took part in it."

It seems, therefore, that the essence of what you complain of on this count lies in the mere fact of Professor Ciardi's having spoken at that particular meeting, without regard to his purpose or any utterance of his.

Your specific complaint—about Professor Shapley—concerns his part in the recent Cultural and Scientific Conference for World Peace in New York. You do not elaborate on that and do not complain of anything he said, nor do you criticize his motives. So it seems that here, too, the offense, in your eyes, is the mere fact of his having presided at that meeting, and his part in its organization, as distinguished from anything said by him or any unworthy motive.

Both the Maryland and New York meetings were on public issues and were open to the press. You do not question the complete legality of either meeting. And yet you seem to say that the two professors committed some sort of grave offense. You seem to base this idea upon the following line of thought: "Communism is not a political movement—but is a criminal conspiracy"; hence if Communists or "fellow travelers" have any material part in a particular meeting, that meeting, although entirely legal and open, is a part of a criminal conspiracy; and hence all persons, including these professors, who engage actively in such meetings, whatever the purpose of the meetings or the motives of the participants or what they said, are involved in a criminal conspiracy.

On this basis, you appear to recommend, although your letter is not absolutely explicit on this point, that these two professors should somehow be disciplined—presumably by dismissal or at least by rebuke.

It is at first hard to believe that you intend to go to such lengths. But on rereading your letter again and again, one is forced to this conclusion. For you seem directly to identify engaging in such public meetings with "other types of conspiracies looking toward other crimes as part of their extracurricular activity" (I suppose, for example, arson or robbery); and ask: "Why then the distinction because the conspiracy is directed toward the forcible overthrow of our government—in short, sedition or peacetime 'treason'?"

I do not see how you can expect reasonable men to think of participation in open and legal meetings on public subjects as the equivalent of secret plotting to commit crime, merely because Communists or "fellow travelers" take part in such meetings. On this line of reasoning, literally thousands of reputable citizens would have offended. By no possibility could Harvard adopt a view which, to put it mildly, is so extreme. To do so would, I believe, call for conclusions which offend common sense and for efforts at repression that would be out of place anywhere in our country and are inconceivable at Harvard.

Concerning your broader proposals for control of the outside activities of all professors, you want all the present agreements for their services so construed and future agreements so drafted that "aiding and abetting sedition or peacetime treason" shall be cause for discipline. Thus you say that in "future contracts, including any required by a raise in salary" there should be "appropriate conditions" on this subject. You also mention that: "Reasonable grounds to doubt his [a professor's] loyalty to our government should disqualify him . . ." and "see no reason" why professors should be treated any differently in this regard than government employees where "'reasonable grounds on all the evidence' to believe an employee is disloyal is a ground for discharge under the president's Executive Order."

From the context it is clear that you would like to have the "appropriate conditions" cover all matters that might in your view furnish the above "reasonable grounds"—including, no doubt, involvement in any meeting materially influenced by Communists or "fellow travelers" and, I suppose, a good many other things. And you evidently want violation of any "appropriate" conditions cause for dismissal or discipline.

In addition you want the authorities to keep a "closer watch on what its professors are doing." On this point you evidently want a watch kept pretty much all the time—presumably day and night, in term and in vacation. For you say that "most of the damage from teachers is done outside of the classroom" and that "it is not reasonable to close one's eyes to such extracurricular activities."

As to the students, you want the Harvard governing authorities to give "official encouragement" to students who organize to oppose communism.

I hope you will agree that this is a fair summary and interpretation of your complaint and recommendations.

II. Harvard conviction and tradition utterly opposed to your program: history and significance of the tradition.

I repeat that the things you ask for will not and cannot be done at Harvard—at least as long as Harvard retains its basic principles and holds by its tradition. And if the day ever came that such things were done at the physical place on which the Harvard buildings stand or anywhere by the Harvard authorities, it would not be "Harvard" doing them; it would be an institution of an entirely different sort, with wholly different ideas and purposes.

The fundamental reason is that for Harvard to take the course you recommend would be to repudiate the very essence of what Harvard stands for—the search for truth by a freed and uncoerced body of students and teachers. And it would be to make a mockery of a long tradition of Harvard freedom for both its students and its faculties.

As to the history of that tradition, while it is much more than eighty years old, it is sufficient, I think, to go back to President Charles W. Eliot's inaugural address in 1869 and follow down from there.

Mr. Eliot then said: "A university must be indigenous; it must be rich; but, above all, it must be free. The winnowing breeze of freedom must blow through all its chambers. . . . This University aspires to serve the nation by training men to intellectual honesty and independence of mind. The Corporation demands of all its teachers that they be grave, reverent, and high-minded; but it leaves them, like their pupils, free."

The tradition so expressed was well understood and applied under President Eliot. It was then carried on and emphasized during the more controversial term of President A. Lawrence Lowell from 1909 to 1933.

In his report for 1916–17 (from which Mr. Conant sent you an extract) Mr. Lowell took notice that the war had "brought to the front" questions of academic freedom, especially "liberty of speech on the part of the professor." He then went on to make so discriminating an analysis of the subject that in the opinion of many, including myself, the writing of those few pages was the most lasting public service of his long career.

As applied to the "extracurricular" activities that you stress, the essence of the report is that "beyond his chosen field and outside of his classroom" the professor "speaks only as a citizen"; that his professorship gives him no rights that he did not possess before; but, on the other hand, it is unwise to restrict those rights because "the objections to restraint upon what professors may say as citizens seem to me far greater than the harm done by leaving them free." Mr. Lowell declared that by accepting a chair under restrictive conditions, the professor "would cease to be a free citizen" and that "such a policy would tend seriously to discourage some of the best men from taking up the scholar's life." "It is not," he emphasized, "a question of academic freedom, but of personal liberty from constraint." Beyond that, he made a point very applicable to what you propose, i.e., that: "If a university or college censors what its professors may say, if it restrains them from uttering something that it does not approve, it thereby assumes responsibility for that which it permits them to say . . . There is no middle ground." And, therefore, he concluded, the University, assuming the sincerity of the professor's utterances on public matters, should take "no responsibility whatever" but should leave "them to be dealt with like other citizens by the public authorities according to the laws of the land."

I have tried to state only the essence of Mr. Lowell's thought as applied to your letter. Doubtless you are familiar with his report and I can only commend a restudy of its closely reasoned pages. The point is that this report, which became famous, stands today as part of the Harvard tradition of freedom of expression, and as a definite guide for Harvard policy.

Coming now to President Conant's term, we find the same basic thought expressed with equal clarity and force. In his address at the Harvard Tercentenary Celebration in 1936, he said:

"We must have a spirit of tolerance which allows the expression of all opinions however heretical they may appear. . . . Unfortunately there are ominous signs that a new form of bigotry may arise. This is most serious, for we cannot develop the unifying educational forces we so sorely need unless all matters may be openly discussed. . . . On this point there can be no compromise; we are either afraid of heresy or we are not."

These declarations of three Harvard presidents are, as you observe, all of a piece. They embody a consistent doctrine that can, I think, be summed up as follows:

(1) *Harvard believes in the "free trade in ideas" of Justice Holmes—a graduate of 1861—which is no more than saying that she believes in the principles of Milton's* Areopagitica (1644), *of Jefferson's First Inaugural (1801), and of Mill's "Essay on Liberty" (1859). She thinks that repression is not wise or workable under our system, that wide latitude for conflicting views affords the best chance for good government, and that in suppression usually lies the greater peril. Harvard is not afraid of freedom, and believes adherence to this principle to be fundamental for our universities and for the integrity of our institutions.*

(2) *She believes that the members of the faculties, in their capacity as citizens, have the same rights to express themselves as other citizens, and that those rights should not be restricted by the University by trying to keep a "watch" on professors or otherwise.*

(3) *She believes that wide limits for free expression by professors are in the interest of her students as well as the teachers. The teachers have rights as citizens to speak and write as men of independence; the students also have their rights to be taught by men of independent mind.*

(4) *Harvard, like any great privately supported university, badly needs money; but Harvard will accept no gift on the condition,*

express or implied, that it shall compromise its tradition of free-dom.

These beliefs are not a matter of lip service. They have been applied in practice at Harvard for a long time. Thus there certainly prevailed at Harvard during the forty years of Mr. Eliot's term, an atmosphere highly favorable to free expression by both students and teachers. I know that when I was at Cambridge 1899–1906, one felt it in the very air that neither the students nor professors were under constraint. The absence of restriction on free expression by faculty and students at that time, and during the early years of Mr. Lowell's term, was implicit rather than something needing constant assertion; but it was nonetheless real.

In later years of the Lowell administration, however, in what has been called the period of "uneasy fears"—much like the present—during and after the First World War, cases arose which provided an acid test for the Harvard doctrine.

The two best-known incidents were those of Professor Zechariah Chafee, Jr., and of Harold J. Laski. They are related in Professor Yeomans' recent life of Mr. Lowell.

In the former case, Professor Chafee wrote an article condemning the conduct of the trial judge in the famous Abrams sedition case. This was in 1920 at the height of the postwar alarm about sedition and Bolshevism. It was the period of Attorney General Palmer's "raids," and of the expulsion of duly elected Socialist members from the New York legislature, in the face of powerful opposition led by Charles E. Hughes. Some Harvard men in New York accused Professor Chafee of inaccuracies in his article and, without specifying exactly what should be done, asked the Overseers to take notice of his conduct. The Overseers' Committee to Visit the Law School took up the matter and there occurred what was known as "The Trial at the Harvard Club." Mr. Lowell appeared and in effect acted as counsel for Professor Chafee. He took an unequivocal position in defense of the professor's right to espouse an unpopular cause, and the net result was a dismissal or dropping of the complaint. That case remains a landmark in Harvard's course.

In the Laski case, Mr. Laski, then a young lecturer at Harvard, spoke up for the side of the police strikers in Boston in 1919. Feeling on that issue was terrific; emotion ran high against anyone taking the strikers' side and there were insistent demands for the dismissal of Mr. Laski. Nevertheless, Mr. Lowell stood firmly for Mr. Laski's right to speak his mind; there was no dismissal and that set another great precedent.

Since then there have been various other incidents in which the principle has been vindicated. Perhaps the very latest was the permission given a month ago to the Harvard Law School Forum to have Mr. Laski (now, thirty years later, Professor Laski of the University of London) speak in Sanders Theater. Because of the Cambridge School Board's objections to Mr. Laski, the Forum had been denied the use of a public school auditorium where its meetings had customarily been held. The Forum then asked for the use of Sanders Theater and, in accordance with established practice on student meetings, the request was granted.

It is, I think, unnecessary to go into more detail. For it is well-established and known that Harvard has a long-declared and, on the whole, well-adhered-to tradition favoring a wide degree of freedom for teacher and student and, therefore, as you must perceive, a tradition utterly at variance with what you recommend.

Mr. Conant mentioned the "significance" as well as the "history" of the tradition.

To my mind, its fundamental significance lies in the thought that the principles back of it are essential to the American Idea—to the workability of our free institutions and to enabling Americans to live satisfactory lives.

The professor's right to speak his mind and to espouse unpopular causes should not be regarded as something separate and apart from the maintenance of our civil rights in general. I think what is usually called academic freedom is simply part and parcel of American freedom—merely a segment of the whole front.

I believe, however, that it is an especially vital segment because it concerns the students quite as much as the professors. If the professors are censored, constrained, or harassed, it affects not only themselves; it affects also those whom they teach—the future voters and leaders upon whose integrity and independence of mind will depend the institutions by which we live and breathe a free air. For if the professors have always to conform and avoid unpopular views whether in class or out, what kind of men will they be? And where will our young men and women go to hear and weigh new ideas, to consider both sides and acquire balance and integrity?

In *The Wild Flag* the essayist E. B. White has defined democracy in a way closely touching this point. "Democracy," he said, "is the recurrent suspicion that more than half of the people are right more than half of the time." This is about it, is it not—the very basis of our system? But how can we possibly expect most of the people to be right most of the time if they are taught by men and women of a sort who are constrained to work under conditions where they may lose their jobs if, pursuant to conviction, they attend meetings that some, or even the majority of the moment, do not approve?

In that inaugural address of Mr. Eliot's, it is also said: "In the modern world the intelligence of public opinion is the one indispensable condition of social progress." And further: "The student should be made acquainted with all sides of these [philosophical and political] controversies, with the salient points of each system . . . The notion that education consists in the authoritative inculcation of what the teacher deems true may be logical and appropriate in a convent, or a seminary for priests, but it is intolerable in universities and public schools, from primary to professional."

But how can we fulfill the "indispensable condition" of intelligent opinion; and how can we have nondogmatic and excellent instruction for our leaders if their teachers are coerced or harassed?

It is impossible; and since I believe that the very existence of our free institutions depends on the independence and integrity of our teachers, the main significance for me of the Harvard tradition is that it powerfully helps to sustain those institutions.

No doubt there are other more specialized significances. No doubt the Harvard tradition has significance because, if abandoned, it would make many good people, members of our faculties, very unhappy. No doubt it is significant because its abandonment would force others—administrators and governing boards—either to resign or, against conscience, to engage in work bitterly hateful to them. These things are true and important. But it is enough for me that the tradition is in harmony with and necessary to the maintenance of the free institutions of America, and to the values that make life in our country most worth while.

III. Practical implications.

I cannot help wondering whether you have thought through the implications of what you propose.

Since you wish to discipline professors for taking active part in meetings such as those at which Professors Ciardi and Shapley spoke, would it not be fair to pass in advance on the kind of meetings professors could safely attend? Would this not call for a University licensing board? And would not such a board have an obnoxious and virtually impossible task?

The very cases you mention illustrate this. The Maryland meeting was called by the Maryland branch of the official Progressive party (the Wallace party), which is a legal organization for whose ticket over a million citizens voted in 1948. The New York meeting was to advocate peace and was sponsored by many reputable citizens whose motives were above question.

If the University should undertake to decide whether or not a professor, in his capacity as a citizen, could take part in these or other meetings, what Mr. Lowell referred to would necessarily occur. If attendance at the meeting were disapproved, the professor would be deprived, under penalty of discipline, of a right enjoyed by other citizens; while if approved, the University would assume the responsibility for endorsing the meeting.

Moreover, I think you will agree that there would be little sense in censoring attendance at meetings and leaving free from censorship speeches on the radio or writings in the press, magazines, pamphlets, and books. Would not your proposals call for a censorship of all these?

Take, for example, the recent book *Military and Political Consequences of Atomic Energy* by Professor Blackett of Manchester University. That is a highly controversial book because it sought to justify the Soviet position on atomic energy control. I have not heard that Professor Blackett's loyalty to Britain has been questioned. But suppose that book to have been written by a Harvard professor, is it not probable that in our more tense and excited atmosphere someone would charge that it raised "reasonable doubts" about his loyalty? I think it would have been quite certain that such a charge would have been forthcoming. And, if so, would it not be fair to the professor, and also necessary to make your proposals effective, that such a book be submitted for censorship before its publication?

Beyond that, however, how could an effective "closer watch" on "extracurricular activities" be maintained unless the watch extended to conversations and correspondence? And how could that be done without a system of student and other informers—the classic and necessary method of watching for "subversive" utterances?

You may not have realized the full implications of what you ask. But if you will stop to consider what would necessarily be involved if your point of view were accepted, you must agree, I think, that these things are precisely what would be required.

What I have just said applies to the professors. But how about the students? Would it be sensible to have the teachers censored and watched while the students remain at liberty freely to speak and write and to attend such meetings as they choose, subject only to the laws of the land? On your philosophy are you not driven on to restrict, censor, and discipline the students also?

What sort of place would Harvard be if it went down this road? It would, I think, not require six months to destroy the morale of both our teachers and students, and thereby our usefulness to the country. I think one need do no more than state the necessary implications of what you ask to demonstrate that nothing could be more alien to the principle of free expression that Harvard stands for.

IV. Harvard money and Harvard freedom.

I want to add a comment on your decision not to subscribe to the Law School Fund. As Mr. Conant wrote you, it has happened before that subscriptions have been withheld because of objections to the acts or opinions of professors or because of disapproval of University policy. This is natural and normal, I think; and it is certainly the right of anyone not to aid an institution with which he is as out of harmony as you now seem to be with Harvard. But it is also true, I am sure you will agree, that Harvard cannot be influenced at all to depart from her basic tradition of freedom by any fear that gifts will be withheld.

An interesting test case on this point came up during the First World War. It related to Professor Hugo Münsterberg, who was a German and very pro-German, and is described in Professor Yeomans' biography of President Lowell. It appears that the press reported that a certain Harvard man had, in Professor Yeomans' words, "threatened to annul a bequest to the University of $10,000,000 unless Münsterberg was immediately deprived of his professorship." Thereupon Professor Münsterberg wrote to the Harvard Corporation offering to resign if the graduate would immediately remit $5,000,000 to the Corporation. The Professor's letter was returned and the Corporation issued, as Professor Yeomans puts it, "one of its rare public pronouncements," as follows: "It is now officially stated that, at the instance of the authorities, Professor Münsterberg's resignation has been withdrawn, and that the University cannot tolerate any suggestion that it would be willing to accept money to abridge free speech, to remove a professor or to accept his resignation."

I think it will always be Harvard policy not to be influenced in any way "to abridge free speech" by the withholding of any subscription. And if $5,000,000 or any sum were offered tomorrow as the price of the removal of Professor Ciardi or Professor Shapley, or of instituting the "closer watch" that you recommend, nothing is more certain than that the Corporation would again reply that it "cannot tolerate" the suggestion.

On this money matter, the practical question has always interested me as to whether Harvard's adherence to this principle has in fact been to her financial detriment. Certainly one can point to some specific cases, besides your own, where gifts have not been made because the possible donors thought Harvard should have disciplined professors or students for their supposed "sedition" or "radicalism." I well remember how much was said on that score during the early days of the New Deal as relating to the activities, actual or supposed, of Professor Felix Frankfurter. So I do not doubt that some gifts have been withheld for reasons of this sort. On the other hand, less is heard, usually nothing at all, of those others who instead of being repelled by the steadiness of Harvard's adherence to free expression, find in it the true glory of Harvard and a principal reason for supporting her finances.

Thus I am quite sure that there are many Harvard men and others who, if they read your letter and were told that Harvard must firmly decline to follow your views, would find in that very refusal a strong reason for adding to their gifts. I think that many such would say: "If Harvard is again under pressure to depart from its tradition but is holding to it as solidly as ever, that is the place on which I want to put my money, because if we want to preserve the essence of the American Idea we must encourage those who adhere consistently to uncoerced teaching."

So I just don't know, and no one can know, whether, on balance, Harvard gains or loses money by its policy in this regard. But, although it cannot be proved, I have a shrewd suspicion that, while Harvard may for a few years, in times of emotion like the present, lose some gifts and bequests by its adherence to free expression, it loses no money at all over a generation by holding to this principle.

In any case, while that is an intriguing question, it is not the real one. For whether the policy gains money or loses it, Harvard, in order to be Harvard, has to hew to the line. That is what Mr. Eliot meant, I am sure, when he said, in 1869, that while a university "must be rich" it must "above all" be free. That choice is as clear today as eighty years ago.

I am under no illusion that this letter, or any similar argument, is likely to affect your attitude in this matter, at least for some time. For my observation in the corresponding period after the First World War was that in a period of alarm, proposals to restrict free expression rest on strong feelings which for the time being override sound judgment. That was certainly true of the above-mentioned successful effort to oust the Socialist assembly-men in New York, and the unsuccessful effort to discipline Professor Chafee. Several years later, I think that some of those who promoted those efforts came to see that they had been impairing the very values which, no doubt sincerely, they purported to preserve. But during the period of stress, they found it hard even to comprehend the other side.

I hope, though, that I may have convinced you that there is another side, and that there is a deep-rooted tradition at Harvard utterly opposed to your view—a tradition that must and will be upheld as long as Harvard remains true to herself.

Grenville Clark

Mr. Allan Knight Chalmers
  Room 1790
    NAACP Legal Defense Fund
    10 Columbus Circle
    New York 19, N.Y.

Dear Mr. Chalmers:

Thank you for your good letter on April 18. Like so many others I have been thinking hard about the future course of our Negro problem, by which I mean especially the best strategy to use in the necessarily long and bitter contest which lies ahead. In part, I have been influenced by a recent reading of Allen Nevins' two volumes called "The Emergence of Lincoln," covering the years 1857–61 down to Sumter. There are, I think, instructive parallels between the developments of those years and what has occurred since the Supreme Court's 1954 decision. I mean in respect of the hardening of Deep South sentiment and action when put on the defensive, together with the slower but ultimately just as deep a hardening of Northern sentiment. In a less extreme form, of course, but still in a very serious way, I think that similar convictions and emotions will operate in the 1960s.

Having in mind that the effort to obtain anything like equal opportunity for our Negro population in the numerous fields in which they are disadvantaged (housing, jobs and pay, voting, education, recreation, etc.) will undoubtedly be long and hard, the key to ultimate success obviously lies in sustaining a *steady, persistent and, if possible, increasing* effort over a long period. In part, this means psychological preparation in much the same way as Churchill, after Dunkirk, made it so clear to the British people that their only chance was to stick it out for an indefinitely long time. However, of equal importance, is the making of long-term strategy plans of a material sort, which largely means a long-term financial plan.

In view of this line of thought, I wonder whether any plan has been formulated to *ensure* some substantial minimum financial support for the NAACP Legal Defense and Educational Fund,

Inc., for some such period as ten years. I don't mean a plan to cover anything like all the money the Fund will need in the next decade which would not be feasible and, even if feasible, not desirable. I mean rather a set of guaranteed subscriptions sufficiently large to provide a substantial nucleus and encouragement, so that even in the hardest circumstances there would be assurance that some substantial work would continue and so that others would be stimulated to sustain and enlarge the work on the basis of a more solid enterprise than could exist without such assurance. The latter is an important point, since there are many people who will give more liberally in support of a plan or institution which they believe to be solidly based and sure to continue. (For example, the older universities.)

More specifically, how about a plan whereby, say, 100 persons from all parts of the country (say 90 per cent white but, if at all possible, 10 per cent Negroes) agree to subscribe not less than $1,000 each per annum for ten years beginning in 1961? My thought is that the subscriptions should be asked on an assumed tax deductible basis and should be legally binding except that the estate of a subscriber would not be liable for any unpaid balance in the event of the subscriber's death before full payment—with the understanding, of course, that any particular subscriber could bind his estate if he chose to do so.

Such a plan would provide practical assurance of at least $100,000 per annum for the ten-year period (i.e., $1 million in all) because, with subscriptions of *not less than* $1,000 per annum, there would be some subscriptions for more than that amount and, since losses from defaults and deaths before full payment would be relatively few, this excess should offset any such losses.

I have no knowledge as to what the Legal Defense and Educational Fund, Inc. has been able to raise in the last few years or what constituency it may have who would be willing and able to subscribe a ten-year fund of this sort. But even if such a constituency does not now exist, I believe that it can be created in view of recently increased understanding of the importance of the problem, both from the standpoint of internal harmony, and from the standpoint of the U.S.A.'s position in world affairs.

It would seem to me that $300,000 per annum will be the absolute minimum amount required by the Legal Defense and

Educational Fund, Inc. during the next ten years, since there is certain to be a constantly increasing volume of litigation relative to Negro civil rights. I have in mind not so much efforts to implement the 1954 decision concerning education (which, however, should be persistently pressed, especially in the border states), but rather the defense of the literally tens of thousands of Negroes who will be prosecuted, probably with increasing severity, for seeking equal treatment in lunch rooms, waiting rooms, parks and beaches, etc. I hope and believe that these active efforts (necessarily involving violation of laws) will continue, and, if so, there will almost surely be a steady and increasing number of arrests, fines, and prison sentences from year to year. It will be of utmost importance that the arrested persons shall *all* be competently represented in court, partly to mitigate injustices against them and partly to demonstrate to others who contemplate similar sacrifices for the cause that they will not be abandoned; and this will cost real money.

In view of the great volume of legal services that will be needed, $300,000 per annum would not indeed go far if the services were charged for at normal rates, having in mind that at least $100,000 of this would have to go for out-of-pocket expense such as travel, typewriting, printing, bail bonds, etc.—leaving only, say, $200,000 to compensate counsel. However, I am assuming that much of the legal work would be volunteered without any charge and that none of the lawyers would expect payment on a usual basis, so that $300,000 a year (with, say, $200,000 for counsel) should stretch quite a way and accomplish as much as $500,000 or more per annum if the legal work were paid for on a normal basis.

I mention all this because what I have in mind is a set of subscriptions which would provide a nucleus of about one-third of the minimum amount required, the balance to be raised from year to year on a shorter subscription basis than ten years. What I am driving at is to encourage and underpin continuity and persistence by providing an assumed substantial nucleus—on the distinct understanding, however, that the intention is to raise in other ways at least twice as much as the amount subscribed by the ten-year group.

Perhaps the above plan is on too small a scale. Perhaps the planned annual budgets should be, say, $450,000 instead of

$300,000 and the ten-year subscribed nucleus $1,500,000 instead of $1,000,000. Certainly there will be an urgent need for $450,000 annually and the only question is as to the practicality of getting ten-year subscriptions for as much as $150,000 per annum and of raising $300,000 more each year. It is perhaps nothing more than a matter of a little better planning and a little more effort to raise the larger sums.

As to the method, whether for a nucleus fund of $100,000 or $150,000 per annum, I should think something like this might work: May there not be about 10 members of the present "Committee of 100" willing and able as a starter to subscribe an average of, say, $1,500 each for ten years (contingent, of course, upon the whole nucleus fund of $1,000,000 or $1,500,000 being subscribed, upon continued tax deductibility and upon the adoption of a ten-year plan calling for raising, if at all possible, $200,000 or $300,000 additional each year)? If such a starting group could be formed, it would obviously be of great help. Each of these initial subscribers might then be asked to suggest, say, ten additional "prospects," and these 100 persons could then be canvassed, producing, let us say, 15 more subscribers averaging, say, $1,250 each per annum. In turn, the new 15 subscribers could be asked to suggest 150 more names; and go on steadily in that way until all the 100 subscribers are obtained. This process might take a year and some efficient person would need to stay right on the job to organize it; but I think some method like this might work better than a wider broadcast appeal or the employment of a money-raising concern.

As to annual campaigns for, say, $200,000 or $300,000, that would be, of course, a wholly different kind of thing and would doubtless require large lists, a fund-raising committee, meetings, etc. But these campaigns ought to be a good deal facilitated by being able to say each year that, say, one-third of the budget had been subscribed in advance.

You may ask why I suggest $100,000–$150,000 per annum for the nucleus subscription rather than some smaller or larger sum. I do so for two reasons: (a) because $100,000–$150,000 per annum seems a practicable amount to get subscribed on a ten-year basis and (b) because such a sum is one-third of what I suppose to be the minimum necessary budget for legal expenses and services over the next ten years, and this seems to me about the right proportion to have assured by a long-term subscription.

You may also ask why a ten-year subscription rather than five years or fifteen or twenty years. Certainly this is not because of any illusion that the effort for equality will even measurably succeed in ten years; for I believe it will need to go on for at least fifty years and, more likely, for a hundred years or even more. The reasons are simply that a shorter period than ten years would not fulfill the purpose, while, on the other hand, it would be very difficult to find subscribers willing to bind themselves for longer than ten years. I would hope, however, that the successful formation of the first ten-year group would supply a precedent for similar ten-year groups decade after decade.

Under such a plan as above outlined, I would be willing to subscribe $2,000 per annum for ten years, i.e., $20,000, and provide for full payment in the event of my death before payment of all the installments. I could not, however, undertake any work in helping to obtain other subscriptions except to send in a small list of "prospects."

I realize that some such plan as this may have often been canvassed and rejected for reasons I don't know about. Or perhaps some similar plan is already in effect. However, there can be no harm in outlining these thoughts and in emphasizing my conviction that the planning and carrying out of a persistent and sustained effort are the key to ultimate success.

Sincerely yours,

(Sgd.) Grenville Clark

P.S. I have written this longhand in the country and am sending it to my secretary at 52 Wall Street to type, sign and mail to you.

G. C.

November 22, 1960

Senator John F. Kennedy
Senate Office Building
Washington, D.C.

Dear Senator Kennedy:

An experience with President Franklin Roosevelt in 1932–33 encourages me to write you.

A few days after Mr. Roosevelt's election in November 1932, I sent him a long letter setting forth my analysis of the situation confronting him and a set of definite proposals to deal with the crisis which then existed. After careful consideration, he told me at the end of January 1933 that he agreed with my view of the need for a bold and drastic program; that he accepted my proposals in all essentials; that the most basic feature, i.e., for radical retrenchment in order to restore confidence, would be embodied in an act to be introduced within a week of his inauguration; and that he would go on the radio (then a novel step) in its support. This was the National Economy Act enacted soon after his inauguration on March 4, 1933 which, as you know, went far to start the wheels again and to open the way for the other measures of the famous "Hundred Days."

The present crisis is, of course, very different from that of 1932–33 since, while of a far deeper and more serious character, it is less immediately apparent and urgent. Yet the two situations have one thing in common, namely, that just as the 1932–33 crisis called for drastic, bold, and creative treatment, so the present one requires a similarly novel, comprehensive, and bold approach. The proposals in this letter are on that premise.

Naturally I cannot expect you to rely on my proposals to the extent that Mr. Roosevelt did, since his confidence in my judgment was based upon an acquaintance of thirty years, including three years together at Harvard, and the 1907–08 year as fellow law clerks in a New York law firm. On the other hand, you know, I think, that I have devoted most of my time for twenty years to the intensive study of the problem of world organization for the prevention of war, and this encourages me to hope that my views will have weight with you.

I submit the following:

1. *Need for a definite and comprehensive program; its main elements.* On the premise you have well stated that peace with freedom is paramount to all other issues, you should, I believe, formulate and personally announce as soon as possible after taking office a *concrete* and *comprehensive* plan including the following elements:

(a) The unequivocal acceptance of universal and complete, rather than partial, disarmament as the definite and considered objective of the United States—it being understood that this total disarmament would be subject at all stages to as effective an inspection system as is reasonably possible and that the accomplishment of each stage be carefully verified before going further. By "universal" disarmament I mean disarmament by each and every nation without exception; by "complete" I mean the elimination of all national armaments right down to the level of agreed-upon police forces for internal order only, strictly limited in number and very lightly armed.

(b) The establishment parallel with the disarmament process of a strong and heavily armed world police force of, say, 500,000 men—this force to be composed of volunteers and not of national contingents, with very careful safeguards against having any undue proportion from any nation or group of nations and in respect of command, disposition, etc., so as to provide every possible assurance against abuse of power by this force.

(c) The establishment of an impartial world judicial, quasi-judicial, and conciliation system, so as to provide fully adequate peaceful means for the settlement of *all* international disputes, in lieu of force or the threat of it.

(d) The creation of a world legislative body with a system of representation which will at the same time be workable in practice and fair to all nations, the powers of this world legislature to be carefully restricted to the end in view, i.e., the prevention of war.

(e) The establishment of an effective world executive body, so weighted and safeguarded as to be free from control by any nation or group of nations.

(f) The establishment of a well-financed world development

authority to mitigate the vast and excessive disparities between regions and nations, which are an underlying cause of unrest and trouble.

(g) The establishment of an effective world revenue system, without which it would be futile to set up the other world institutions for the elimination of war.

Elaborately detailed proposals for these and other auxiliary world agencies are set forth in Professor Sohn's and my book *World Peace through World Law*, which you have seen and have been good enough to comment upon favorably. It is, however, in no way necessary to accept the particular detailed proposals of the Clark-Sohn plan. What is necessary is to realize that peripheral, partial, and halfway measures will not meet the situation and that if genuine peace is to be achieved, nothing less will suffice than a *comprehensive* and *adequate* plan along the general lines of that above summarized. You will doubtless receive an abundance of counsel contrary to the above—advising caution, "gradualism," "arms control" (whatever that means) rather than total disarmament, etc. I urge you to reject all such overcautious and timid advice on the ground that it is as clear as crystal that nothing less will suffice than a *comprehensive* plan for enforceable world law in the limited field of war prevention.

Having once reached that conclusion, you will, I feel sure, also conclude that each one of the above-mentioned main elements is indispensable and that it is no more sensible to expect genuine peace without *all* these essential world institutions than it would be to expect a watch to keep time without all its essential and interrelated parts.

2. *Four key positions.* Although it is indispensable that you shall personally lead the new effort for disarmament and genuine peace, it goes without saying that capable and loyal associates will be important. My suggestion here is that the position of our chief delegate in the long disarmament negotiations which must ensue may prove of no less importance than that of secretary of state and ambassador to the United Nations. The position should, therefore, be upgraded and the man appointed should, if at all possible, have no less ability and reputation than the secretary and the ambassador. As I see it, the leadership in the Senate on this

subject will be of no less consequence. It can and probably should be separated from the position of official leader of the Senate. Above all, as in the case of the three other positions, belief in the cause of total disarmament under enforceable world law should be the prime requisite.

3. *The new disarmament negotiations; inclusion of Communist China.* With regard to the method and machinery for the new negotiations which must be started as soon as possible, I believe that it would be unwise to seek the withdrawal of any of the ten conferees on the recent Ten Nation Committee, but that it is essential to add five or six other nations, including, above all, mainland China. As to China, everyone knows that no worthwhile disarmament plan can come into force without the participation of that nation with its more than 600 million people; and, this being so, it is no more than common sense to bring China into the new negotiations from the start. For when one knows in advance that the agreement sought in a difficult negotiation can never become effective unless assented to by a certain important interest, it is elementary in my view that this interest should be asked to participate in the negotiation from the outset rather than be asked later on to assent to an agreement in the formulation of which it has had no part. In such case, it is almost inevitable that the excluded party will say: "If you wanted my assent and knew it to be essential, why didn't you invite me to participate instead of asking me now to sign on the dotted line? You can go to the devil." Having in mind also that China, as you know, has already given explicit notice that it will not feel bound to assent to any disarmament agreement negotiated without its participation, it would, in my view, be simply stupid to carry on further negotiations without China's active participation as a conferee. I believe also that it will be wise and necessary during your administration to resume regular diplomatic relations with mainland China and to bring her into United Nations membership. But these measures can wait a while and are separate and distinct from inviting China's participation in the new disarmament negotiations—which is a matter which cannot wait and will need to be decided by you very shortly. Once the inclusion of Communist China has been agreed upon, it should not be too difficult to agree upon four or

five other nations in order to provide better representation for all geographical areas and for neutrals.

4. *Subordination of military influence.* In order to achieve disarmament under world law, it is absolutely essential that the military be put and kept in their proper place, i.e., as subordinate to the civil authority in the making of policy. On this point also, I invoke the precedent of President Franklin Roosevelt, who, although paying all proper attention to military advice, drew a clear line in respect of national policy within which military officials must stay. Under the Eisenhower administration this line has become blurred and military officers have often expressed opinions and sought to influence policy on questions beyond their proper scope and for which their training did not qualify them. By and large, professional military men (with rare exceptions such as General MacArthur) oppose or deprecate disarmament, not because they are any more callous or inhumane than others, but simply because, in view of their training and belief in the importance of their profession, they cannot be expected to acquiesce in and much less to advocate the abolition of that profession. As you have well put it, they and others have a "vested interest in armament." The President alone can see to it that our military people keep within proper bounds; and it is of utmost consequence that he do so.

* * *

By coming to grips with the problem of disarmament and peace through a program of this sort, I believe it entirely possible within four years to work out the main features of a great world treaty which would end the arms race and establish the world institutions essential to genuine peace—so that the next president could see the plan well on its way toward realization.

On the other hand, with any less comprehensive program, I would anticipate the same frustrations and failures in respect of progress toward peace that have characterized the past eight years.

You have two roads to follow. One requires a willingness to pioneer and the intelligence to see that nothing less will suffice than a great and novel plan. The second derives from lack of understanding of the revolution that has occurred in human affairs and is the road of avoidance, hesitation, and half measures. One road leads to great and constructive achievement; the other leads at best to frustration and at worst to catastrophe.

I have much confidence that you will take the former road and wish you well.

Sincerely yours,

(Sgd.) Grenville Clark

About the Authors

Simeon O. Adebo, formerly Nigeria's ambassador to the United Nations, has served also as under secretary general of the United Nations. Once a member of the board of directors of the Institute for World Order of New York, he has been active in the world peace area both in America and abroad. His home is at Abeokuta, Nigeria.

Patrick Armstrong has made a large contribution in the area of world peace, and has served for many years as a member of the Parliamentary Group for World Government in Great Britain.

Roger N. Baldwin was a Harvard graduate of the Class of 1904. A teacher and writer, he was one of the founders and former director of the American Civil Liberties Union and is a long-time defender of individual rights.

Stringfellow Barr, author and lecturer, was president of St. John's College from 1937 until 1946, and president also of the Foundation for World Government from 1948 to 1958. In 1952 his book *Citizens of the World* was published.

Kingman Brewster, Jr., law graduate, author, and educator, attended the first Dublin Conference in 1945 and presided at the second Dublin Conference in 1965. He is currently president of Yale University.

David F. Cavers, educator, a graduate of Harvard Law School in 1926, has practiced the law, served widely as a legal consultant, and has been a distinguished professor at the Harvard Law School for many years. He lives in Cambridge, Massachusetts.

Joseph S. Clark, lawyer and public servant, was mayor of Philadelphia from 1952 until 1956, and then served two terms as U.S. senator from Pennsylvania. Once president of World Federalists, USA, he now plays a leading role with the Coalition on National Priorities and Military Policy.

J. Garry Clifford, historian and teacher, is an associate professor of political science at the University of Connecticut. He wrote the book *Citizen Soldiers: The Plattsburg Training Camp Movement, 1913–1920.* He is the official biographer of Grenville Clark.

James B. Conant, scientist, distinguished educator, and writer, was president of Harvard University from 1933 until 1953. He also served as U.S. high commissioner for Germany and as U.S. ambassador to the Federal Republic of Germany. He lives at present in Hanover, New Hampshire.

Norman Cousins, editor, lecturer, and author of many books, has long been associated with World Federalists, USA, and the World Association of World Federalists. He is currently editor and publisher of *Saturday Review* and continues vigorous activity in the world peace area.

Alan Cranston, once a foreign correspondent, is a past president of World Federalists, USA. He held public office as controller in the state of California and is now senior U.S. senator from that state. His writings include *The Killing of the Peace* and *The Big Story.*

John S. Dickey, educator, practiced law in Boston, Massachusetts, served with the Department of State, was special assistant to the coordinator of inter-American affairs, and was attached to the U.S. delegation at the United Nations Conference of International Organization in San Francisco in 1945; he is president emeritus of Dartmouth College and lives in Hanover, New Hampshire.

John M. Dinse practices law in Burlington, Vermont, with the firm of Wick, Dinse and Allen, and handled legal matters for the Clark family, some of whom have resided in the Burlington area for more than a century.

Harold W. Dodds is president emeritus of Princeton University. Distinguished author and teacher, and the recipient of numerous honorary degrees, he continues to live in Princeton, New Jersey.

Lewis W. Douglas, former congressman, director of the budget, and ambassador to Great Britain, commuted between New York City and Tucson, Arizona, until his death in 1974.

Henry J. Friendly, lawyer and a founder of the firm of Cleary, Gottlieb, Friendly, and Hamilton, is now chief judge of the U.S. Court of Appeals, Second Circuit, in New York City.

Lloyd K. Garrison, lawyer and public servant, was formerly dean of the University of Wisconsin Law School and once president of the New York City Board of Education. He practices law in New York City with the firm of Paul, Weiss, Rifkind, Wharton and Garrison.

The Rev. Gerard G. Grant, S.J., teaches at Loyola University of Chicago and has led World Federalists, USA, in the Chicago region along with other activities in the world peace area.

Jack Greenberg, a lawyer and active in civil rights work for many years, is the director-counsel of the Legal Defense Fund and the author of *Race Relations and American Law*.

Erwin N. Griswold, formerly dean of Harvard Law School, recently the solicitor general of the United States, now practices law with the firm of Reavis, Pogue, Neal and Rose and lives in Washington, D.C.

Sir Alexander J. Haddow, one of the world's foremost cancer specialists, a member of the American Academy of Arts and Sciences and of the Academy of Medical Sciences of the USSR, works at the Royal Cancer Hospital in London, where he resides.

W. Averell Harriman, scholar, author, one of America's most distinguished domestic advisers and foreign diplomats, has been ambassador to the USSR and later to Great Britain. He most recently wrote *America and Russia in a Changing World.*

James P. Hart, once chancellor of the University of Texas, and for many years an associate justice of the Supreme Court of Texas, currently practices law with his son and lives in Austin, Texas.

Mary Kersey Harvey, editor, journalist, and writer, formerly with the *Saturday Review* and *McCall's* magazine, is now editor of *Center Report*, a bimonthly publication of the Center for Democratic Institutions at Santa Barbara, California, where she lives.

General Lewis B. Hershey served as director of Selective Service from 1941 until 1970. He has been recently special assistant to the president on matters relating to the military draft. He is also an author, and resides in Bethesda, Maryland.

Elizabeth Jay Hollins is an author and the daughter of Grenville Clark's closest friend, the late Delancey Kane Jay.

Harry B. Hollins, formerly director of the World Law Fund, is currently chairman of the executive committee of the board of directors of the Institute for World Order.

John M. Korner, once with the firm of Root, Clark, Buckner and Howland, now lives in western Pennsylvania after years of duty abroad in the Canal Zone, Cuba, and South America.

Cloyd Laporte, summa cum laude graduate of Harvard in 1916, entered law practice with Root, Clark, Buckner and Howland, and later was a partner with the firm Dewey, Ballantine, Bushby, Palmer and Wood until his death in the summer of 1974.

Louis Lusky, lawyer and author, a former law clerk to Justice Harlan Fiske Stone, entered law practice with Root, Clark, Buckner and Howland, later practiced law in Louisville, Kentucky, and is now professor of law at Columbia University.

John J. McCloy, lawyer, veteran of the famous Plattsburg training camp of 1915, has held numerous government positions, including that of assistant secretary of war, U.S. military governor and high commissioner to Germany, and special presidential adviser on arms control and disarmament. He is currently chairman of the board of the Chase Manhattan Bank of New York.

William L. Marbury was a member of the Harvard University Corporation from 1947 until 1970. A member of the law firm of Piper and Marbury of Baltimore, Maryland, he currently lives in that city.

Henry Mayer began his legal career with the Root, Clark, Buckner and Howland firm in 1915 and still practices law in New York City. His son, Martin Mayer, published a biography of Emory Buckner in 1968.

Stanley K. Platt, for many years an active leader of World Federalists, USA, is with the investment counseling firm of Platt, Tschudy, Norton and Company, Inc., of Minneapolis, Minnesota, and presently resides in that city.

Robert H. Reno, a graduate of Yale Law School, practices law in Concord, New Hampshire, has been involved in numerous world peace activities, and led the primary campaign of Congressman Paul McCloskey for the presidential nomination in New Hampshire in 1972.

I. A. Richards, educator and author, was professor of English at Harvard University from 1939 to 1963. An active world federalist, he lives in Cambridge, Massachusetts.

Francis E. Rivers, distinguished attorney and jurist, active over many years in the area of civil rights, was formerly a justice in the New York City Civil Court, and currently resides in New York City.

Carlos P. Romulo, one of the founders of the Republic of the Philippines, former ambassador to the United Nations, is a distinguished public servant, editor, and author, and is at present with the Department of Foreign Affairs in Manila.

Einar Rørstad, educator and former head of *En Verden*, the Norwegian world federalist organization, recently spent two years in India, and has now returned to live in Oslo, Norway.

Lyman V. Rutledge, for several years pastor of the Dublin Community Church, now resides in retirement in Kittery, Maine.

Louis B. Sohn, educator and co-author of *World Peace through World Law*, is professor of law at the Harvard Law School, and has served as adviser to both the State and Defense Departments.

Samuel R. Spencer, Jr., educator and writer, was formerly president of Mary Baldwin College in Virginia, and is currently president of Davidson College in North Carolina. He is the author of *Decision for War, 1917*, and *Booker T. Washington and the Negro's Place in American Life*.

C. Maxwell Stanley, resident of Muscatine, Iowa, is president of the Stanley Foundation, and has long been active in the world federalist movement, serving twice as president of World Federalists, USA. He is the author of *Waging Peace*.

Edward P. Stuhr, investment counselor, is vice president and honorary director of the Fiduciary Trust Company of New York, and resides in New Jersey.

Grenville Clark Thoron, said to be one of the thirteenth successive generation of his family to be born on Manhattan Island, formerly with the Smithsonian Institution and for a year in India for Yale University working in paleontology, now writes and does historical research in Cambridge, Massachusetts.

Lyman M. Tondel, Jr., lawyer and lecturer in law, currently practices law in New York City with the firm of Cleary, Gottlieb, Steen and Hamilton, and lives in Tenafly, New Jersey.

Edric A. Weld, educator and retired minister, was headmaster of the Holderness School, Holderness, New Hampshire, and now lives in Dublin, New Hampshire.

Paul Dudley White, one of America's most honored cardiologists at home and abroad, belonged to the Academy of Medical Sciences of the USSR and also visited the People's Republic of China in 1971. He died at age eighty-seven in October of 1973.

William Worthy, a distinguished reporter and journalist, especially renowned for his visits to Cuba and China in the 1950s and 1960s, currently lives in Boston, Massachusetts.

Charles E. Wyzanski, Jr., formerly law clerk to the two distinguished judges, who were brothers, Augustus and Learned Hand, has been a U.S. district judge in Massachusetts since 1941.

Muhammad Zafrullah Khan, distinguished jurist of Pakistan, has served as head of the International Court of Justice of the United Nations and been active in world peace affairs.

Index

A.B.C. (A Better Chance) program, 153
Academic freedom, defense of, 12, 139–41, 150, 157, 161–64, 204–5
See also Ober, Frank B., correspondence
Acheson, Dean, 14, 21, 197
Adebo, Simeon O., 227
recollections of Clark, 229–31
Albright, Dr. Fuller, 191
Aldrich, Winthrop, 36, 37
Allen, Dr. Arthur, 191
Allison, Henry, 200
Ambedkar, 256
American Bar Association:
Bill of Rights Committee, 10, 19, 21, 27, 56, 83, 108, 110, 120, 128, 273
Gold Medal awarded to Clark, 5, 61, 97, 119
American Civil Liberties Union, 120
American Scholar, article on Clark, 110, 117
Ames, "Del," 11
Amory, Cleveland, 144
Anti-communism, *see* Ober, Frank B., correspondence
Arant, Douglas, 26–27
Arms Control and Disarmament Agency Act, 39
Armstrong, Patrick, 214, 218
recollections of Clark, 245–46
Arnold Arboretum controversy, 13, 26, 96, 124, 150–51
Atomic weapons control, *see* Disarmament, support for
Attlee, Clement, 23, 96, 152, 179, 186–87

Aub, Dr. Joseph, 191
Austin, Warren, 21

Baker, Newton D., 15
Baldwin, Roger N.:
recollections of Clark, 120–21
Ballantine, Arthur A., 70, 92
Bank of Manhattan, 93
Barkley, Alben W., 86
Barnette case, *see West Virginia State Board of Education* v. *Barnette*
Barr, Stringfellow:
recollections of Clark, 247–48
Baruch, Bernard, 9, 223
Bass, Robert P., 3, 21, 253
Baxter, James Phinney, 12
Beale, "Joey," 118
Bell, Laird, 270
Bell, Ernest ("Doc"), 26
Benson, Frank, 182
Berman, Harold, 167
Bessey, E., 69
Bibb Manufacturing Company v. *Pope*, 79–81
Biddle, Francis, 126
Bill of Rights, respect for, 82–83, 101, 140
See also American Bar Association, Bill of Rights Committee; Civil rights, defense of
Bill of Rights Review, 83, 116
Bird, Francis W., Jr., 69, 70
Black, Hugo, 24, 91, 129, 130, 134
Blacks, rights of, *see* Racial equality, support for
Bolté, Charles, 21
Bowers and Sands, absorbed by Root, Clark law firm, 75

311

Bowie, Robert, 167
Bowles, Chester, 256
Brandeis, Louis D., 88, 90, 105, 179
Brewster, Kingman, 5, 12, 167, 238, 253
  recollections of Clark, 159–60
Bridges, Harry, 124–26
Bridges, Styles, 253
Buchan, John (Lord Tweedsmuir), 22, 173
Buckner, Emory R., 10, 13, 16, 70, 75, 76, 78, 79, 81, 82, 89, 92
Buckner and Howland, 70
Budd, Kenneth, 20
Burke, Edward, 85, 86, 198, 210
Burke-Wadsworth Selective Service Bill, see Selective Training and Service Act of 1940
Burlingham, Charles C., 14–15, 85, 86
Burnham-Clark family, 34
Byrd, Richard E., 15, 179

Canfield, Franklin, 25
Cannon, Le Grand B., 69
Carnegie, Andrew, 72–73, 158
Carroll, Philip, 11
Carter, Ledyard and Milburn firm, 16
Cavers, David F.:
  recollections of Clark, 165–68
Chafee, Zechariah, 12, 27, 110, 272, 285, 291
Chalfont, Lord, see Jones, Alfred Gwynne
Chalmers, Allan Knight, 116, 122
  Clark letter to, 292–96
Chase National Bank v. E. W. Clark and Company, 35–36
China, People's Republic of, Clark views on, 7, 24–25, 133, 300
  visit attempted, 6, 134, 153
Chou En-lai, 7, 24

Churchill, Winston, 180
Ciardi, John, 279–80, 288, 290
Civil Aeronautics Act of 1938, 91
Civil rights, defense of, 10, 19, 23–24, 96, 101, 108–11, 116, 120, 124–35, 272–75
  See also American Bar Association: Bill of Rights Committee; Racial equality, support for
Claflin, "Bill," 163–64
Clark, Dr. Donald, 191
Clark, E. W., and Company, 34–36
Clark (E. W.), Dodge and Company, 34, 69
Clark, Edward White, 34
Clark, Enoch White, 34
Clark, Fanny Dwight (Mrs. Grenville), 6, 10, 16, 40, 96, 100, 139, 140, 144, 152, 158, 174–77, 182–84, 191, 201, 204, 212, 222, 225, 255, 258
Clark, George C., 35
Clark, Grenville, Jr., 212
Clark, Hattie, 35
Clark, Joseph S., Jr. ("Joe"), 22, 23, 27
  recollections of G. Clark, 33–34
Clark, Joseph Sill, 34–35
Clark, Julian B., 102, 103, 146
Clark, Kate Avery Richardson, 35
Clark, Louis Crawford, 34
Clark, Louisa, see Spencer, Louisa Clark
Clark, Mary, see Dimond, Mary Clark
Clark, Mary Brush (Mrs. Grenville), 41, 191, 201, 215, 250
Clark, William, 33–34
Clark family, 33–35
Cleary, Gottlieb, Steen and Hamilton, 13, 96
Clifford, J. Garry, 9–29
Colby, Bainbridge, 75–76

Committee to Defend America by Aiding the Allies, 197
Compton, Randolph P., 214–16
Conant, James B. ("Jim"), 12, 13, 42, 57, 94, 141, 150, 163–64, 197, 279, 283, 284, 289
recollections of Clark, 161–62
Conant, Patty, 12, 141
Conference on Science and World Affairs (COSWA), 232
Connally, Thomas T. ("Tom"), 85
Cooke, Jay, 34
Coolidge, Calvin, 15
Cousins, Norman, 21, 50, 215–18, 237, 253
recollections of Clark, 3–8
Cowles, John, 237
Cranston, Alan, 5, 21, 22, 26, 159
recollections of Clark, 252–64
Cranston, Geneva, 260, 261
Cuban missile crisis, 6, 22, 28, 133

Dartmouth Conferences on disarmament, 5, 158, 214
Davis, John W., 14, 72
Day, Edward M., 11
Dean, Arthur H., 39, 40
Derby, Ethel Roosevelt, 180
Derby, J. Lloyd, 70, 187, 268
Derby, Richard, 11
Dickey, John S., 12
recollections of Clark, 146–54
Dies, Martin, 124
Dilliard, Irving, biography of Clark, 110, 117, 139
Dimond, Dr. E. Grey, 7, 25
Dimond, Mary Clark, 7, 25, 185
recollections of Clark, 170–82
Dinse, John M.:
recollections of Clark, 102–4
Disarmament, support for, 4–6, 21, 22, 38–40, 43, 46, 48,

61, 62, 141, 142, 194, 199, 241–42, 245, 249, 298–301
Distinguished Service Medal awarded to Clark, 60
Dodds, Harold W., 12, 57, 150
recollections of Clark, 139–45
Dodge, Robert, 26
Douglas, Lewis W.:
recollections of Clark, 195–99
Douglas, William O., 129
Dowling, Noel, 86
Draft of a Proposed Treaty Establishing a World Disarmament and World Development Organization (Clark and Sohn), 48
Dublin Community Church, endowment of, 200–2
Dublin Conferences, 3–5, 27, 46, 61, 62, 106, 117, 159, 182, 228, 238–40, 247, 248, 253, 255
Dublin Declaration, 259
Dulles, John Foster, 21, 24, 38, 132
Dumbarton Oaks Conference, 61
Dwight, Fanny, *see* Clark, Fanny Dwight

Eaton, Fredrick, 22
Eichelberger, Clark, 218
Einstein, Albert, 181–82, 243–44, 256
Eisenhower, Dwight D., 12, 22, 39, 301
Eliot, Charles William, 161, 236, 279, 282, 285, 287, 291
Eliot, George Fielding, 272

Farley, "Mike," 26
Federal Union, Inc., 247
Federation of Free Peoples, A (Clark), 22
Ferry, Mansfield, 70
Fiduciary Trust Company, 93, 211

Finletter, Thomas K., 253
Fischer, Louis, 255
Fitzhugh, Dr. Greene, 191
Flanders, Ralph, 22
Flynn, William J., 75, 76
Foord, Dr. Andrew J., 11, 191
Ford, John, 81
Ford Foundation, 21, 166–68
Foundation for World Govern-
    ment, 248
Frankfurter, Felix, 16–19, 57, 88,
    90, 91, 110, 118, 129, 152,
    158, 181, 210, 290
Frankfurter, Marion, 19, 181
Freedom Ride cases, 27, 111–12,
    116, 152
Friendly, Henry J., 105, 111, 216
    recollections of Clark, 88–91
Frost, Robert, 12, 180–81
Fulbright, J. William, 7, 38
Fuller, "Lon," 165
Fund for Peace, 214–15

Gaitskill, Hugh, 181
Gandhi, Devadas, 256
Garrison, Lloyd K., 9
    recollections of Clark, 98–101
George, Walter, 85
Gérard, Francis, 52
Gibson, Ernest W., 270
Gobitis case, see Minersville
    School District v. Gobitis
Gottlieb, Leo, 79
Grant, the Rev. Gerard G.:
    recollections of Clark, 239–40
Greenbaum, Edward S., 163
Greenberg, Jack:
    recollections of Clark, 122–23
Grew, Joseph Clark, 34
Grew-Clark family, 34
Griswold, Erwin N., 7, 165–67
    recollections of Clark, 155–58
Griswold, Harriet, 158
Gromyko, Andrei, 256

Habicht, Max, 49, 187–88
Haddow, Sir Alexander J.:
    recollections of Clark, 232–33

Hague, Frank, 27, 83, 110, 116,
    273
Halifax, Lord and Lady, 179
Hall, James P., 105
Hall, Livingston, 156
Hammarskjöld, Dag, 250
Hand, Augustus N., 80, 98
Hand, Learned, 98, 160
Harlan, John M., 19, 90, 111,
    180
Harriman, Averell, 25
    recollections of Clark, 59–62
Harrington, the Rev. Donald S.,
    95, 118
Hart, James P.:
    recollections of Clark, 105–6
Hart Schaffner and Marx, 78–79
Harvard Corporation, 4, 10–13,
    16, 42, 94, 96, 120, 140,
    150, 151, 155, 156, 161–64,
    197, 257
Harvard Law School Fund, 157,
    279, 289
Harvard Law School International
    Legal Studies Program, 165–
    68
Harvey, Mary Kersey:
    recollections of Clark, 214–18
Heffner, Richard D., article on
    Clark, 43, 217
Henderson, Ernest, 94
Herrick, Dr. W. W., 191
Hershey, Lewis B.:
    recollections of Clark, 209–10
Herter, Christian A., 38, 39
Hines, John F., 197
Hoadley affair, 75–76
Holliday, William, 21
Hollins, Elizabeth (Betsy) Jay,
    28, 220–23
    recollections of Clark, 183–84
Hollins, Harry, 28, 184–86, 188,
    218
    recollections of Clark, 220–25
Hollins, Stephanie, 187
Holmes, Oliver Wendell, 4, 284
Hoover, Herbert, 10, 15, 92, 179

Hopkins, Ernest J., 12
Hornblower, Ralph, Jr., 147
Howland, Silas W., 70
Hudson, Manley O., 45
Hughes, Charles Evans, 130, 179, 272, 285
Hull, Cordell, 277
Humphrey, Hubert H., 39
Hutchins, Robert Maynard, 12, 179

Institute for International Order (Institute for World Order), 223
Intemann, Alfred C., 69, 106
International Law of the Future (Hudson), 45
International Legal Studies Program at Harvard Law School, 165–68

Jackson, Elmore, 193
Jackson, Robert, 126
Jacobson, Dr. Bernard, 191
James, Alexander, 238
James, Henry, 12, 163
James, Mary Brush, *see* Clark, Mary Brush
James, William, 41
Jay, Betsy, *see* Hollins, Elizabeth (Betsy) Jay
Jay, Delancey Kane, 11, 14, 26, 92, 183, 184, 186–89
Jehovah's Witnesses flag saluting case, *see Minersville School District v. Gobitis*
Jessup, Dr. Everett C., 188–89, 191
John XXIII, Pope, 238
Johnson, Lady Bird, 27
Johnson, Lyndon B., 7, 27, 134
Jones, Alfred Gwynne (Lord Chalfont), 245

Katzenbach, Nicholas, 22
Kennedy, John F., 6, 21–23, 38–40, 57, 61, 62, 207, 220, 253
Clark letter to, 297–302
Khrushchev, Nikita, 21, 23
Kidder Peabody and Company, 34
Killing of the Peace, The (Cranston), 252
King, Martin Luther, 29
Knickerbocker Club, 10, 94, 96
Knox, Frank, 17, 95, 198, 263
Korean war, views on, 148
Korner, John M.:
recollections of Clark, 69–73

La Guardia, Fiorello, 18
Landis, James M., 126
Landon-Roosevelt campaign, 140
Laporte, Alphonse, 25
Laporte, Cloyd, 25
recollections of Clark, 78–87
Laski, Harold J., 179, 285–86
League of Nations, 251–54
Leale, Loyal, 106
Lee, Dr. Theodore H., 191
Lindbergh, Charles A., 180
Loeb, William, 24
Long, Benjamin H., 11
Longworth, Alice Roosevelt, 180
Lovett, Robert, 20
Lowell, Abbott Lawrence, 13, 16, 42, 94, 161, 179, 272, 279, 283, 285, 288
Lowell, Ralph, 164
Lusky, Louis, 24, 27, 128–31
recollections of Clark, 108–12
Lyman, Theodore, 11

MacArthur, Douglas, 301
McCall's magazine article on Clark, 43, 217
McCarthy, Joseph, and McCarthyism, 12, 22, 24, 26, 141
McCloy, John J., 12, 21–23, 39, 40, 57, 62, 152
McCloy-Zorin agreement, 22, 48, 62
recollections of Clark, 63–65

McDuffie, John, 195, 197
McKinley, William, 42
McNamara, Robert, 7
McVitty, Marion, 218
Mahony, Thomas, 21, 257
Mallalieu, Lance, 218
Maloney, Genevieve, 54, 95, 255, 257
Manchester *Union-Leader*, 24, 130
Mao Tse-tung, 7, 24, 25, 77
Marbury, William L., 12
  recollections of Clark, 163–64
Marshall, George, 15, 20, 21, 198
Mayer, Henry:
  recollections of Clark, 74–77
Mayer, Martin, 13, 76–77
Mehren, Arthur von, 167
Mendenhall, Thomas, 33–34
Meyer, Cord, Jr., 5, 21, 26, 253
Minersville School District v. *Gobitis*, 19, 110, 273
Missisquoi National Wildlife Refuge, 146
Monadnock, Mount, Committee for the Preservation of, 26, 57
Morison, Samuel Eliot, 12
Moses, Robert, 179
Mowrer, Edgar Ansel, 253

NAACP Legal Defense and Educational Fund, 11, 56, 96, 101, 113, 116–18, 122, 123, 153, 158, 225, 292–96
Nasser, Gamal Abdel, 182
National Committee for Independent Courts, 15, 54, 84
National Economy Act of 1933, 16, 297
National Economy League, 15, 25, 196
National Emergency Civil Liberties Committee, 133
National Emergency Committee of the Military Training

Camps Association of the United States, 15, 25, 209
National War Service Act, Citizens' Committee for, 27
Naval convoys to Britain, Clark letter to Willkie on, 270–71
Nehru, Jawaharlal, 22, 96, 182, 256
Nevins, Allen, *The Emergence of Lincoln*, 116, 292
New Deal, support of, 16, 17
Niebuhr, Reinhold, 12, 179
Nixon, Richard, 133
Nobel Peace Prize, nomination for, 7, 29, 214–18, 236, 248
Nye, Gerald P., 83

Ober, Frank B., correspondence, 12, 157–58, 162
  text of, 279–91
O'Brian, John Lord, 12
Osborn, Earl D., 223
Owen, J. Roberts, 3

Pacem in Terris encyclical, 238, 239
Palmer, John McAuley, 14, 15
Paramount insolvency proceedings, 90, 93
Park, the Rev. Charles E., 200, 202
Patterson, Robert P., 17, 20, 70, 163, 164
Paul VI, Pope, 22, 238
Peabody, Endicott ("Chub"), 26
Peace through Disarmament and Charter Revision (Clark and Sohn), 46, 47
Perkins, Frances, 124–26
Perry, Ralph Barton, 12
Pershing, John J., 15, 60, 64, 71
Petersen, Howard C., 20, 25–26, 163, 198
Plan for Peace, A (Clark and Sohn), 21, 46, 142, 188

Planning for Peace resolution, 38–39

Platt, Stanley K.:
recollections of Clark, 237–38

Plattsburg movement, 10–14, 16, 17, 20, 22, 25, 55, 56, 59–60, 62, 64, 70, 92–93, 95, 113, 114, 118, 141, 184, 197, 203
Clark-Roosevelt letter on, 266–69

Pomfret School, 10, 173

Porcellian Club, 10, 57–58, 177

Powell, Wesley, 127

Princeton Conference, 243–44, 256

Quinn, Edward F., 70

Racial equality, support for, 43, 56, 96, 101, 111–19, 122–26, 152–53, 158, 225, 292–96

Railroad reorganization and rates, work on, 79, 90, 92

Rajagopalachari, C., 185

Rankin, "Tom," 26

Reno, Robert H., 24, 28, 46, 218, 257
recollections of Clark, 127–31

Richards, Dr. L. F., 190

Richardson, Elliot, 7

Richardson, Kate Avery, *see* Clark, Kate Avery Richardson

Rickenbacker, Eddie, 180

Rights publication, 133

Rivers, Francis E.:
recollections of Clark, 113–19

Roberts, Owen J., 3, 61, 253

Rock Island litigation, 92

Romulo, Carlos P., 22, 228, 255
recollections of Clark, 249–51

Roosevelt, Franklin D., 10, 11, 15–21, 26, 42, 54, 84–87, 93, 95, 140, 152, 161, 163, 179, 196, 210, 263, 297, 301

Roosevelt, Theodore, 10, 42, 64, 254
Clark letter to, 266

Roosevelt, Mrs. Theodore, 179

Root, Elihu, 11, 17, 42, 152, 253, 254

Root, Elihu, Jr., 13, 42, 64, 69–71, 81, 92, 96

Root, Clark law firm, 17, 25, 27, 36, 42, 54, 69–74, 78–79, 89–90, 92–93, 95, 98, 99, 105, 106, 108, 110, 128, 155, 156, 254

Rørstad, Einar, 29
recollections of Clark, 234–36

Rørstad, Lillemor, 235–36

Royce, "Alec," 80

Rusk, Dean, 7, 39

Rutledge, Lyman V.:
recollections of Clark, 200–3

Saltonstall, Leverett, 160

San Francisco Charter, 277

San Francisco Conference, 47, 147

Saturday Review, article on Clark, 217

Schlesinger, Arthur M., Jr., 39

Scott, Austin W., 155

Seabury, Samuel, 14

Selective Training and Service Act of 1940, 7, 11, 12, 14, 15, 17, 18, 20, 21, 54–56, 60, 64, 91, 94, 113, 115, 163, 197–98, 209–10

Shapley, Harlow, 279–80, 288, 290

Shattuck, Henry L., 12

Sheehan, William, 29, 215, 217, 218

Sherley, Swager, 197

Sherwood, Robert E., 270

Smith, "Al," 180

Smith, Dr. George, 191

Smythe, Robert D., 253
Snow, Edgar, 6, 24, 25
Snowman, Dr. Richard, 191
Sohn, Louis B., 5, 24, 28–29, 38,
    61, 96, 112, 149, 156–57,
    167, 180, 214–16, 226, 229,
    232, 241, 248, 256, 259, 299
    recollections of Clark, 45–52
Soviet Union, Clark views on, 4–
    6, 14, 26, 154, 193–94, 276–
    78
Spencer, Louisa Clark, 40, 184,
    187
Spencer, Margaret, 201
Spencer, Samuel R., Jr., 18, 26
    recollections of Clark, 53–58
Stanley, C. Maxwell:
    recollections of Clark, 226–28
Stanley Foundation conferences,
    227–28, 241, 250
Stevenson, Adlai, 21, 220
Stewart, William, 25
Stimson, Henry L., 10, 11, 14,
    16–21, 26, 53, 57, 58, 60,
    72, 85, 95, 114, 152, 158,
    198–99, 210, 252–53, 263,
    278
Stone, Harlan F., 27, 128
Streit, Clarence, 21, 46, 188, 247
Stuhr, Edward P.:
    recollections of Clark, 211–13
Supreme Court packing plan of
    Franklin D. Roosevelt, 11,
    15, 16, 25, 54, 56, 84–87,
    113, 114, 163
Surrey, Stanley, 167

Thacher, "Archie," 20, 64
Thomas, Norman, 23, 110, 116
Thoron, Grenville Clark:
    recollections of Clark, 206–7
Tondel, Lyman M., Jr.:
    recollections of Clark, 92–97
Tracy, John, 147
Treaty of Versailles, 251

Truman, Harry S., 20, 25, 26,
    254
    Clark letter to, 276–78
Tweedsmuir, Lord, see Buchan,
    John

Union of Free Peoples proposal,
    142
Union Now (Streit), 247
United Nations, Clark views on,
    21, 22, 37, 46–48, 61, 100,
    121, 142, 147, 203, 216,
    218, 226–30, 238, 241, 249–
    51, 255–56, 277
United World Federalists (UWF)
    (World Federalists, U.S.A.),
    20, 37, 158, 185, 215, 218,
    226, 227, 247
Universal Military Training Act
    of 1920, 210
Uphaus, Willard case, 19, 23–24,
    27, 28, 111, 127–31

Vandenburg, Arthur H., 85, 276
Vatican, contacts with, 22, 238
Versailles treaty, 251
Veterans' compensation, efforts to
    revise, 195–97
Vietnam war, opposition to, 7,
    25, 27, 134, 207, 220

Wadsworth, James, 26, 198, 210
Wallace, Henry A., 23
    Progressive party campaign,
    280, 288
Welch, Joseph, 26
Weld, Edric A.:
    recollections of Clark, 204–5
Weld, Gertrude, 204
Wendel estate litigation, 90
West Virginia Board of Educa-
    tion v. Barnette, 19, 110
Wheeler, Burton K., 85
White, Dr. Paul Dudley, 7, 24,
    41, 152, 207, 232, 233, 258
    recollections of Clark, 190–91

Whitehead, Alfred North, 12, 182
Wight, Ruth, 28, 49, 50, 51, 187, 216, 217
Willkie, Wendell L.:
Clark letter to, 270–75
Wilson, Harold, 23, 77
Wilson, John A., 105
Wilson, Woodrow, 10, 64, 74, 258
Winant, John G., 179
Windegger, Fritz von, 21
Wister, Owen, 173
Wood, Leonard, 13–15
Woodring, Harry H., 17
Woodrum, Cliff, 197
World Association of World Federalists (WAWF), 187, 215, 227–29
World Disarmament and World Development Treaty, 50
World economic development, support for, 48, 228
World federalist movement, 10, 12, 20–23, 87, 160, 226–28
See also United World Federalists
World Federalists, U.S.A., *see* United World Federalists
World Government, Parliamentary Association for, 232

World Government, Parliamentary Group for, 232
World Law Fund, 6, 11, 28, 62, 218, 220, 224, 225
World law movement, 4, 5, 21, 39, 42, 43, 55, 143, 148, 153, 166, 181, 203, 228, 242, 253, 259
See also World Law Fund
World organization proposals, 45–50, 56, 60–62, 64, 100, 142, 153, 158, 193, 259, 278, 298–99
World Peace through World Law (Clark and Sohn), 5, 21, 25, 27–29, 38, 47–52, 61, 96, 112, 143, 149, 180, 185, 214, 220, 223, 226, 229, 234, 235, 241, 248, 257, 299
World police force, advocacy of, 298
Worthy, William:
recollections of Clark, 132–35
Wyman, Louis C., 127, 130
Wyzanski, Charles E., Jr.:
recollections of Clark, 124–26

Zafrullah Khan, Muhammad, 228, 241